# Sublime Lunacy

# Sublime Lunacy

## People, Places & Pleasures

An Anecdotage

# John Cooke

**ISBN 978-1-79478-869-5**

Second Edition

Other Books by John Cooke

The Restless Kingdom (Facts on File)
Safe Keeping (Lulu & Amazon)
Focus on Nature (Dent) (co-author)
Oxford Book of Invertebrates (OUP)(co-author)
Lament for Democracy and other Essays
(Lulu & Amazon)

Cover Picture:
Balinese Child's Barong Painting

# DEDICATION

This book is dedicated
to succeeding generations
that they too may enjoy
a life as rich as mine.

# CONTENTS

# CONTENTS

# CONTENTS

# FORWARD

The gentle kiss of a fine vintage is frequently all that is needed to lift a distant, long-dormant memory into consciousness and add it to the archive of anecdotes that make up this volume. As I enter my dotage, the failing memory of old age has swallowed many contenders for inclusion, but the remainder stand as testament to a rich and enjoyable life. A few of the episodes recounted here have already appeared in print elsewhere, but have nevertheless been included in the belief that they merit repetition. Also included are unvarnished personal revelations and opinions that in my younger days might well have been suppressed, but are here laid bare as part of the historic record of self.

Uncomfortable writing at length in the first person, I have employed a literary device, and entrusted the task of gathering this residue of my life to Sandy Lea, a fictional *alter ego* and amanuensis, who has witnessed, and indeed partaken in, the events here documented.

It seems pretentious to dignify each brief section of these jumbled reminiscences with the title of 'Chapter'. As an alternative, ''Discursus''—defined as "wandering or logically unconnected statements"—appears far more apposite.

Envisaged as light bedtime reading by my descendants and friends, this is an ephemeral contribution to a history otherwise soon destined to vanish without leaving more than transient digital key prints in the sands of time yet to come.

SUBLIME LUNACY

# PREFACE

History, silently moving forward, embraces each of us and relentlessly adds everyone to its ever-growing inventory of ancestors. Great and small, we are carried irreversibly and, however unwillingly, into the past, accumulating millennium by millennium, like anonymous fossils on the bed of an ancient sea. Time stretches out behind us into the past as a great, boundless desert. Here and there occasional features, dimly recalled from distant school days, protrude like Shelly's vast and trunkless legs of stone. Thus we may recognize major catastrophes such as the Black Death or the destruction of Pompeii, and identify notable individuals like Alexander the Great, Genghis Kahn or Julius Caesar. Likewise important cultural landmarks such as the invention of printing or the discovery of gunpowder may also claim our attention.

But history, of course, is not only in the past, for it also stretches forward in time, and we should not be blind to those landmarks yet to come—landmarks of which we can only dream, and then very imperfectly. Fresh discoveries and inventions are awaiting their turn upon the world stage, together with catastrophes and celebrities; the latter, after a brief burst of fame and acclaim, probably destined to settle anonymously into timeless oblivion.

Only those afflicted with both pathological short sightedness and a total lack of imagination, could agree with

Henry Ford that "history is bunk." At the very least history possesses the ability—albeit frequently neglected—to warn us against making yet again the same mistakes that plagued our predecessors.

To me the infinite complexity of history is both fascinating and rewarding. To keep a map of history, however inadequate, pinned in place within the quicksands of memory, I had drilled into me in childhood a few salient dates. Being English, it is not surprising that foremost among these was 1066, when Duke William of Normandy, following the footsteps of his Viking ancestors, successfully invaded the Saxon kingdom of King Harold at Hastings. For others, brought up elsewhere in the world, it might perhaps be the death of Shah Abbas of Persia (1629), the eruption of Mount Tambora on Sumbawa (1815) or the year of the first 'divine wind' or *kamikaze* that saved Japan from the Mongol hordes of Kublai Khan (1274). The date itself is irrelevant, provided only that it is memorable. The crucial thing is to have sound temporal moorings to which one's historical highpoints may be secured.

Late in life I have found that my limited knowledge of antiquity comes to my aid in a wholly new and unanticipated way—one that seems particularly apt in this digital age. Somewhat surprisingly history helps me to keep track of the innumerable, readily forgettable, passwords and PIN numbers that lie in wait to trip me up on those embarrassing moments when they suddenly evaporate from memory at the supermarket check-out or ATM

# PREFACE

I am plagued, I should perhaps explain, by a form of numerical dyslexia, in which figures as such have little meaning and easily vanish or transmute when not written down. However, so deeply ingrained are a few of the key dates of English history, painfully impressed in childhood, that I have only to recall the battle of Bosworth Field (1485), the death of Queen Elizabeth the First (1603), or the Great Fire of London (1666), for example, to be able to reinstate many vanished numbers when they are needed. The same approach can even serve from time to time for telephone numbers—thus the death of Cardinal Woolsey in 1530 invariably reminds me of the last four digits of my French telephone number. Of course, the world is rarely so well ordered that events and the requisite dates coincide exactly, necessitating the interpolation of an extra step—a corollary such as "five years after the death of Queen Anne" for the PIN 1719, which has little in its own right to recall (unless the publication of Robinson Crusoe carries special meaning). In the United States "1776 plus ten" (also the first ascent of Mont Blanc) would serve to preserve PIN 1786 if needed. The potential is endless. These examples, I would emphasize, are completely hypothetical and bear no relation to numbers I actually use with bank accounts and other such sensitive matters.

I mention this reliance on dates, because it also helps me to locate myself firmly in the historical landscape, giving me a temporal context to which I am able to relate. My parents were essentially Victorian, albeit rather modern in outlook. Father was born slightly less than two years before

Victoria's death (1901) and my mother barely a year after it, so for them the Victorian age and *mores* naturally lingered on at least through their childhoods. Even when I was a teenager, my mother still claimed to believe that visiting the cinema on a Sunday was immoral!

Although dead now for quite some years, my parents remain in my memory as living, vivacious characters on a contemporary stage. It is only when I consider how my parents' parents must have appeared to them eighty years on, that I begin to get a sense of historical perspective. Thus my grandfather was just four years old when the Crimean war ended in February 1856—and soundly beaten by his father to impress upon his young mind just how auspicious an occasion this event was. Perhaps even more remarkable, my father, as a young doctor in the 1920s had a patient whose father had fought at the Battle of Waterloo in 1815. To me this brings home just how recent so much of what we consign to history really is. It delighted me recently when the identity of King Richard III's remains, hastily interred in 1485, were located beneath a corporation car park in Leicester, their identity confirmed by DNA testing, so wondrously uniting ancient and modern.

These casual meditations on the vagaries of history were recently prompted by a young person expressing ignorance and surprise at events that had occurred during my lifetime—events that remain as fresh and vivid to me today as when they first occurred some decades ago. I foolishly, for example, take it for granted that everyone knows at least as much as I do about the Second World War, and hence it was in sheer disbelief that I recently learned that there are now officers serving in the Royal Air Force who claim complete ignorance of the Battle of Britain. (For those likewise stricken by amnesia, the heroic sacrifice by a small band of pilots who successfully thwarted Hitler's planned subjugation of the British Isles). So fast does time pass us by!

However, it came as no little surprise—indeed something of a shock actually—to realize that so much of my own personal story is no longer contemporary, but has already passed well into the pages of history. As I am persuaded by friends that history would be enriched in some small measure by my own life experiences being recorded for my descendants, I have yielded to the clamouring and allowed a few events from a not uneventful life to be committed to paper—or as a first step, to digital memory.

History sometimes creeps up on us without warning, bearing unexpected gifts. Just such an occasion was the discovery of a letter from the Queen—actually the late Queen Mother, for it was written towards the end of the Second World War. It surfaced amongst my father's papers, concealed with other treasures in an old plastic shopping bag. I will not expand upon the circumstances, for they have been fully described elsewhere[1]. Suffice it to say that it lay included in a horde of correspondence between my mother in war-torn

---

1    *Safe Keeping: Voices from a vanished World.* 2019

England and my American foster mother in Connecticut—
ninety-seven long, articulate letters that cast a fascinating
spotlight into the deeper recesses of a drama-filled childhood.
Her majesty was writing to thank American foster parents for
their generosity in providing sanctuary to British children at a
time when Nazi invasion had seemed almost inevitable.

The prelude to the discovery of this treasure trove,
in which the expression of royal gratitude was discovered,
was an exciting transatlantic crossing in 1940. Today I look
fascinated at children five years of age, finding it difficult to
visualize them in the circumstances that I encountered at
that age. Even more impossible to visualize are the emotions
my mother must have experienced. I see it as if it were only
yesterday—my mother, two sisters and I huddled next to our
appointed lifeboat in mid-Atlantic, swept by wind and spray
as depth charges hurled columns of water into the air, to the
accompaniment of deep, sonorous explosions. In the midst
of this apocalyptic chaos our attention is drawn to a torpedo,
fired from the invisible U-Boat attacking us. It was traveling
directly towards us. By good fortune it passes harmlessly a
few feet under our stern. Strangely, at the time fear did not
penetrate my armour of excitement. I cannot say the same for
my mother, for whom it must have been the realization of her
worst fears, truly the immanent arrival of Armageddon.

This event would prove to be a dramatic introduction
to the wartime sojourn described in the mother-to-mother
letters. I will not dwell here on the litany of misdeeds reported,
although my mother did feel obliged to ask on one occasion

PREFACE

"I wonder if you can substantiate the story of John knocking out the school janitor?" Although I had not, the question was not wholly unreasonable, given my penchant for mischief; a quality encapsulated in the Indonesian word *nakal*, meaning 'endearingly wicked'.

But these letters, for all their wealth of detail, cover only three crowded childhood years. There have since followed many more rich and exciting ones, the recollection of which will periodically be reclaimed from the dusty attic of memory by a casual passing remark or in response to gentle prompting from Bacchus. They range from a visit to the underworld of the ancient Greeks from which, like Hercules, I returned unscathed, to an embarrassing evening with the royal family of Japan. From journeys on foot through Africa, to imprisonment in a Macedonian jail; from climbing adventures on cliffs and buildings to nocturnal excursions in search of rare insects on mountaintops, and a confrontation with heavily armed nomads in a remote Anatolian volcanic crater. How many eight-year-olds have had to endure the conviction that they had inadvertently killed somebody? How many biologists have subsequently discovered that their fieldwork was undertaken in an uncleared minefield? Given the multitude of near escapes, I am thankful that I was not born a cat—nine lives would never have sufficed!

# SUBLIME LUNACY

## Discursus One
# Introduction

John was in meditative mood as he slowly poured himself another glass of port after dinner. "If I were to have the opportunity of living my life over again," he observed, "I do not think I would make any major changes. After all, it could have been a great deal worse. Of course, there could also be some improvements—easing the burden of lost opportunities perhaps, revisiting the dreams of what might have been, and particularly avoiding those embarrassing moments of inadequacy that still weigh silently upon my conscience—but taken over all, it's not been too bad" "Moreover," he added, "think of all the Hollywood re-makes that were so much worse than their originals." Reflecting on his words, I felt obliged to agree. Among all my wide circle of friends and relatives, few if any would appear to have led such a rich and diverse a life. Even so, as John would appear to bear not the least resemblance to Dr Johnson, it had never occurred to me that I might one day find myself cast in the role of his Boswell—that is, until one warm summer evening some years ago in France. My recollection of the occasion has not faded with the passing seasons.

We have dined long and well, to which the empty bottles ranged along the great trestle table on the terrace stand mute but eloquent testimony. The sun hangs lazily above the horizon, seemingly loath to leave us, as it so often does in this part of Europe. Above us looms the dark mass of the château, its one remaining tower casting long shadows across the flagstones, a stark reminder that this was once a baronial stronghold. Below us the French countryside stretches out in every direction as the birds and insects sing their final paeans to the departing day above the valley of the river Creuse.

The conversation is brisk, effervescent and volatile as usual, flitting easily from topic to topic, like a butterfly exploring blossoms, pausing briefly to sip nectar here, before moving on to draw more deeply elsewhere. A passing remark is all it takes. Suddenly, a Proustian beam of remembrance will penetrate the darkness, and in the accumulated debris cluttering the attic of his memory, light upon some dormant image that has long lain undisturbed. Released from its bondage of forgetfulness by the delicate kiss of a fine vintage, another story surfaces—and then another still.

I no longer recall—if indeed I ever understood—what particular remark had caused the conversation to move to Libya that evening—was it Greek mythology, oil, or revolution perhaps? I know not, but I recall vividly the scene that triggered my determination to start recording a few of his anecdotes before Father Time comes calling and obliterates all trace of them.

It was part of a longer narrative—one that like so many others, involved a journey in search of spiders, for natural history in general, and spiders in particular have been his passion since childhood. John told of a visit to a desert oasis renowned in ancient times as the fabled Garden of the Hesperides. Here, in a cool cavern deep underground, he had stood on the banks of the subterranean stream believed by the ancient Greeks to be the River Lethe. In the eternal darkness he strained, he said, to catch a glimpse of Charon ferrying the souls of the damned across the waters of forgetfulness to Hades—but without success. Neither, he assured us, did he see three-headed Cerberus. However, as evidence, that like Hercules before him, he had returned safely from the underworld, he brought back a blind white crayfish that would later be recognized as a species hitherto unknown to science and christened at the Natural History Museum in London with the sonorous name *Typhlocaris lethe.*

# SUBLIME LUNACY

## Discursus Two
# Master of the Ordinance

I have known John for many years—we share the same birthday—and I have been party to his deeds, and misdeeds. Yet it is only since that memorable evening in France that I have tried consciously to recall the high points of his enviably diverse life. Even so, the river of forgetfulness has already reclaimed far too many anecdotes worthy of note.

As a child—and his childhood, I should stress, extended far in adolescence, if not well beyond—he was shy and withdrawn. By his own admission he was Kipling's Cuchundra, the Musk Rat who never comes out into the middle of the floor, but always creeps round by the wall. He sought the shadows, insecure in company, always anxious to avoid the public gaze. I find it difficult to reconcile this awkward youth with the seemingly self-assured and confident image that he now projects onto the world.

John has always had a fine disregard for convention and at one time seriously considered assuming his mother's maiden name for no better reason than that her side of the family seemingly possessed more colourful ancestors. He identified particularly with Sir Henry Lee, the Elizabethan nobleman of whom John Aubrey, the diarist, wrote:: "He was never married, but kept woemen to reade to him when he was a-bed".

Diplomat, poet, and courtier, Sir Henry of Ditchly Park in Oxfordshire was Queen's Champion and Master of the Royal Ordinance. His tomb, in Spelsbury Church, is surrounded by the kneeling effigies of his mistress, Anne Vavasour, and his children. The inscription, reports Aubrey, reads;

> "Here lies that good old knight Sir Harry,
> Who loved well, but did not marry.
> Whilst he lived and had his feeling,
> She did lie and he was kneeling.
> Now he's dead and cannot feel,
> He doth lie, and she doth kneel."

John's mother, Vera, long harboured the conviction that it could only have been through some clerical carelessness or administrative oversight in the far distant past that had allowed the Ditchly estate to be mistakenly bequeathed to some other—and in her eyes at least—less deserving branch of the family.

Even among the unconventional university wives that thrive in North Oxford, his mother stood out from the crowd. Trained as a singer in Florence, she had a love of the stage, and was in frequent demand by the many dramatic productions with which the Oxford summer is blessed. I can see her now, clad in full nun's habit, setting off on her motorcycle, wimple flapping in the breeze, clutching a lighted cigarette between fingers brightly adorned with vivid nail polish to appear in some Restoration Comedy."

Her professional training had given her a voice that was clear, even if normally soft. However, she also possessed a stage whisper that rendered the telephone utterly redundant.

# INTRODUCTION

It was a formal occasion in the Great Library at Blenheim Palace—a meeting of the British Medical Association—at which many university dignitaries were present, all clad in full evening dress.

As sometimes happens in gatherings such as this, there can be a passing moment, a mere second or two, when all conversation suddenly ceases. It was in just such a transient instant of silence that her eyes alighted upon the unwelcome figure of the Estates Bursar of St. John's College. St. John's (sometimes unkindly referred to as St. Rachman's College, in memory of a notorious London slum landlord) owns much of North Oxford, and the bursar was embroiled in a somewhat acrimonious dispute involving the family home. Every head in the substantial crowd turned to look as a lone female voice echoed from one end of the library to the other announcing "My God! There's that bastard!" She apparently enjoyed the moment rather more than the object of her contempt.

However, John's mother was not wholly immune to embarrassment, and would recount how one day during the war she had encountered the wife of the hospital administrator, a somewhat self-important lady, sensitive to her non-academic status. It is always said that in Oxford one can dress as one likes, provided one never apologises. Seemingly ignorant of local custom, the Administrator's wife is profusely apologetic for her appearance. "Oh," gushes John's mother, "we all look ragbags in wartime, don't we?"
"I mean," came the cold response, "that I've just had all my teeth out!"

# SUBLIME LUNACY

## Discursus Three
# Fairy Godmother

The deep well of memories into which John dips at intervals—often in response to some light prompting from Bacchus—disgorges its contents very haphazardly, the topics shifting unpredictably from moment to moment, the sequence being generally dictated by sheer, illogical whimsy and flights of fancy. As this has been the form in which I have heard his stories repeated, it seems only right to retain them thus, but out of respect for my readers I have taken the liberty of attempting some slight semblance of chronological and geographic order.

John has told me several times that he himself had always intended to commit the high points of his life to paper, but as he put it, sloth and indolence supervened, and the years slipped by. He had originally been urged by his aunt Dorothy, his father's sister, to set down his African experiences—the first of his many travels. In truth he did once start, but the enterprise ground to a halt when his laptop computer was stolen in Indonesia after fifty-thousand words had been lovingly entrusted to its memory as Dorothy approached her century—and sadly the work was not resumed before she passed on at one-hundred-and-two

Fairy godmother and periodic financial ambulance, Dorothy had travelled widely herself. As a sixteen-year-old before the First World War she had crossed Canada alone, a feat more extraordinary then than it would be considered today. Undoubtedly the travel bug was sown by her father, a remarkable gentleman who as a sea captain had travelled the world under sail. His constant companion on his voyages was the Encyclopaedia Britannica, which he would read nightly while at sea. He lived well into his nineties and seemingly never forgot a word that he had read.

As a young man in the middle of Queen Victoria's reign, he had purchased a tailored dark suit, but greatly resented the cost. Over the years, as he and his suit aged, he would periodically unstitch it and use the disassembled pieces as patterns to create a new one. Like a game of sartorial Chinese Whispers, with each cutting the pattern would lose some of its precision. Towards the end of his life, as he had shrunken and the tailor's original craftsmanship had become increasingly diluted by constant copying, his clothes took on the appearance of having been a Salvation Army donation.

Dorothy's father, John's grandfather, who had been sailing off the island of Krakatoa when it vanished in a massive volcanic explosion in 1882, was born during the Crimean War and four years old when it ended. So that he would not forget so auspicious an occasion, his father had dragged him from his downy bed and beaten him soundly—a somewhat brutal *aide memoire* by modern standards. The family was staying with Dorothy and her father when the Second World War ended. Having heard his story, Dorothy's niece—John's sister Jean—prevailed upon her grandfather to administer a similar reminder on her younger brother. John, a sound sleeper, claimed to have retained no memory of the event by the following morning, wondering later whether it might have been a beating more symbolic than actual.

During the First World War Dorothy's father and his vessel had the misfortune to be captured by a German Cruiser. As captain, he recognised the responsibility he owed to the owners of his vessel in accounting for its loss. He therefore demanded from the commander of his German Nemesis a proper receipt for the ship, setting out the circumstances of its loss. It is a tribute to the code of honour still observed even in wartime by the German warrior caste that such a receipt was formally written and presented. This unique historic document now resides in London's Imperial War Museum— which has somehow managed to misplace it, as I discovered, when I wanted to check the names of the vessels involved.

Although Dorothy made periodic visits to her sister in what was then Rhodesia (now Zimbabwe), staying at the Leper Hospital founded by her brother-in-law at Ngomahuru, this hardly counted in her eyes as travel. She continued to live with her father and care for him until the end of his life. Only then, in late middle age, did she resume real travels.

On one occasion she was returning on leave to England from the school she had started near Ibadan in Nigeria. However, on reaching the coast instead of turning right and heading North, as geography might suggest, she turned left instead and headed South down the coast of Africa. She had just started up the Congo River when the Korean War broke out—an event of which she was to remain in ignorance for some months. In time she emerged from the headwaters of the Lualaba, a tributary of the upper Congo. Crossing Lake Tanganyika, she passed into what at that time was still British East Africa and made her way slowly down the Nile, with the expectation of finding a steamer to carry her back to England when she reached Alexandria.

There was no ready passage home, however, when she arrived at the Mediterranean coast because all shipping was headed to Korea with supplies for the military. The British consul in Cairo demanded that she wait in her hotel for an indeterminate number of weeks until a berth became available. For someone of her temperament such veritable incarceration was unthinkable and she determined to explore those parts of Cairo not normally covered by Baedeker. It was on one such excursion that she found herself abducted while travelling in a taxi and taken deeper into the slums than planned. It was only when the taxi was forced to pause briefly at a crossroads that she was able to leap out. Marching furiously through the crowds, clearing a way with her parasol, which she wielded like a sabre, she eventually found her way back to the hotel. On hearing of her adventure, the consul promptly found her a passage!

Despite not having children of her own, Dorothy had in innate understanding of child psychology. How else could she have devised such an immediate cure for hiccups? She would take a half-crown coin (a significant sum in those days) and set it down on the table, saying: "If you hiccup again, you can have it." No matter how hard the child tried to hiccup to gain this prize, the urge always evaporated.

Over the years, as we sat drinking together at the Château d'Alogny and elsewhere, John recounted many other stories of his Aunt Dorothy—an eccentric in the finest English tradition, and who by war's end, after volunteering improbably for factory work, was a skilful riveter of airplane fuselages. In her late eighties she was still living alone in Crewkerne down in Somerset, but would periodically drive to Oxford to visit her brother and his family. On one such occasion she arrived somewhat later than expected—not an unusual event in itself—and by way of explanation said casually that while driving on back roads across Salisbury Plain in her little Morris Minor she had found herself caught up in the noise and turmoil of a full-blown military exercise. Tanks were rolling at high speed in every direction and helicopters swooped low overhead. "What" exclaimed the assembled company in horror, "did you do?" "Oh" she said nonchalantly, tucking her travelling rug tighter around her knees "I just wound up my window."

SUBLIME LUNACY

## Discursus Four
# In Convoy

John is the first to admit that his early childhood had been thoroughly conventional—and perhaps by modern standards even a little spoiled. Following the custom of the times in middle-class Oxford society, he was consigned to the care of a Norland nanny, employed at the then-going rate of £50 per annum His world was the nursery, the large town garden—in which browsed his resident herd of imaginary cows—and the University Parks, to which he would walk daily to feed the ducks.

It was, he recounted, on one of these excursions at the age of four that he and Nanny apparently met an old lady walking her dog, a Dachshund. A recent sojourn at Nanny's parent's farm, combined with life within a medical family had imparted a somewhat precocious familiarity with animals and their anatomy. "My" he observed, "What big 'shudders' your dog has", clearly confusing dogs and cows. "Oh no", he announced on closer inspection. "It's a penis!" Such a word was hardly known outside the medical fraternity, and never heard in polite society.

John recounts that when he was about eighteen months old, his sister Jean was seen carrying him up the garden, dripping wet and swathed in green slime. He had fallen into a water tank in the greenhouse and his noble sister had pulled him out and saved him from drowning. She for long basked in the *kudos* resulting from this deed, but eventually, more than twenty years later, admitted that it was she who had pushed him in in the first place.

This childhood idyll amid North Oxford's spring blossoms came to an abrupt end early in 1940. As Hitler's armies marched triumphant across Europe, announcing England as the next objective, the spectre of war loomed ever nearer. Across the Atlantic, a small group of faculty at Yale University, many with close Oxford connections, set up a committee to offer sanctuary to children from Oxford and Cambridge—but one of many similar schemes initiated within the United States to save European children.

The invitation reached Oxford early in June 1940. Parents had to decide rapidly whether the risk of being torpedoed by the numerous U-boats then operating in the Atlantic was outweighed by the very real prospect of having one's children brought up as little Nazis. It was an impossibly Pyrrhic decision.

Perhaps the most remarkable aspect of the whole venture was that only three weeks elapsed between the invitation arriving and the enormously extensive and complex arrangements completed for 105 children to board a ship bound for Canada. John has already told the story of that voyage[2], and the ensuing years of exile, but I cannot resist the urge to repeat some of them here. Describing the transatlantic crossing he wrote:

---

2       Safe Keeping – Voices from a vanished world. 2019.

"It is dusk before I can escape my mother's vigilance. Warily I creep towards the foredeck, anxious that no one sees me, for this is forbidden territory. Carefully I reach under the rail and lower my baited line over the ship's side, never doubting that the morning will bring a noble catch.

Early next day, before anyone else is awake, I dress quickly and slip out of the cabin. The ship seems deserted—only the dull throbbing of the engines follow me as I move cautiously, level by level upwards. I am soon on deck, fighting a chill ocean wind. The ever-shifting grey-green Atlantic swell, dotted with lines of foam, vanishes into the light mist that surrounds us. Nobody sees me as I move towards the *Antonia's* bow—and nobody would have known what had happened if I were to disappear overboard.

My line is still where I had left it the previous evening, firmly tied to a convenient stanchion. I start to pull it in, but something is holding it back—I must have caught something huge. Curious, I peer over the rail. However, the ship's side curves back sharply beneath me and the waterline remains hidden.

A cold fear still knots my stomach, and chills run down my spine each time I re-live the scene. The image refuses to fade. A small boy is on the outside of the ship's port-side rail, hanging on by his left hand. Facing aft, he leans out as far as possible above the cold, swirling waters, straining for a better view.

I discover in dismay that my line no longer reaches the water, that no great fish is holding it taut. Impossibly tangled and knotted, it now clings firmly to the ship's side, snagged on some protruding piece of metal. Disappointed, I realise that fishing is a lost cause. The details of that mid-ocean expedition will remain a secret for over forty years— my mother forever spared the worst of it."

## Discursus Five
# Dear Vera – Dear Gacie

Of his wartime sojourn in Connecticut John would recount many tales. It was a rich and generally happy experience, recently made more immediate and vivid by a remarkable discovery. Following his father's death, shortly before his hundredth birthday, many family papers and heirlooms had been shipped to France, and now lay in confusion amid the debris of unfinished renovation work in the recently purchased ancient tithe barn in Saint Pierre-de-Maillé.

"I was rummaging aimlessly though half-emptied boxes, periodically transported in my imagination back to my childhood home, when I came across an old plastic shopping bag that bore the insignia of a well-known Oxford supermarket. Unpretentious and almost overlooked, it proved to contain a priceless treasure, a magic window into my childhood more graphic, more powerful than anything I could possibly have imagined.

Lovingly preserved by my mother, but long lost in storage after her death, were her own personal mementos of my distracted childhood, now brought to light after remaining hidden for sixty years and more. Letters and pictures, programs and cuttings lay in confusion. I discovered, for example, that in September 1938, at the age of three, I had played the dual roles of 'Dream Elf and Page' in a dramatic production written and produced by my elder sister Jean and her cousin Daphne. Here was the evidence—a handwritten program for an "Entertainment to be performed at 3:30 pm."

At first I looked no further than the collection of early school reports—reports that reflected painfully little academic merit, but indicated that at least I was gradually participating better in class activities. Nor was I really surprised to learn that at an earlier age, during my first nursery school Band Class, I had "conducted beautifully," sang London's Burning ("on and on"!), and played my tambourine "with far more vigour than was necessary"!

However, closer inspection was to reveal something of far greater interest and significance. Jumbled together in disorder, like Tutankamun's treasure, lay a confusion of letters—the complete correspondence, it transpired, that had passed between my mother in England and Grace Bacon, my foster mother in Connecticut. As I rummaged, I would occasionally discover letters that I myself had written—or more accurately that I had dictated, taken down on the typewriter at high speed by Grace Bacon as I galloped on. The improbable circumstances under which the two halves of this correspondence would come to be miraculously united and preserved in one place remains a mystery.

As I dipped casually into the pile, picking up pages at random, I frequently found myself unable to continue reading for the tears that kept welling up unbidden. It became so profound and emotional an experience, peering into the forgotten corners of my past, that I soon found myself quite unable to continue. Quietly I returned the letters to their resting place, but knowledge of their existence continued to haunt me."

Prompted by the discovery of these wartime letters, which in time he came to prepare for publication under the title 'Safe Keeping – Voices from a Vanished World', John found himself drawn ever more back into his childhood, re-living many events that had remained deeply buried beneath the accumulating silt of later adventures and mishaps. Amid these echoes from the distant past, I recall several worthy of repetition.

On first arriving in America in mid-July, 1940 the family had been invited by their hostess, Susan Keith, to spend the rest of the summer with her at her vacation home overlooking Squam Lake in New Hampshire. Some thirty years later, when John had returned to America with his own young family, aged Susan Keith invited them back to Pine Ledge again, although she herself was no longer living there. Arriving long after dark, John soon found a pair of large stone gateposts that he had been reminded marked the driveway. The front door was unlocked, but no lights were on. The house seemed strangely unfamiliar and did not in the least resembled his memory of it, but long years had passed, it was dark and he was tired. After putting the children to bed he started to explore. There were many books in the house, but none bore the names of either Keith or Bacon, and gradually the suspicion grew that this might not, in fact, be Pine Ledge after all.

"It was midnight before I set off through the trees with a small flashlight. Up the road some distance, I soon discovered another pair of stone gateposts. Surreptitiously

I crept along the drive, fearful of being identified as an intruder. The house was in darkness, but something distantly familiar about its silhouette in the moonlight tempted me to try the front door. It too was unlocked. Suddenly, in the feeble beam of the flashlight, past and present fused. I was back!"

With considerable anxiety he returned to the sleeping family. Scenes of Goldilocks, and of the three bears returning to their rumpled beds, flashed before him as the children were bundled, half asleep, into the car. The covers were quickly smoothed to conceal their presence and, fearful lest they meet the rightful owners in the driveway, the family hastily withdrew with only sidelights showing.

As dawn broke the next morning, there was Squam Lake, just as he had remembered it, spread out before them, the magic in no way diluted by the passage of thirty years. He says he often wondered whether the neighbours ever noticed the brief intrusion and puzzled over the identity of their mysterious nocturnal visitors.

# Discursus Six
## Nakal

Over dinner one evening John admitted that like many small boys, he would often find himself in trouble—more by accident rather than design—for he was, he said, what in Indonesian is called *nakal*—endearingly wicked.

"There was one occasion was when I feared—nay was certain—that I had inadvertently killed somebody. The journey home from school each day involved a walk from the bus stop of about a mile. The route followed a tree-lined country road before branching off across wasteland, where I had found my first praying mantis.

I had been to the circus a short while before and was very impressed by the man who threw knives and tomahawks at an attractive, under-dressed young lady without hitting her. I was not much interested in the young lady, but desperately wanted to master the art of throwing a knife with great accuracy.

The trees along the roadside provided admirable targets as I walked home after school, and I was quite pleased with my progress. On most attempts my knife embedded itself blade-foremost in the chosen tree, and week-by-week my confidence grew. One day the appearance of a car in the distance prompted me to wonder about the parameters involved for hitting a moving target—a purely academic exercise, let me emphasise. Fully intending to hit the nearest tree, I carefully judged the speed of the car and decided that if I wished to hit it, I would throw the knife...now! My calculation proved to be disastrously accurate. Unconsciously compensating for the car's speed, I completely missed the target tree, however, and was horrified to see my knife pass through the car's open rear window. I also caught a glimpse of someone sitting in the back seat.

In an instant there was a squeal of tires as the car skidded to an abrupt halt. Even before it stopped moving, I had turned to flee. I was not far from a new, partially-completed freeway—the Wilbur Cross Parkway—beneath which ran a network of drains and tunnels. The closest opening was in part of the system I had not explored, and in my panic I soon became disoriented underground. When I eventually found a way out, it was on the wrong side of a sizable pond—actually a river—quite some distance from home. Anxious for sanctuary, I decided to swim across as dusk fell, and had then to creep back to the house, cold and dripping wet, by a circuitous route through the woods to avoid being seen. That evening, having changed un-noticed into dry clothes, I listened with particular attention to the radio, expecting at any moment to hear reports of the unprovoked attack—and possible death—of an innocent passing motorist or his passenger. Wracked by guilt and overcome with anxiety, I passed a desperate week until it became clear that the police were not out in force looking for me. I never did become particularly skilled at knife-throwing and have always resented the loss of my prize throwing knife after that."

This episode was not, John assured me, the first time that an innocent mistake had had unfortunate repercussions. It was in First Grade at the Foote School in New Haven that his reputation was irredeemably blackened. He had only recently joined the school, a shy, somewhat timid little boy. In the playground one day he discovered a large stone—or was it half a brick? Knowing it shouldn't be there, he promptly disposed of it over the fence and out of harm's way. Sadly there was a little girl playing out of sight below on the other side, and she protested very loudly when hit on the head. It was not, he assured me, a serious wound, but it did require stitches. From that moment on he was dubbed "that horrid little evacuee."

His reputation, at least among the teachers, took another blow a year or two later when he was discovered up a tree in the playground raining lighted matches onto the ground below. It was, in fact, a lifelike re-enactment of the London blitz for the benefit of his assembled classmates. The teacher overseeing recess that day, with a singular lack of understanding, belligerently demanded that he come down immediately to face unspecified retribution. Fearful of what this might involve, John had climbed a bit higher into the tree, whence the infuriated teacher attempted to follow. Little boys weigh less than teachers and can climb in safety to slender upper branches. To the unrestrained delight of the onlookers the furious teacher ventured too far into the canopy and fell painfully and with total lack of dignity onto the playground beneath when a branch snapped under his weight. It was fortunate that the head mistress, Win Sturley, understood the motivation, and being a better psychologist than her member of staff, exacted no punishment other than a stern warning not to repeat the offence.

# SUBLIME LUNACY

## Discursus Seven
# Divine Intervention

John was reminiscing about his return journey to England shortly before the D-Day invasion in the spring of 1944. Anticipation of this voyage had precipitated an acute crisis that was manifested in serious behavioural problems at school. These were eventually traced to a deep fear of being torpedoed again. The prospect of travelling on a fully operational warship eventually quieted these anxieties.

"I was one of about twenty small boys travelling on a Royal Navy aircraft carrier from New York to the Clydeside port of Greenock. We had been placed in the care of a young officer, who clearly had no understanding of children and how to handle them. With earnest solemnity we were instructed exactly what, and what not, we would be permitted to do; where, and where not, we might go on board. It was made abundantly clear that any transgression would be met with dire retribution.

To a mischievous nine-year-old this was a challenge too good to pass up. There were lamentably few parts of the ship to which we might legitimately go—naturally they were the least interesting. Over the course of the voyage there would be very few compartments on that carrier with which I did not become intimately familiar. In retrospect, it proved excellent training for a later incarnation, when I became a pilot in the Fleet Air Arm during my two years of National Service.

The engine room, where I was made welcome by

the stokers and other denizens of the ship's nether world, was naturally a prime destination. To someone already fascinated by mechanical devices, it became a source of endless pleasure and delight. I also found a warm, embracing nest in the thick asbestos insulation covering the boilers.

The greatest prize, however, was to gain access to the hanger deck, an area from which we were quite specifically banned. Terrible punishments were threatened to those who ignored the ban, but the beatings I received never outweighed the delights to be found there—except once!

I had gained entry to a Grumman Avenger on the hangar deck, and after spending some time in the cockpit, made my way up into the machine gun blister above. Once inside, a small metal flap could be pulled up to form a floor. After about twenty minutes of shooting down imaginary German aircraft it was time to leave. However, I was quite unable to find the catch that would release the metal flap beneath me. Try as I might, there was no escape, and so I remained trapped, in mounting apprehension.

After what seemed an eternity, the hangar deck suddenly sprang to life. To my horror I could see planes being rolled onto the elevator and taken up to the flight deck. This was not a possible consequence of my disobedience that had ever crossed my mind, and was beyond all imagination. In due course, my plane too was lifted into the daylight, without anybody noticing my presence. Only when the rightful occupant tried to enter, in preparation for the sortie about to take off, was one very frightened little boy discovered.

The punishment that this episode attracted is one of the few beatings, out of a very considerable total, of which I have specific recollection, for the pain endured for several days in the form of extensive bruising. But there then followed the most wonderful Divine Intervention.

The mess deck where we ate had long tables running athwart ship. The sea was calm and the wooden partitions that divided up the tables in rough weather were not in use. The officer responsible for my discomfort was seated at the head of the table, and I was required to be seated painfully close to him on his right side. Suddenly, without warning, the ship made a violent change of course, heeling over sharply to port. In disbelief I watched as the entire contents of the table started to move, gathering speed as plates, glasses, cutlery and water pitchers swept down to engulf my nemesis. As food and table settings poured into his lap, he overbalanced backwards, to vanish beneath a mountain of wet, gooey spaghetti and other debris. In that moment I knew that there was a God—and that she was on my side."

The crossing had taken almost three weeks when they finally disembarked in Greenock. By the time they boarded the packed train to London, night had fallen, and as there were no vacant seats, the boys were forced to stand in the corridor. John's only memory of that long nocturnal journey was of being surrounded by friendly soldiers and sailors, who plied him constantly with cigarettes, asking all the time about life in America. He is in no doubt that he obliged with a suitably embellished fantasy.

The long letter from Gacie, his foster mother, detailing for his mother the normal routines of his life in America, by some happy stroke of fate would not arrive in Oxford until several weeks had passed. He took full advantage of this opening so happily offered. After arriving home he was put into the bath and thoroughly scrubbed to remove the ingrained dirt of the journey—and the strong smell of tobacco. Clean, nay polished, he was left in the nursery while his mother went to the kitchen to get supper. When she returned, he was neatly clad in pyjamas and dressing gown, riding on the rocking horse—and smoking the cigarette that he swore he always had before retiring.

> "My mother was placed in a very difficult situation. Much as she had to exercise some restraint and discipline, she was also very conscious of the need to humour me through this difficult transition, where so much was new and strange. By being too strict, she might risk alienating my affection. Without the knowledge of my normal routine in America, she was prey to my wildest flights of fancy, at a time when I had but limited regard for the truth."

## Discursus Eight
## **Square Peg**

The conversation over dinner would sometimes turn to differences between the English, French and American school systems, and not infrequently John would feel prompted to expand upon the difficulties that he himself had experienced in trying to settle back into Oxford at war's end.

The England to which he returned was suffering privation and hardship after the long, tumultuous years of war. It was not hard, he said, to adapt to shortages and rationing, to the lack of fuel for heating and travel. What was hard, however, was the sudden immersion in an alien educational system, dominated by the study of a dead language of which he had no prior knowledge, and of mysterious sports, whose rules and ethos remained—and indeed were destined to remain so permanently—utterly beyond comprehension.

The Dragon School in Oxford was no ordinary educational establishment. With some 400 boys and 20 girls, it was acknowledged to be a tough environment for newcomers, but with an academic record second to none. On his first morning he sat through two consecutive Latin lessons. It is hard to describe, he said, the feeling of utter helplessness. He had, after all, never heard of Latin—had no notion, he said, of what a latin might be—and indeed, the whole concept of foreign languages was alien having barely heard anything but English spoken. Everybody else in the class had been doing Latin for at least two years, possessed a sizable vocabulary and understood the basic concepts of Latin grammar.

"You would not believe how alienated and miserable I felt. Latin would continue to haunt me to the end of my school career. In those days admission to Oxford required a working knowledge of one ancient as well as one modern language—in my case Latin and French. The fact that I passed Latin Responsions, and was hence able to enter Oxford, was a tribute to the teaching skills of a certain elderly Mr Goldie, to whom I was sent by my anxious parents for special tuition. The examination itself was made no easier by the girl sitting in front of me, who on looking at the paper, burst into tears, and continued sobbing piteously for the next two hours until the exam was over.

Mr Goldie had been an undergraduate at Christ Church around 1890, and was the archetypal don. In retirement he lived in a flat in Wellington Square that was lined from floor to ceiling with stacks of books on seemingly every subject. On one occasion the conversation drifted to Ancient Egypt, a subject in which I had at one time immersed myself as a child. I may have mentioned to Mr Goldie that when confined to bed with some childhood ailment I had set my poor father an examination on hieroglyphics—a subject of which he was wholly ignorant.

It took only a moment before Mr Goldie, searching the packed shelves, had located a large tome filled with hieroglyphics. Quite casually he took it down— and began translating unseen from the Egyptian Book of the Dead. Of course, I was unable to check how accurate his translation was, but it sounded good to me.

But this was not his only achievement. He would, he told me, take regular walks in the University Parks—as I myself had done since childhood. He brought out shoeboxes filled with clay pipes—beautiful, long stemmed XVIIth and XVIIIth Century pipes that he had casually collected while on his walks. Needless to say, I have never seen the trace of even a single clay pipe on my perambulations there.

One day he opened the door to me in a state of some excitement. Wellington Square has in its centre a garden area for residents. That very morning, while taking a short stroll, he had spotted a beautiful dish half buried in a flowerbed behind a pillar-box. It proved to be a museum-quality Anglo-Saxon piece. What it is to have a keen eye and a prepared mind!"

Assimilation into the rarefied atmosphere of the Dragon School was unquestionably difficult, but John has no problem in admitting that in retrospect, every trauma experienced was in a good cause, and bore rich fruit. There were several boys who had returned from America at the same time, and it was inevitable that they should band together, for all must have suffered, to a greater or lesser degree, the same problems of integration.

Naturally shy, he hated to be the centre of attention. Yet it was inevitable that he be conspicuous. Tall for his age, gangling, ignorant of Latin, of sports, of the school traditions, he was a very square peg in a finely engineered round hole. To all this was added the fact that he spoke in a strange Yankee tongue riddled with words and expressions that nobody understood, and that he wore outrageous clothes—plaid lumberjack shirts and dungarees, while everyone else was in utilitarian blue mechanic's overalls—and his hair sported not only an American crew-cut, but in a moment of excessive patriotism he had shaved in a V-for-victory that resulted in an early Mohican crest. Children can be unbelievably cruel to one another, and he found himself the butt of many jokes.

It was not until the exceptionally harsh winter of 1946-47 that his American background was to prove truly advantageous. With ice and snow lying everywhere, the unheated classrooms became ever less habitable. Accepting the principle of making lemonade when engulfed by lemons, the school abandoned conventional teaching and devoted itself to outdoor activities better suited to the winter conditions. Each night the teaching staff would work long hours to create skating rinks on the lawns and playing fields. The snow would first be rolled flat, and enclosed within a shallow rim. Newspapers were then carefully spread out flat and repeatedly sprayed with water. Gradually a substantial layer of smooth ice was build up, and on arrival in the morning the boys would be urged to skate. It remains a mystery how the school mustered so many pairs of skates in the post-war austerity, but John had his own highly prized American hockey skates.

Raised in a cold New England with a pond next to the house, skating had become his second nature. Here at last was a sport in which he possessed skills far superior to most, and so for days on end he played endless ice hockey. Having thus attained status in this highly sporting and competitive environment, he found himself finally accepted and able to participate to the full, enjoying school for the first time ever. No longer victimised and picked on, his schoolwork miraculously improved.

Compared with most English prep schools, the Dragon was exceptionally laid back. Masters were universally addressed, and referred to, by their nicknames, and did not enjoy undue respect. John's father never recovered from hearing him say to a master "Don't be so silly, sir!" Nevertheless, there was a code of discipline that demanded adherence. Mostly a matter of common sense, transgression would invite almost certain retribution, which in serious cases would result in physical punishment. A congenital rebel, John was frequently punished, but rarely unfairly. Beatings, he observed, teach self-control, "for tears would have been an admission of defeat". And besides, the pain was only transitory and soon forgotten—until the next time.

The school enjoyed extensive river frontage along the Cherwell, a tributary of the Isis, the local Oxford name for the Thames. A good swimmer, he was allowed down to the river's edge unsupervised. Those who had not demonstrated an ability to swim across the river and back fully clothed were, most prudently, not permitted within fifty feet of the water without a master present.

One evening, long after school, he was found alone standing on a diving board high above the water holding the long Dinka fishing spear his aunt Dorothy had brought back from one of her African journeys. He knew perfectly well that at that hour the river was out of bounds, so he claims he held no resentment when Francis Wyllie administered a firm rebuke, strongly reinforced with a gym shoe, on the place provided by nature.

Not all misdeeds brought retribution, and some were even handled with sympathetic tact and understanding. John's eldest foster brother Tom, who had been drafted into the American army, was one of the very few survivors of the Malmedy massacre. Here, on Belgium's border with France during the 'Battle of the Bulge', a group of eighty-four unarmed American prisoners-of-war were taken into a snow-covered field and executed on December 17, 1944 by soldiers of the 1st. SS Panzer Division. After surviving extreme hardship, including immersion for hours in a freezing water-filled ditch, Tom was re-captured and force-marched to a POW camp, losing toes to frostbite along the way. For months nobody had heard anything of him, and there was a growing suspicion that he might even be dead.

One day a phone call was received from a US military hospital in Cirencester, a Cotswold town not far from Oxford. Tom, it transpired, had been rescued from a German prison camp, and flown to England. It was, of course, still wartime, and with petrol severely rationed, travel was difficult. Being a doctor, John's father was able to keep his car on the road, and by stretching the rules a little, felt able to drive the family to see Tom. He was barely recognisable. Emaciated, frost bitten and stricken with tuberculosis, he nonetheless made rapid progress in hospital, and in a few weeks time was allowed to come and convalesce with the family in Oxford. As a gift, he brought John a wonderful souvenir—a large SS dagger emblazoned with a swastika.

Thrilled with his new acquisition, John could not resist taking it to school, where it received the anticipated envy of all the boys who saw it. All was well until he rather ostentatiously unsheathed the 12-inch blade and used it to sharpen his pencil. Firmly, but without rancour, the dagger as removed until the end of the day. The school, recognising the source and emotional significance of the gift, took no retaliatory action. It was returned intact—but with a strict injunction against it ever being brought to school again.

Long after he had left the Dragon, John's sister Jane joined the exclusive band of Dragon girls—daughters of staff members and sisters of old Dragons. Few concessions were made to the fair sex, and Jane took up boxing along with the boys. She also played rugger, another rather un-ladylike pastime. It was on the rugger field that she suffered her ultimate indignity—being tied by the opposing team to her own goal posts by her long red pigtails.

The Dragon staff was a strange lot, composed largely of men unsuited by age or infirmity for military service. Many had fought in WW1 and carried the scars, both mental and physical. 'Fuzz' Francis had lost half his face in a wartime injury, and he provided a valuable lesson in learning to see past disability to the person within.

A generally beneficent teacher, Nikko' was a disciplinarian of the old school, who had little tolerance for deliberate flaunting of the relatively liberal school rules. He was known to be someone who should not be crossed. Those who incurred his displeasure paid dearly for their misdeeds. Each master had his preferred weapon when it came to administering a beating—a regular occurrence that rarely provoked any comment. In the case of Nikko, his weapon was particularly evil (or efficacious, depending on one's viewpoint). It was the ramrod of an old muzzle-loading rifle. Thin and extremely flexible, it carried a silver tip that would wrap firmly around the malefactor's bottom, adding a painful bruise on the hip in addition to the transverse welts. One soon learned not to misbehave in Nikko's presence.

'Tubby' Haig had apparently received a head injury that made him prone to apoplectic temper tantrums. It did not take much to precipitate a "bate", as it was called, and it was always a worthwhile entertainment in class. The trick was to arouse Tubby's ire, and then misdirect his rage onto some poor blameless boy sitting near the front of the class. In purple-faced fury, veins bulging, Tubby would grab the victim by his hair and pound his head violently against the desk. Today such behaviour would undoubtedly result in a court case, if not a government enquiry, but at the time it was just considered an innocent diversion from algebra.

## Discursus Nine
## **Radio Control**

The Dragon master who was to have the greatest, most lasting impact on John was neither old nor infirm. Gerd Sommerhoff was of mixed Dutch and Austrian parentage. He had come to Oxford just before the war to write a book, but because of his ancestry found himself interned as an enemy alien before it could be finished. Returning to Oxford following his release towards war's end, he took a supposedly temporary job teaching science at the Dragon while finishing his book 'Analytical Biology'. He proved to be a brilliant and inspiring teacher. Later, after teaching how to teach science for many years, he ended his career in Cambridge seeking a mathematical and logical understanding of living systems.

His first act at the Dragon was to create an informal, out-of-hours 'Science Club' in which members embarked on a series of practical experiments in a chosen field, which when completed would merit the award of a 'star'. Competition to acquire stars was intense as members worked their way through increasingly complex and revealing courses. Starting with simple cat's-whisker crystal sets, they gradually acquired sufficient practical knowledge of electronics to build radios containing several valves.

Then came the very first transistors. Gerd managed to acquire a few of these strange new devices and together club members set out to discover their uses. They had to abandon all that had been learned about the familiar voltage-controlled circuits of the old-fashioned valves, and master the totally new and strange principles of current-regulated circuits to work with the mysterious transistors.

A major benefit of transistorised circuits was their small size, which enabled the building of more complex radio-control systems for the model aircraft they constructed. Specifically, it allowed graduated control of flaps, ailerons and rudder. Under Gerd's instruction the club built a plane with an eight-foot wingspan that he had designed. Taking it for its maiden flight to the barren expanse of Port Meadow, it performed perfectly—until it perversely broke free of its wirelessed instructions and vanished over the distant forested slopes of Wytham Woods. It would be several weeks before the wreckage was finally located and the engine and electronics successfully recovered.

Having worked his way through a long series of chemical and physical experiments, thereby amassing a significant number of stars, John says he became the first boy to tackle the microscopy course. A major part of this was learning to fix, section, mount and stain samples of biological tissue. He chose to serial section an entire earthworm, having previously having had the pleasure of dissecting one. It was a daunting undertaking that occupied several weeks, but in the end he possessed a fine set of microscope slides that would later become part of the undergraduate invertebrate practical course he was to teach at Oxford years later.

"Gerd provided a most wonderful foundation in science. Not only did boys acquire, for example, sufficient understanding of atomic theory to carry them through to the 'O-level' examination, if not beyond, but it instilled an instinctive appreciation of the majesty of nature, and taught the importance of logical reasoning and the 'scientific method'."

John's membership of the Science Club had initially been delayed for the best part of a term because, he said, his father, with a lamentable regard for the truth, had listed on the application form that among his interests was "Chemistry – particularly explosions". While undeniably true, it represented only part of his scientific horizon.

As an eight -year-old in Connecticut one of John's favourite pastimes was his chemistry set. The chemicals supplied were all supremely safe and frustratingly devoid of any pyrotechnical potential. However, once back in Oxford this defect was successfully addressed through developing friendships with local pharmacists. The pitiful fireworks available at war's end to celebrate Guy Fawkes Night were soon supplemented, to the amazement and admiration of friends and neighbours.

"Gerd died in 2002 at Trinity College, Cambridge, where he was an acclaimed pioneer in the arcane world of theoretical neuroscience. When an article on science teaching at the Dragon appeared without any mention of Gerd, I was told, on enquiry, that the school had forbidden mention of his name, because long after his death, he had been mentioned in an alleged school sex scandal. Regardless of possible wrongdoing, and in the absence of any proof, I shall continue to honor his memory as a remarkable and outstanding teacher.'

SUBLIME LUNACY

## Discursus Ten
# Parson's Pleasure

One day, over a relaxing glass or two of wine, John talked about 'Parson's Pleasure', a now-defunct men-only nude bathing area in a fenced-off section of the River Cherwell as it passed through the University Parks. Women were required to disembark ands walk round, but on occasion a punt would pass through still bearing female passengers—usually visible only as beady eyes peering out from beneath a pile of cushions. Once the intruders were spotted, the bathers would either dive into the water, roll over, or cover themselves with a towel. On a day that has passed into university folklore, one elderly don simply wrapped his towel around his head, remarking later when questioned: "In Oxford, I am known by my face".

This reference to Parson's Pleasure was a prelude to further anecdotes related to a scientific childhood, for on his return from bathing he would pass the university's Department of Inorganic Chemistry in South Parks Road. Here he would make regular stops, developing useful friendships with a changing galaxy of graduate students. Time and time again he would be given pieces of laboratory equipment through the open ground-floor window to be taken home concealed in his bicycle basket.

Obtaining chemical reagents was often, he said, a major bottleneck. Some could be begged from his graduate student friends, but others came from the local pharmacist, Cousins Thomas in the Banbury Road, where he would sometimes help to fill prescriptions—doubtless permitted out of deference to his father, despite his tender age.

From time to time, also around twelve years old, he would volunteer to help in the pharmacy at the Radcliffe Infirmary, the local hospital. In those long-gone days he would be given barbiturates and amphetamines whenever he asked for them, together with bottles of caffeine citrate, which he claimed, provided a lift without the trouble of brewing coffee. Such drugs caused few raised eyebrows and were treated quite casually. There was an occasion when three separate schools in Oxford called John's parents during the morning, each suggesting that their child should be collected and taken home as he or she was persistently falling asleep in class. It turned out that his mother had carelessly confused the saccharine tablets, used in the days of sugar rationing as a sweetener, with her phenobarbitone sleeping tablets. Both were small and white, but possessed of very different properties.

For a doctor's house, John felt there were very few conventional household medications—even an aspirin could sometimes be hard to find. On the other hand there was always a supply of ether, used mainly to remove the sticky residues of adhesive dressings. At a time when fireworks were still unobtainable after the war, his ether bombs were always a huge success. These were made by filling metal cartridge cases, particularly 20mm cannon shells, with ether and firmly sealing them with a tight rubber or cork bung. Placed above a small flame, they would suddenly explode with a gratifying roar as a column of flame shot ten feet or more into the air.

For the most part his chemical experiments passed off with surprisingly few mishaps. Even his most monster explosion, although it caused some anxiety, brought no retribution. Buried in a flowerbed in the back garden, it was detonated from behind a low earth bank one evening when his parents were out. Fortunately he was wearing a steel helmet as he lay face down on the grass. The force of the explosion was substantially greater than anticipated—the new formulation was an unqualified success.

The tremendous roar was followed by the distant sound of broken glass from many directions. The only house in the neighbourhood whose lights did not immediately go on was his own. Looking at the crater—three feet across at least, and over a foot deep—he realized the power he had unleashed. Feverishly he filled in the hole to restore the flowerbed to its original pristine condition and crept back to his room and quickly into bed. For an hour or more he lay there in the dark, waiting for a knock at the door as the police came calling. Remarkably not one window in his house was damaged, and he was never questioned. However, he did not tempt fate again with a repeat performance.

The chemical mishap that put a sudden end to his experiments was wholly accidental and almost ended in tragedy. His father had a patient come to see him who was already in a very poor state of health. Instead of being shown into the dining room, which normally served as a waiting room, the patient was ushered into the drawing room to recline on a sofa instead of upright chairs. John's laboratory was in the cellars beneath the drawing room, to which it was connected by a space designed to accommodate heavy wooden counterbalanced sliding shutters.

A new, and hitherto untested, pyrotechnic mixture had been left uncovered on the workbench. An hour or two later, it suddenly ignited spontaneously, filling the room with dense, acrid smoke. This soon filtered up and into the drawing room, where the already feeble patient was found semi-comatose, struggling for breath. The episode was deeply regretted, but his father was adamant—no more chemical experimenting.

> "To this day I still wonder what caused the mixture to ignite, but as the list of ingredients sitting next to the beaker was destroyed in the fire—fortunately not a big one—I have been unable to re-create the conditions in which the fire started."

Spontaneous ignition, however, was not an unfamiliar phenomenon. Through the Dragon School science club he had learned the wonderful properties of a mixture of finely divided aluminium powder and iodine crystals. Left uncovered, the mixture would gradually absorb atmospheric moisture. At a certain moment, determined by the humidity, the mixture would suddenly ignite, giving off clouds of beautiful deep purple iodine vapour. Small quantities of the mixture could be left in inconspicuous locations about the school, later causing much entertainment. Likewise nitrogen tri-iodide was a favourite substance to scatter about. Once dry, it would detonate with considerable force, to the accompaniment of little purple clouds of iodine vapour, when walked on. Who can be surprised that small boys dream of becoming chemists?

## Discursus Eleven
# Organ Donors

J ohn would often remark, both with gratitude and surprise, on the lack of parental restrictions he enjoyed in childhood. As we sat together drinking chilled vin rosé by the river one day he began:

"Looking back, I am quite surprised by the degree of freedom we were allowed. No one questioned our going down to the railway tracks, whether to collect engine numbers or flatten pennies under the wheels of passing trains. No one advised us against riding alone along the canal towpath, although, even then, there was some risk from the strange characters that one encountered there. It became an area with which I would be very familiar for it adjoined the great open expanse of Port Meadow, a marvellous place to ride, and over which I would frequently gallop on horseback at full speed.

I was never a collector of engine numbers, for it seemed to me a very silly pastime—although it had its uses. Sometimes I would join a group of keen train spotters and go up to London. Here we would travel the underground to visit as many main-line train stations as possible in the hope of seeing some special locomotive like the Flying Scotsman. In reporting our adventures afterwards we never mentioned the shifty-eyed men who would occasionally attempt, with bribes and considerable insistence, to lure us away from our friends.

Later, as a young teenager I would make regular journeys to London. Here on Thursday evenings I would listen entranced to my trumpeter idol, Humphrey Lyttleton at his Jazz Club in the cellars beneath 100 Oxford Street, forever regretting my inability to play like he did. Again, my parents never placed barriers in my way, although they must have had some inkling of the dangers that lurked in the darker alleyways of Soho and London's West End.

My collector's instinct was not blunted, but simply diverted into areas I found more interesting than engine numbers. When I was about twelve years old I had my appendix removed. The offending organ was presented to me in a bottle, which resided on my bedside table until I left hospital. This strange little anatomical specimen, however, resonated with my curiosity, and I set about seeking other organs. My father had an old friend at the Radcliffe Infirmary, Alistair Robb-Smith, who was a pathologist, and through him I built up a representative collection of major human organs, while Dr Antoinette Pirie, a senior figure in the Eye Hospital not only donated specimens from her department, but helped me to understand the structure of the eye by providing large cow's eyes for me to dissect under her tutelage.

Not surprisingly I was intensely curious about all aspects of medicine, and it was assumed that I would eventually follow my father into practice, although ultimately I would find myself more interested in the insect vectors of disease than the well-being of patients. I remember vividly the day my father had a patient with Bilharzia a rare condition in Oxford before the days of universal air travel. With great excitement I was invited to view the offending schistosome parasite found in the last, bloody drops of urine.

It was reported that when about ten years old, I was found instructing the professor of obstetrics, who had come to dinner, in the finer details of childbirth, having recently read A 'Manual of Midwifery' from my father's library."

The imminent arrival of his daughter in France prompted John to recall her previous visit, when he had been persuaded to join her on a 15-kilometre ride through the countryside on horseback. Forgetting how many years it had been since he last rode, it had been a somewhat painful experience as unfamiliar muscles were unexpectedly summoned into service.

"I was forced to acknowledge that I was no longer as young and indestructible as I once had been. Riding with my father was one of my early pre-war memories, and later, by the age of eight, it had become a passion.

My foster parents had arranged for me to spend a few happy weeks at Fenimore Camp, set in Mohican and Deerslayer country overlooking Lake Otsego near Cooperstown in upstate New York. Here I learned how to shoot, to camp and canoe. Reluctant to take my feet off the bottom, I was slow to swim—until one of the counsellors deliberately threw me in where the water was too deep, since when swimming has become second nature. Under the stern eye of Colonel Koritsky, a Polish Cavalry officer, I became a passable rider, and not unknowledgeable about the care of horses. I was heartbroken when the colonel suddenly died after choking on a chicken bone at dinner one day.

After my return to Oxford I discovered a riding school close to the house, and after demonstrating my abilities, I was allowed complete freedom to ride alone. Port Meadow, a huge expanse of common land beside the river, was my favourite spot, and here I could gallop unrestrained—and endure some spectacular falls.

It was a moment of acute embarrassment, not to say anxiety, when returning to the stable one day my horse bolted as I was about to exchange bridle for halter. She galloped out onto the Woodstock Road, a major North

Oxford thoroughfare, and then proceeded to explore the gardens of several large Victorian houses, leaving a trail of destruction through flower beds and vegetable patches, before being recaptured with the help of passers-by."

"My daughter, like so many girls in England, was a keen rider from an early age. Next to Dove House, our home in the village of Church Hanborough, we had a couple of loose-boxes, so when she was offered an injured horse to care for, there was no hesitation. Having been hit by a car, the horse was destined for the knacker, but under Kate's care, made an unexpected recovery. Rising at 4:30 each morning, she would muck out the stable and groom the horse before heading for school, so initiating the course she was to follow in later years. One day, while driving through the countryside, I caught sight in the distance of a horse at full gallop, soaring over hedges and fences, the rider's long blond hair streaming out behind. Drawing closer, I recognised with no little horror that it was Kate. I had no idea that she had become such an accomplished rider. Small wonder then that in time she would find herself working for Garfield Weston, the Canadian philanthropist and caring for his polo ponies, on which incidentally, Prince Charles played."

She has continued her love of horses into middle age, and regularly serves as a fence judge at 3-day events.

## Discursus Twelve
# Respect

It is usually after a good meal that John's reminiscences of times past resurface. We were enjoying our postprandial port one day, when his mind returned once again to memories of his childhood.

"In retrospect, we children were raised in an extremely nurturing environment, in which our views and opinions were sought—and listened to. In many ways we were treated as equals, and never spoken down to or addressed condescendingly. Conversely, we were expected to behave in a responsible, adult manner. For whatever reason— idleness, emotional stress or sheer perversity—my school work was far below the standard expected. This was brought home to me forcefully whenever school reports arrived—sometimes as frequently as every fortnight. The dreaded envelope would appear on the breakfast table with the morning post, and inevitably would be followed by a summons to my father's study. It was clear that his pain was as great as mine, and I was overcome with guilt. Time and again I would promise to do better, and time and again I would apparently fail. The resulting mantra, which I heard on many occasions, would run: "Do you really wish to spend the rest of your life as a shop assistant?" In time the full horror of this oft-repeated spell sank in and had the desired effect, but it was a long time coming. The turning point did not occur until well into my public school career at Shrewsbury, when a few words of genuine praise for a well-written essay were to transform my work. I shall never forget the thrill that ran through me when I received back my comparison of the poetry of Pope and Dryden. I had worked hard, and with great enjoyment on the project. Written large across the top of the page, in Jasper Knight's delightfully idiosyncratic style were the words: "Alpha plus plus – right excellent good, i'faith!" From that moment on I began to write with confidence and pleasure, and the resulting improvement quickly spread to other subjects."

John's parents were the first to acknowledge that although widely read and generally well-informed, they were far from infallible. So it was that whenever during a meal that a question was asked to which the answer was unclear, the appropriate works of reference would be brought to the table. It was rare, said John, for a meal to end without both volumes of the Shorter Oxford English Dictionary, Whitaker's Almanac, E. Chobham Brewer's Dictionary of Phrase and Fable or Fowler's Modern English Usage lying open among the dishes.

The subject of infallibility on at least one occasion led on to that of short-story writing. John is in no doubt that 'Saki' (H.H. Munro) was the most skilled short-story teller in the English language—a point on which he remains absolutely dogmatic. He was first introduced to 'Saki' at school, when Michael Heseltine (later destined to become Deputy Prime Minister in Margaret Thatcher's Conservative government) would read to the other boys in his bedroom. And the link to infallibility? It was "The Lumber Room" in which a small boy declares that there is a frog in his cereal at breakfast one morning. His elders and betters all rebuked him and insisted that there couldn't possibly be a frog in his cereal—but they were incontrovertibly wrong. There was indeed a frog in his cereal—he knew it because he had put it there himself—and the fallibility of grown-ups was well proven.

"English Grammar was a subject with which I long struggled," announced John one day. "The roots of my antithesis lay in Fourth Grade, while in America. I felt (quite wrongly, I should add) that being English, I already knew the language adequately, and needed no further instruction in it. I reacted with unusual stubbornness to the dry, formal teaching of English grammar, and one day responded with a violent and wholly unreasonable outburst of temper. As a result I was suspended from school for several days. The most painful part of the whole episode lay in the irony that the teacher involved was my favourite, and her son was one of my best friends. It was small compensation that this embarrassing interlude, perhaps the darkest cloud to hang over my educational history, had taken place during the winter, allowing me more time to skate—and also more time to contemplate my misdeeds.

I was indeed fortunate that both the school principal, Win Sturley, and my foster mother were compassionate and blessed with understanding. Recognising that there must be some underlying cause for the sudden and marked decline in my school work, of which this outburst was but the climax, they sought the cause. There had recently been discussion of my returning to England as the tide of war was rendering the invasion of Britain ever more remote, and I was adamant that I did not want to go. Gentle probing revealed that I still retained vivid memories of being torpedoed on the journey to America, and that my behaviour was linked to acute, but suppressed, anxiety about the same thing happening again on any subsequent voyage. Once the cause was uncovered and suitable reassurances given, my schoolwork recovered as quickly as it had declined. The turning point came when the opportunity arose at the crucial moment for me to travel back to England on board an operational Royal Navy aircraft carrier, an inducement no small boy would be able to resist

Ironically, the only person able to teach English grammar in a way that seemed to make sense to me was Paul Brodsky, a teacher at the Dragon School, who being Hungarian himself, had learned the subject as a foreign language and so had insights and understandings beyond those of a native English speaker. A similar situation arose years later when, as a graduate student at Oxford I felt it wise to take a course in scientific German. This was given by Nikko Tinbergen, whose Nobel Prize for his researches in Animal Behaviour did not excuse him from teaching mere graduate students. Being Dutch, Nikko had learned German as a foreign tongue, making him a far better teacher than the one I had gone to previously, who undoubtedly spoke good German, but was wholly ignorant of scientific terms in either German or English. It has always struck me that Oxford was squandering its resources by using Nobel laureates to teach peripheral courses to graduate students."

John has always regretted his inability to master foreign languages easily, for it had not escaped his notice that those who were fluent in several tongues were generally intellectually gifted—and also possessed of superior musical abilities. His failure to become fluent in any language apart from his mother tongue did not, however, lessen his curiosity concerning languages. It was the compound German word

Eiablageflussitkeit that first ignited a desire to learn more of this scientifically and philosophically important language. Any nation that could create a special word for the fluid in which a spider's eggs were enveloped as they were being laid, clearly had a culture of more than passing interest. Likewise, the discovery of a Turkish word meaning "to begin to blow from the south-east" hinted a linguistic repository of more than passing interest. In retrospect it probably referred to the start of the khamsin.

> "We stumbled across this improbable, but potentially valuable verb while driving across a rather barren stretch of the Anatolian plateau, and became absorbed in exploring it possible uses. At first it was just a case of reciting its simple grammatical forms—I begin to blow from the south-east, you begin to blow from the south east, he begins to blow from the south-east, etc. etc. Once the conventional past, present and future tenses had been covered in full, it was the turn of the more challenging subjunctives, gerunds and gerundives, when such matters were still retained from schooldays. Quite a few miles of un-noteworthy scenery had passed by before our fund of grammatical minutiae was exhausted."

It was while telling us about some of the improbable words he had encountered that John suddenly recalled his surprise when he found the reflexive swahili verb *kuchamba*, in his dictionary. It apparently means "to scrub one's testicles'!

# SUBLIME LUNACY

## Discursus Thirteen
# Unconformity

The transition from prep school to public school is a major event in the life of any small boy, particularly for those who have never been away from home before. One goes from being a person of significance, perhaps even some importance (if only by dint of seniority) to being a total nobody, the lowest form of animal life. As John observed:

> "Shrewsbury was probably a bit more advanced than some other public schools at that time, but it was still a repository of out-dated Victorian rules and attitudes. The absurd artificiality of the carefully-nurtured environment of exclusivity was revealed by the need for every new boy to learn—and be tested on—the slang vocabulary and traditions peculiar to the school. Boys had, for many years past, given up wearing the ridiculous little caps that had been required while Victoria was on the throne. Nevertheless, as a mark of respect, when ever we passed a master, or wished to speak to him, we were still required to touch the back of our head, whereon had perched the cap worn generations earlier."

Even so, progress had been made. Just a year or so before John arrived at Shrewsbury in 1948, an old tradition in his house, Moser's Hall, had been abolished. Junior boys were no longer required to warm the toilet seats in the unheated outside bathrooms in advance of their use by senior boys. Fagging was still a fact of life. For the first two years you were at the beck and call of the older boys, be it polishing their shoes, ironing their CCF[3] uniforms or making them toast. Sometimes the demands could be more personal and less pleasant in nature.

The most senior members of the house, the monitors, shared a large, comfortable study, well-heated with a gas fire. If any monitor required some service to be performed, he would open the door and call "Doooowuuuuul"[4]. All junior boys were required to drop whatever they were doing and run to 'headroom'. The last arrival was then ordered to perform the task at hand. It was, of course, grossly unfair, as those whose studies were farthest away would tend to find themselves called upon with disproportionate frequency.

The logic underlying the persistence of fagging, now regarded as institutionalised bullying, was simple. Most boys in the school came from privileged backgrounds and were destined in time to become leaders. It was held that one was more likely to treat those over whom one had jurisdiction with consideration if one had first hand experience of being an underling.

"My limited boarding experience at the Dragon during my last term, served me well, and I suffered little of the home sickness I witnessed in others, and apart from the unwelcome and distasteful highly personal attentions of my first study monitor, the first two years passed relatively uneventfully. The overriding mantra of the public school system was conformity. Individuality was frowned upon, and pressure endlessly applied to erode away any incipient signs of deviation from the expected norm. I never have

3      Combined Cadet Corps – Playing soldiers.
4      From the Greek δοῦλος, doulos, a slave.

conformed readily. To disdain cricket and football in an
excessively sporting environment; to be an outspoken
atheist in a pious Christian fraternity—not to mention to
go grubbing about for spiders in the undergrowth, are all
sure ways to find oneself somewhat marginalized."

John has never had any reticence about his disbelief in, and
antithesis towards, organised religion, but neither does he
parade his opinions. He claims he cannot recall when he
first rebelled, but it might well have had its roots in hated
Sunday school, from which he was soon granted respite, so
voluble were his objections. Certainly by the age of ten he had
begun, I clearly recall, to question seriously the assumptions
on which were based the religious instruction to which we
were both subjected. It is impossible to retrace with any
certainty the steps by which doubt became crystallised into
active opposition. Certainly the conventional image peddled
to children of their destiny being dependent on the whim of
a benign old gentleman sitting on a cloud plucking his harp
in his nightshirt lacked credence from an early age. With time
the catalogue of theological improbabilities grew inexorably.

"My father was happy to proclaim his disbelief, but would
attend christenings, weddings and funerals for form's
sake. Of my mothers true beliefs I have no clear picture,
although I recall with pain the hurt she expressed when
I once insisted on going to the cinema on a Sunday. I'm
sure her Christian Science upbringing still coloured
her thinking, even though she had abandoned the faith
when she shamelessly married a doctor. Her liquor-free
upbringing was painfully manifested when she (for the
first and only time) shook the vintage port bottle."

The discovery that there are over four thousand (or is it over eight thousand?) recognised religions also helped fuel John's doubts. Each and every one of them, he would point out, is convinced that they alone hold a monopoly on truth, with members of every other religion being considered misguided heathens. At best only one in four thousand of these religions could be right, and given such odds, what probability exists that any might be true? In this statistical argument he found satisfying support for his opinion.

"Had it not been for the tradition of confirmation I might well have escaped detection as an unbeliever. Confirmation at around the age of fourteen or fifteen was a school tradition, and necessitated special instruction. For many boys, I discovered, the religious aspects of confirmation were of little significance. The real attraction lay in the fact that it was a ceremony that could generate handsome financial rewards from elderly distant relatives. I refused to be tempted—any more than I was tempted by the evangelical hot dogs and hamburgers offered at campfire revival meetings at seaside holiday resorts. When it was noticed that I did not attend confirmation classes, I was roundly and repeatedly questioned as we lay in bed talking after the lights were out. Always an outsider, abhorring participation in the shifting tribal cliques and alliances so commonplace in institutional settings, I was generally in a minority of one. My bland assurance that God was a concept born of ignorance and superstition, and that it held no place in my universe provoked outrage among those who had been conned into the straightjacket of conventional belief in childhood and lacked the wit to question what they were told. They sought solace in running with the pack".

Arguing when heavily outnumbered has few rewards. In order to silence his assailants John reluctantly agreed to go to the school chaplain and give voice to his doubts in the presence of higher authority. Few of those who taunted him believed that he would comply and were duly surprised when he gave a detailed account of the meeting a few evenings later. It was, in John's eyes, a rather pathetic encounter, and he felt saddened at having caused obvious pain. The only advice that the poor Rev. Furnival could give was to pray—a manifestly absurd suggestion to one already questioning the existence of any deity. John's schoolfellows claimed victory through having forced the confrontation.

"On the other hand it was perfectly clear to me that I had triumphed and had no need to reassess my position. If I had not already formed my negative opinion of the church and its proponents, I would most certainly have done so a while later after becoming the victim of sexual assault by a young visiting clergyman. A deity unable to restrain the baser instincts of its own concupiscent bishops and lascivious priests clearly lacked the moral authority claimed for it by its adherents. Sadly the priest's name has been erased from memory, even though the event has not. He would appear regularly at the house on the pretence of helping with the termly dramatic productions, and I have no doubt that I was not alone in being subjected to his advances. Already worldly, I was not so much shocked or traumatised as simply disgusted. I also realized that I had a duty to protect others from his attentions. The question was how to make his actions known to the school authorities, for it could be both distasteful and humiliating. An opportunity arose when D. N. Clark-Lowes, the senior chemistry master, with whom I was friendly, one day found himself unexpectedly teaching our class English. Embedded in an essay—I forget the precise topic—I made reference to; "An old member of the school, now in holy orders, whose frequent visits back to Moser's Hall were anticipated by the younger boys in the house with less than unalloyed pleasure."

My arrow found its mark. I was quietly questioned and word quickly travelled back to my housemaster, A.H.Phillips. The offender was never seen again at the school, but as I never heard anything further, I must assume that no retaliatory action was taken. Over the years I have on several occasions made feeble attempts to recall the man's name so I could file a formal complaint with both church and civil authorities, but so far it remains buried with other unpleasant memories.

In the same way that I uphold the concept of consensual sex of any flavour between consenting adults, so too I am happy for believers to practice their own particular flavour of religious belief in private, provided that in so doing they do not infringe on the freedoms of those holding different opinions—most particularly my own. The imposition of religion on children too young to understand or form a sound opinion of their own, however, I hold to be a form of child abuse that should be roundly punished. Nowhere do I feel this more strongly than in the absurd nonsense preached by fundamentalist creationists, who are both wilfully ignorant and deceitfully opinionated. Their position is so manifestly untenable that one is at a loss to understand how they ever win converts. That they are able to flourish is a sad indictment of the inadequate, anti-intellectual US school system.

The full exposition of my position on matters religious has been clearly expressed (and far more cogently than I could ever do) by Richard Dawkins in his admirable book 'The God Delusion'.

As an aside I should add that Richard and I were friends in the zoology department at Oxford years ago, where we were active participants in a lunch club that Richard had initiated. Each week a member would prepare some exotic delicacy to be shared with the group, which met in one of the huts on the old department roof.

Richard's numerous books have given enormous pleasure over the years, none more so than his 'Ancestor's Tale', which is a marvellous exposition of the animal kingdom's diversity and evolutionary history. Each time I read it I am overcome with regret that I abandoned Academia."

SUBLIME LUNACY

## Discursus Fourteen
# A Society of Equals

John will not infrequently quote entries from his Chinese dictionary to make a point. It is not, he will emphasize, a dictionary in the conventional sense, but rather extracts from a volume produced by an early visitor to China, who clearly had difficulties with the language. There is, for example, a word that apparently means "to stand still or gallop at full speed." It also contains a wealth of philosophical terms, such as "the state between emptiness and nothingness", "the sound of a stone," and the observation that "when the lips are lost, the teeth will grow cold", as well as such useful verbs as "to throw the literati into a pit." John found it easy to relate to "the student not succeeding and giving himself over to liquor" and "to dislike offending one's superiors, yet be fond of making insurrection".

It was after quoting several such entries that John suddenly lapsed into a strangely reflective mood of self-analysis.

> "As far back as I can remember I have recognised that within this single body there has long existed more than one personality, two bickering inner demons at the least, two schizophrenic identities that are diametrically opposed to each other, but forced to cohabit within a single brain."

The root of this inner conflict lay, it seems, in two inescapable realities—the recognition that he was born into a somewhat privileged life, mixed inextricably with an affinity and respect for the poor and oppressed. Absorbed by other interests, John long abhorred politics and was content to conform to the group opinions of those with whom he mixed. This complacent view of society, untarnished by familiarity with the living conditions of the masses, continued unchallenged into public school life. Here, nurtured in a hothouse of privilege, he continued blind to the realities of life until one memorable day, when an inner conscience was unexpectedly ignited.

"A young master, in the course of his geography lessons, introduced the class to the elements of Communist philosophy. While I have no doubt that he had been instructed to do this—it was the time of the 'Cold War'—he contrived to make the basic principles of Marxist belief sound remarkably attractive, so fuelling a dichotomy in my perception of the world. I have often wondered since whether it was a deliberate act on his part as a closet communist, or merely a happy accident.

It was about the same time that I encountered practical democracy in the flesh: a peaceful self-regulating society of equals. A close friend of my mother's had a daughter, slightly older than myself, who was cosmopolitan and intellectually gifted. Through her I was introduced to the London circle in which she moved—a firmament of professors, architects and artists that included familiar left-wing names such as J. D. Bernal—and through them I was invited to join an unusual young person's sailing club on the Norfolk Broads."

The Theta Club had been started just after the war, and was located in the village of Thurne—more accurately in an old converted WWII landing craft aptly named The Ark, which was moored in a small dike a short walk from the village. The Ark served as dormitory, galley and living room. Each day, while most took off sailing, two members would be detailed stay 'home' to clean, cook and do whatever other chores were needed—such as periodically digging a pit to empty the chemical 'Elsan' toilet, accommodated some distance away across the field. It was a self-governing community with minimal adult supervision or interference. Skippers—those with acknowledged sailing skills—were leaders in this classless soviet, and organised the daily schedule and made sure all necessary duties were accounted for, assisted by 'Mates', the first rung on the ladder to skipperdom.

> "For the first time I found myself in a true community, in which everyone was equal, and tasks were undertaken for the common good. Skinny-dipping among the dunes at Winterton on the coast was likewise a liberating escape from the snickering sexual *mores* of an all boys school. I still cherish the vision of Diana, an exquisite nut-brown maiden, dark hair blowing in the breeze, standing proud on a dune top looking unselfconsciously out to sea—the first time such a vision had been vouchsafed."

It was also a revelation to undertake housekeeping tasks, catering and cooking for the assembled company when they returned after a day's exploration. Ever ambitious, John embarked one day on making a steamed pudding with orange marmalade sauce. This necessitated finding a container of sufficient size in which the pudding could be steamed. A galvanised garbage pail, well-scrubbed worked well. To cover the pudding in its bowl he resorted to a large green bandana, but on serving it before the hungry crowd he was shocked to find that the dye had run and his masterpiece emerged a bilious greenish hue. Even so, it was consumed with gusto.

"My sense of self-esteem, hitherto negligible, received a valuable boost when I was promoted first to 'Mate', in recognition of my sailing abilities—soon thereafter reinforced further by being acclaimed a 'Skipper' by the assembled company. Here was evidence that seriously undermined my almost pathological self-doubt."

John's special joy were the three 'Tiddlers', remarkable craft designed by, and built for, one of the founding adults. Small and manoeuvrable, they were just eight feet overall, but sported a 22 foot mast, making them inherently unstable. Blunt-nosed, they were designed to plane at speed, and with a balloon spinnaker in addition to jib and mainsail, this happened frequently. Handling the five sheets single-handedly was a challenge. Even more challenging was sailing without getting wet. Successful 'Tiddler' sailing often meant hanging far out to windward, when a sudden loss of wind could send the unprepared backwards over the side.

The self-confidence that accrued from the Theta Club experience marked a turning point in John's school life, and brought the necessary self-respect to withstand the rigours of two years military 'National Service', and to benefit fully from the freedoms offered by university life.

## Discursus Fifteen
# Eight-legged Orthodoxy

John formed few close friendships while at Shrewsbury, for there were not many like-minded individuals whose company he found congenial, and whose conversation stimulating. The one striking exception was George Lampel. He and his Jewish parents had escaped from Hungary a year or two before the war and for a time had lived in Oxford before settling in Leeds.

"I was very impressed that George had personally witnessed the occasion of the only war damage in Oxford. 'Lord Haw Haw', the English traitor William Joyce, who broadcast Nazi propaganda from Bremen and Hamburg, had warned "Citizens of Oxford, look your last upon your dreaming spires, for tomorrow they will be no more." It was, therefore, all the more remarkable that Oxford sustained minimal war damage—although it would later emerge that Hitler planned to make Oxford his capital. George and his family had been walking along the banks of the River Cherwell when an injured allied bomber swept in only a few feet above them and crashed into the stables of a large house on the other bank. It turned out that the house, at the end of Linton Road, was the family home of the distinguished scientific Haldane family. The nearest bomb damage to Oxford was a small railway bridge near Thame—almost certainly a German plane jettisoning its load at random on the return flight home."

This mention of the Haldanes triggered a flood of memories, for John's parents were old family friends. J.S. Haldane, patriarch of the family, was a distinguished physiologist best known for his work on respiration. When he died in 1936 his equally famous son, JBS Haldane, approached John's father to arrange that JSH's brain be shipped to America to be examined by a researcher studying the brains of exceptional people.

> "Shipping human remains across the Atlantic, even for legitimate scientific study, is no simple matter. This my father soon found out. It is also not cheap. It cost my father around £60—more than Nanny's annual salary— and the bill was never settled. I think what grieved my father most was the fact that nothing was ever published on J.S. Haldane's (or anybody else's) brain to justify the expense. It rankled with him to the end of his life,"

Widely read, and with a penetrating scientific mind, George Lampel was a boy of great ability, but like John himself, alienated from the mainstream of school culture. Together they read Elliot, Auden, Spender, McNeice, James Joyce and more. The libraries would become their sanctuary, where on occasion they even so lost themselves as not to attend the hated compulsory chapel services. However, a failing for organ music would sometimes lure John back on secular occasions. The workings of the organ proved a great attraction, and he would sometimes gain unauthorised entrance to explore its capabilities. John often lamented not having been made to study the keyboard, for he has always resented not being able to play Bach well.

"Nothing united George and me more than our shared love of natural history, and we would spend whatever time we could searching for insects and other wildlife. On our early excursions into the countryside we had noticed that cow pats of different ages appeared to harbour different beetle species, and so we set about investigating this succession of fly and beetle communities. It was in the course of this study that we became aware of the many and diverse spiders that also crossed our path. Whereas the identification of insects, at least to family if not generic level, was not too difficult, information on spiders was extremely hard to find. Gradually the spiders came to dominate our collecting trips, and we started to scour bookshops and libraries for any volumes that might help us to identify our captures. A turning point occurred during the school holidays after I had found in Blackwell's, the great Oxford bookshop, a copy of the rare two-volume work by W.S.Bristowe entitled "The Comity of Spiders". This summarised all that was known about spider biology and in addition gave detailed information, such as existed, on the geographical distribution of spiders in the British Isles. At two guineas[5], it was a major investment, but absolutely invaluable. A well-timed attack of jaundice confined me to the school sanatorium for several weeks, thereby giving me an uninterrupted opportunity to read and digest my new purchase in the closest detail, so making me *de facto* an 'expert' on spiders.

We received neither help nor encouragement from

---

5       £2.20 in decimal currency. Current price £350 – if it can be found.

our biology master, Bertie Fowler. A strange character, always seemingly depressed, I think he began to feel threatened by our growing expertise in a field of which he was ignorant. Moreover, we had got off to a bad start when I had the temerity to argue when he rebuked me for sharpening my pencil in a way different from that which he advocated. It has always remained a source of regret that I was never able to break down his reserve and enjoy the mutual respect and comradeship that I came to develop with some of the other masters.

One of the few books on spiders available was a not very impressive volume in the 'Wayside & Woodland' series, written by Theodore Savory. It wasn't long before we started to spot apparent errors; statements that did not agree with our own observations. Savory, we discovered was a schoolmaster in London, and we eventually felt compelled to write to him, pointing out where we disagreed. Fortunately Savory's love of spiders overrode any sense of injury, and we received a warm and courteous reply, essentially welcoming us to the tiny coterie of British spider enthusiasts, which at the time comprised at most no more than half a dozen individuals. Savory was the first to acknowledge that we might have been correct in our criticism, passing on the sage advice that we should never believe implicitly all that we read in books. He also stressed the importance of observing the behaviour of live spiders. "One live spider in a jam jar", he said, "will teach you more than a hundred dead ones pickled in alcohol."

As they became more knowledgeable about the world of spiders and the people who studied them, George and John felt a tremendous need to gain access to the scientific literature, not least to be able to identify spiders from different parts of the world. John managed to become a reader at the Radcliffe Science Library in Oxford, despite not being a member of the university—doubtless his father being a Fellow of Merton College contributed to this privilege. He recalled vividly having to swear that "I bring not into the library, nor kindle therein any fire or flame." He also became a regular visitor to the Entomology Department in the University Museum, where he was delighted to find that Savory had presented a small collection of named British spiders. These he intended as a collection that could be examined by the public, thereby saving from undue use and damage the great collection amassed by Octavius Pickard-Cambridge, squire and rector of Bloxworth in Dorset, one of the two greatest world arachnologists in the previous century. No matter how detailed a written description may be, there is nothing like having a named specimen to confirm an identification.

"George and I also began competing in the acquisition of books and papers on spiders. We had discovered two booksellers in Holland, A. Asher & Co and Antiquaariat Junk, who both held large numbers of offprints. The amount we could buy was limited by our available funds, but between us we amassed the foundations of a library that would eventually grow to several thousand items.

I also started to write to individual authors around the world asking whether they had any spare copies or off-prints of their publications. Bill Bristowe, at that time Director of Personnel at ICI,[6] was one of my targets. He responded with an invitation for George and me to visit him at his very fine home near Tonbridge. After a delightful weekend, we left heavily burdened with the duplicate books and papers he showered on us, thereby cementing a friendship that would last until his death — and extend on to his daughter Ginny in Australia.

Bill Bristowe was a remarkable man. After reading for a science tripos[7] at Cambridge he went into industry. He became expert in several fields apart from spiders, writing among other things a history of Thailand, a book on islands, and countless scientific articles. One of my favourites was on "Insects and other invertebrates as human food in Siam" In it he gave the Latin, Thai and Cambodian names, together with instructions on how best to cook them. He finished by describing the taste. In the case of the 'Siamese edible Spider' (*Melanopeus albostriatus*) the preferred method of preparation was to singe off the blue-black body hairs over a fire, this giving it "A crisp exterior, with a soufflé-texture inside, and a flavour resembling a mixture of lettuce and potato." I never confirmed this myself, as I always enjoyed keeping the spiders alive when I found them.

His *magnum opus*, 'The Comity of Spiders', had been written on the train as he commuted daily to London, a true testament to his focus and dedication."

On one occasion, perplexed by his inability to find a copy of Chyzer & Kulczynski's Araneae Hungariae, and desperately

---

6      Imperial Chemical Industries,

7      Cambridge bachelor's degree

wanting a copy of this large folio volume with its beautiful illustrations, John wrote to the State Zoological Library in Budapest, asking if they had any suggestions as to where a copy might be found. To his surprise and delight, they sent a copy as a gift. In the next forty years he never once saw a copy offered for sale anywhere. It was a rare and beautiful prize.

There was an embarrassing occasion when a letter arrived at the school addressed to "Idler Loobe". From its contents and origin it was clearly intended for John, and he became the butt of many jokes for his inability to sign his name legibly—a signature that has only deteriorated further with the passage of time.

The discovery of new or unfamiliar species is always a source of pleasure, one that John has enjoyed on many occasions.

"My first such experience occurred, appropriately enough, in the Entomology Department. I was sitting at my microscope examining some pickled specimens, when a group of visiting school children appeared. At the same moment a small, unfamiliar Jumping Spider appeared on the microscope stage. I rather ostentatiously made a show of capturing it in a small glass vial, and then examining it. It proved, eventually, to be *Euophrys (Pseudophrys) lanigera*, an extremely rare species that had only been found previously in Britain at one location—the Natural History Museum in London: a most curious coincidence. Investigating further, I found that the preferred habitat was among the slates and flashing on the museum roof, where it eventually proved to be quite common. It has since turned up on buildings in many parts of Britain."

Leaving the school premises during term was not easy. Even a visit to the town for some legitimate purpose required written permission—although this did not much discourage illicit trips. We soon discovered which pubs had rear entrances through which we could escape should a master be spotted coming in through the front door. However, it was possible to go out legally at weekends with parents or family friends. One had only to write in the book that lay in the housemaster's hallway, giving details of the proposed absence. George and I were enthusiastic weekend travellers, taking our bicycles on extensive collecting trips. To do this we evolved a system for recording our excursions in the housemaster's book. We would bracket our names together and add "out with friends". If questioned, I would be out with my friend and he would be out with his. Fortunately this exercise in logic was never tested, and I am certain that the housemaster, 'Bounce' Phillips (who had been at Oxford with my father) was fully aware of what was happening but did not wish to discourage our obvious enthusiasm".

It was required that when the school first soccer XI was playing against another school, all the boys should be on the touchline to provide encouragement. It was a cold and boring exercise in their eyes, so George and John would position themselves close to one of the large trees along the touchline and gradually strip off bark to examine the fauna living underneath. Small, dark erigonine spiders were welcome, but the discovery of a pseudoscorpion was always an occasion for celebration.

Through their reading they learned of a peat bog some distance away that had yielded rare and interesting butterflies. Whixall Moss became a locality that beckoned strongly but proved terribly elusive. Lying on the border with Wales less than twenty miles north of Shrewsbury, there was no easy way to get there. An opportunity came when the school declared a one-day 'whole holiday', whose specific purpose was to get boys out into the countryside. A bus took them to Wem, but after that they had to hitchhike, the last few miles on the back of a farm tractor in the rain.

Their patience was richly rewarded. Whixall Moss proved to be a place of exceptional interest, and filled with arachnological delights. Giant *Dolomedes* raft spiders were common, as was *Argyroneta aquatica*, the only spider to live under water. Even though time was severely limited by the demands of transportation, they still found many species that were new to them.

"It would be some time before we finally identified the greatest prize, *Pirata uliginousus*, a species at that time unrecorded from Britain. We knew we had made a contribution to knowledge and settled down in ecstasy to write our first scientific paper. When about to publish, we were dismayed to learn that Eric Duffey, a research student at Oxford had also found the same species the year before. What made his discovery particularly galling was the fact that he had found it on my doorstep in Wytham Woods just outside Oxford, where I too regularly went collecting. Eric's paper was already in press and so we had to accept playing second fiddle. It was a disappointment, to be sure, to be pipped at the post, but it did not dampen that special excitement of identifying our first species new to Britain— an excitement that would continue unabated as my list of new species grew in the years following."

Forty years or more since first going to Whixall, John was gratified to learn that the whole area has since been recognised as a site of exceptional scientific interest and is being rigorously conserved. The harvesting of peat, carried on by hand for generations, did some damage, but the sudden appearance of giant machines to dig peat on a commercial scale threatened to destroy the whole delicate balance of this ancient relict bog. Just in time, government intervention prevented disaster and the damage done by peat cutting is now being gradually healed and the endangered communities of wildlife are returning.

Although in his eighties now, and somewhat impeded by the ravages of age and infirmity, John still cherishes the dream of a pilgrimage that he feels he should undertake. In the South Indian state of Kerala he is drawn to the village of Kodumon, for here is found Chilanthiyambalan, an ancient temple in which spiders are venerated. Dedicated to the Goddess Durga, the warrior form of Parvati, Goddess of love, beauty and fertility, victims of skin diseases and spider bites come on pilgrimage to be cured.

Believed to be the world's only spider temple, John feels it should be a place of pilgrimage for all devotees of what he calls the eight-legged orthodoxy—to distinguish it from the six-legged heresy of entomology. .

## Discursus Sixteen
# Anonymous Alcoholics

In 1952 Shrewsbury School celebrated the four-hundredth anniversary of its foundation by Edward VI. It was a busy summer as the school prepared for a royal visit. Not only was John to play in the school band and serve as bugler for the CCF parade, but he was called upon to organise a suitable program to entertain the Queen and Prince Phillip as they toured the biology building, and he entered into the latter task with enthusiasm. Much time was devoted to creating a massive demonstration of arthropod classification, and he also set up a large cage of breeding locusts. To add colour, he ordered a large assortment of pamphlets from the natural history museum in London, which were left out for visitors. The question of budgets had never come up in the course of planning, and the school was mortified to receive a sizable bill from the museum to cover the cost of their pamphlets happily taken away by visitors.

It had been laid down that when the royal party entered the building, all the boys would be elsewhere. Only the senior masters concerned were to accompany them. However, shortly before their arrival it was discovered that a large number of locusts had escaped and were flying about the laboratory. Nobody knew how Her Majesty might react to locusts becoming entangled in her hair. It was imperative that the escapees be rounded up and returned to their cage immediately. Before John had finished, the royal party entered the building and would shortly be coming upstairs. He was trapped—and not a little anxious as to how the discovery of his presence might play with the school authorities. He was just closing the cage door on the last of the errant locusts when Prince Phillip suddenly appeared and set course towards him. His initial horror of the situation was quickly transformed by the Duke's easy manner as he engaged him in conversation about locust life histories and related matters. Although Bertie Fowler looked daggers at the time, there were no adverse repercussions.

"Despite my avid interest in natural history, there was for a time talk that I might read chemistry at university, it being a subject I found easy and in which I could shine without too much effort. Unlike natural history, which requires no special equipment or space, chemistry was a subject that could only be pursued in the laboratory. I had reached a level in the school where I enjoyed a certain degree of freedom, and could use certain free periods for chemical activities. I prepared a variety of obscure compounds, and spent almost a whole term synthesising aspirin and vitamin A (probably unsuccessfully). But there remained many experiments I wanted to try that would not have been looked on sympathetically by the school. Foremost amongst these was the synthesis of alcohol. Alcohol is normally produced by fermentation and then distilled. However, the laws of Great Britain are very strict on such matters, and the distillation of alcohol without proper permits decidedly frowned upon by HM Customs & Excise."

"I discovered that it was possible to make alcohol without distillation by passing acetaldehyde vapour and hydrogen gas over reduced nickel at an appropriate temperature, but the necessary apparatus was unlikely to remain operational for long without attracting unwelcome attention. It was purely by chance that I discovered one day a back door into the chemistry laboratory that was rarely if ever used. Struck sharply in the right place, it would spring open. Using this knowledge, I was able to spend many happy wet weekends, when natural history fieldwork appeared less attractive, undertaking a range of illegal chemical experiments, of which alcohol production was the most rewarding. There were insufficient quantities of platinum compounds to make the recovery of metallic platinum worthwhile, however for a time the school seemed content to replace the hydrogen cylinders I emptied, but eventually the supply dried up, and so did my production line. The alcohol that dripped out of the end of my apparatus tasted terrible, being heavily contaminated with acetaldehyde. Various methods were tried to remove the offending flavour, but it never wholly vanished. The only solution, were the alcohol to become marketable, was to disguise the taste with something stronger. A fat volume in the library provided an assortment of recipes for creating chemical flavours, and soon I had a market, albeit rather small, for my line of horrendous synthetic fruit-flavoured liqueurs. Like my earlier cigars, I was far too prudent to consume my own brew."

Nevertheless, life at Shrewsbury was by no means wholly teetotal. It was in no way related to today's scourge of 'binge-drinking', and I do not believe that any of us ever became seriously intoxicated."

The horror of a hangover was still several years away. John, and many of our friends, came from families in which modest consumption was a normal activity. Offered a glass of wine, sherry or a liqueur when appropriate, alcohol was never felt to be an illicit pleasure. This toleration was not shared by the school authorities, who thereby turned alcohol into a prized forbidden fruit.

"I seldom felt the need to consume much, but somehow George and I acquire a reputation as 'dealers' and would be asked to supply those whose needs were more strongly felt, but were afraid to risk the consequences of being caught in a pub. We had found a country pub two or three miles away where purchases could be safely made, and we occasionally made forays on weekends to satisfy the demands of our clients. There was a memorable occasion when we had mistaken the time, and were forced to run home along the Shrewsbury by-pass to make call-over, sweating profusely with the mass of bottles in our raincoat pockets weighing us down and clanking loudly for all to hear.

I suspect alcohol (and cigarettes) were a greater problem in some other houses at Shrewsbury. In Churchill's Hall it was reported that the scion of a leading jam manufacturing family had excavated a secret room beneath his study, to which he and his close friends would retire to enjoy themselves—like the Hellfire Club at Medmenham Abbey two hundred years earlier. This Xanadu was only discovered through a fault in the wiring."

## Discursus Seventeen
# Close Encounters

It was a hot summer afternoon in France, and we had bicycled to a spring that bubbles up from some deep underground fissure beside the river Anglin. Clear and cool, it was a spot we visited frequently to gather drinking water of unparalleled purity. A short distance away, rock climbers were demonstrating their athletic skills on a small limestone cliff, and this unleashed a flood of John's climbing memories.

"My parents tell me", John began languidly, "that when I was three years old, workmen were repairing the roof of the family home on the Woodstock Road in Oxford. It is a large house on four floors, and as my father turned into the driveway one day he was appalled to see a small figure at the top of a very tall ladder, about to clamber onto the slates. Not wanting to distract me, he resisted the urge to call out, and could only watch in horror. Fortunately, one of the men working on the roof caught sight of me and very gently picked me up and carried me down."

Having once again caught the attention of his listeners as they relaxed in the long grass beside the spring, John continued to reminisce:

"It was probably because of my height that I found it easier than most to climb into inaccessible places. By scaling a tree just outside the school grounds I was able to gain access to the roof of the Dragon School's Old Hall, and its surrounding classrooms. It was quite an elaborate roofscape, with many dips and gullies, which largely concealed me from view. Here among the rooftops I discovered a valuable hoard of errant tennis balls that had been propelled from the playground below and become trapped. These could be retrieved for profit and provided a valuable supplement to my meagre pocket money. Of course, such ascents were severely frowned upon, not least presumably because of risk and liability issues—to say nothing of the damage to slates and tiles"

The subject of climbing and risk led the conversation on to close encounters. Several of us recalled occasions when death had come unpleasantly close. It was not a conversation that John found easy to ignore, and in due course he asked: "Did I ever tell you about my first posthumous scientific paper?" In truth, he had!

While at school he had stumbled upon a small advertisement from a dealer in Brazil, offering to supply butterflies and other tropical insects. John immediately wrote asking whether it was also possible to supply spiders and other arachnids. A few weeks later a mysterious packet covered in exotic foreign stamps arrived in the post, bearing the following, inscrutable warning: "Somehow poisonous also."

Inside was a large, beautiful, very aggressive spider. It turned out to be a female *Phoneutria fera,* one of the most poisonous of all South American spiders. "I felt," said John, "like Conradin in Saki's Sredni Vashtar, harbouring an all-powerful deity in total secrecy".

"Some months later the spider, in its glass-topped box, was accidentally knocked from its place of honour on the desk and fell to the floor. "Instinctively," said John, "I reached down to retrieve it. Suddenly I felt a burning pain in my left hand, and looking down found my spider with its fangs deeply buried in the second joint of my index finger." In her fall, she had landed part way down on the leg of the desk, and her ill temper aroused, had lunged at the passing hand."

The pain was excruciating, and gradually spread up his arm, before finally settling in the lymph glands under his armpit. The accident could not be concealed, and naturally provoked considerable parental concern. "Do something, call somebody," my mother wailed in genuine panic." By that time already one of the few spider experts in the country, John assured her that there was only one person in the world knowledgeable about *Phoneutria* venom. "Call him, call him" came the anguished refrain. "Well," he responded, "he's an unfrocked Nazi priest living somewhere in Brazil, and I don't have his phone number." This did little to assuage maternal anxiety!

With his father's professional help, John set about documenting the course of his envenomation for posterity. Hour by hour the symptoms were recorded; pulse, respiration, temperature, blood pressure, together with a subjective assessment of the pain. After two days the pain began to subside, although the site of the bite remained sensitive to the slightest touch, which would send violent spasms shooting up his arm. With true scientific devotion the episode was written up for publication. It was destined to be his first posthumous scientific paper, "but fortunately", he added, "it was never published."

"Probably on more occasions than I realise," John observed, "climbing has come close to killing me. One experience in particular has left a lasting impression. The Dragon school had suggested that my homework might be better if I stayed to do it in the supervised company of the boarders. At home there were too many distractions and the work was frequently skimped. My excuse that the wind had blown my homework out of my bicycle basket en route to school one morning was received with the disbelief and derision that it deserved—I never have successfully mastered the art of creative mendacity.

So it happened that I would have to walk home from school in the dark. Along the way I passed through a stone archway leading into the North Oxford Victorian housing development known as Park Town. Some ten or twelve feet above the road, I noticed a small metal box fixed to the wall, and climbing up the conduit running to it I was able to access the timer that controlled the nearby street lights. Several times I could not resist the temptation to alter the settings so that the lights were off by night and on by day.

One night, climbing up in the dark, I opened the box and put my hand in, only to find that the timer had been removed—probably in the belief that it was persistently malfunctioning. Instead of touching the timer, I unwittingly touched the bare electric terminals. A massive shock surged through my body, from one arm to the other across my chest, and several minutes later I regained consciousness lying in the gutter across the street. It had been a miraculous escape. Although I have been told that street lights run on 480 volts, I suspect the timing control was only the standard British 240 volts, which is nevertheless sufficient to kill. Needless to say, I have never fiddled with a street light since!"

Years later, as an undergraduate at Oxford, John miraculously survived a catastrophic fall while climbing on the Three Cliffs in the Llanberis Pass in North Wales.

"It was on Carreg Wastad ('The Grave Stone'), although I can no longer recall with certainty the name of the route. I was seconding, and had ascended two full rope lengths (240 ft.) to the crux of the climb. This consisted of two smooth rock faces at 90 degrees to one another. Although there was a piton in place, as a purist I refused to use it for direct aid. A light rain had started to fall, making the rock somewhat slick, but as I was supported from above, the prospect of a small error was of no concern—I would be left suspended in safety.

Suddenly I lost contact, and the rock face up which I was climbing began to move upwards, and in that moment time virtually stood still. As though in slow motion, pitch by pitch moved by me until I passed through a tangle of tree branches, hit a sloping rock face and ricocheted off into space. I have a clear memory of the early part of my descent, when my life did indeed pass before me, but then only the faintest memory of flying like a rag doll down a scree slope before losing consciousness. I came-too briefly as I was carried down to an ambulance, and only regained consciousness some hours later in Bangor hospital. Only later was I told that my companion was dead, having himself fallen too.

It was an accident that should not have happened. We were both experienced climbers, and normally a second losing contact with the rock would have been insignificant.

For this reason my friend Hugh Banner, an outstanding climber, undertook to discover the reason why on this occasion the outcome was so tragic. The clue was a lone nylon sling still in position where the leader had been belayed. In re-creating the accident, Hugh came very close to being killed himself. Using a sack of rocks to simulate the weight of a second, Hugh discovered that the geometry of the belay was such that a weight on the rope bore down on the karabiner or snap-link securing the leader's waist line to the sling. Although equipped with a safety sleeve to prevent the gate being accidentally opened, the sleeve had not been closed and the climbing rope pulled down on the gate and opened it, allowing it to detach from the sling. A moment of carelessness in not securing the safety sleeve had resulted in a tragic and unnecessary death. Hugh's careful re-enactment of the circumstances explained several earlier accidents in which experienced climbers had been killed or injured."

Released from hospital a week later, bruised and shaken, John was met by another climbing friend, Chris Bonnington, who would later become a leading figure in the mountaineering world.

"Chris was adamant. If I did not return immediately I would lose my nerve and never climb again. When he suggested we climb 'Cemetery Gates', an exposed and very challenging route up a ninety-degree open crack my protest were over-ruled and I found myself on one of the hardest climbs of my life. It was just as well. A few days later I was in the Alps with OU Mountaineering Club companions, happy to tackle several classic routes. However,

I did receive a pointed reminder that I had only recently survived a potentially deadly fall. I had become aware of some discomfort in the back of my thigh, but chose to ignore it. I was half way up a moderately challenging rock face on the Dent du Requin when a massive haematoma that had been slowly filling for days out of sight, suddenly burst, pouring several pints (as it seemed) of fluid down the rock. The hospital in Chamonix was staffed by delightful nuns wearing the large, unwieldy wimple of their order. Under their care I soon recovered and was able to continue climbing. It was only after becoming a father a few years later that I finally succumbed to mounting pressure and gave up overtly challenging gravity."

SUBLIME LUNACY

## Discursus Eighteen
# Her Majesty's Service

Although his military career was short-lived, John's two years of enforced naval service between school and university were not uneventful, and gave rise to many stories, some of which seem worthy of repetition.

"Like all national servicemen," he began one evening, "I entered on the lower deck and was subjected to that special oppression and contempt that the regular sailors reserved for conscripts like us. I had resented the prospect of what at the time I considered as two wasted years, and decided that volunteering to be trained as a Russian interpreter would keep my mind active and might equip me with skills valuable in later life. At the time I was wholly unaware of the duties that National Service interpreters might be called upon to perform. It was many many years later that I learned that a major source of espionage data was collected from the remains of torn-up one-time code pads that the Russians were using in lieu of toilet paper. In the event, I am very happy that I never learnt Russian!

After basic training I was interviewed in relation to my application to go for language training. It was an interesting interview, which ended with the words: "So you want to study Russian—have you ever thought of flying?" Given my well-known lack of linguistic ability, it was just as well. In the event, my future was decided for me. My father was also a pilot—in the First World War. In those days flying was in its infancy and its military value still apparently under-valued. For reasons that escape me, flying was considered the job of the cavalry. Consequently my father wore jodhpurs and boots to become airborne. It was a singularly dangerous occupation, the life expectancy of an airman at the front being just one week. It was indeed fortunate that father had not reached the front by the time that the armistice was declared."

As an after thought John added: "In those days things were made to last. When father finally gave up horsemanship his military riding boots were still in excellent condition and his Scottish ancestry rebelled against simply abandoning them. Instead, he had the tops cut off to convert them into a pair of stout brown shoes. These he continued to wear into his late nineties."

The flying aptitude tests to which John and his fellow-trainees were soon subjected took several days to complete at RAF Hornchurch on the outskirts of London. How anyone passed the tests is a mystery, for they all went into London and drank far more than was prudent, returning at breakfast time next morning feeling like death. Could it be that tolerance to alcohol, he wondered, might be one of the qualities being tested for?

Flying school was shore-based at HMS Siskin, located at Gosport, near Portsmouth, in one of the forts built to withstand Napoleon's anticipated invasion. If one had to be in the military, this was undoubtedly a good place to be.

"We were", he explained, "regarded as lunatics, many destined for a short life, and in consequence were allowed unusual freedoms and relief from the petty restrictions that make service life so irksome. Indeed, our class of a dozen trainee pilots would be noteworthy for losing half our number in fatal accidents. Being for the most part midshipmen, we lived in comfort in the officer's mess, where we wined and dined exceptionally well.

After we had moved on, I later learned that the mess secretary had been grossly over-charging the admiralty by inflating the number of personnel being catered for, and that subsequently the standard of service had been severely curtailed.

We underwent a wide range of training, much of which has served me well in after years. It was rightly believed that pilots should understand how their aircraft functioned and why they could remain airborne. Consequently we stripped down engines and rebuilt them, were taught the theory of carburettors, and the principles of aerodynamics. We studied meteorology and radio communications, weaponry and survival skills—it was a thoroughly worthwhile experience.

Work ended quite early each day, after which I was able to go hunting spiders in the long summer evenings. This did not go down well with my superiors, who were constantly assessing us for OLQ—officer-like qualities—and grubbing about in the undergrowth did not improve my rating. It was on one of these excursions into the surrounding heathland that I found myself being shot at. Fortunately my assailant had remarkably poor aim. He must also have had very bad eyesight, for upon confronting him in some consternation, he dismissed me by saying only that he had thought I was a rabbit! Being some six-foot-five in height, I make a very impressive rabbit."

Anticipating all eventualities, the class had to be prepared to bail out of their aircraft over water. Wearing immersion suits, they were taken out into the Solent by motor launch and pushed over the side. For some the sensation of bobbing about in the open ocean all alone was unsettling, but John was fortunate in having already had the experience in a course of SCUBA training.

The immersion suits, which were worn when flying over water, included an opening through which one could urinate. A length of rubber hose, it had to be tied tight with string when not in use. Those who did not check this before departure would become uncomfortably aware of their oversight when cold water began to flood into their supposedly waterproof suits.

"The highlight of the immersion exercise was the appearance of a helicopter zooming in low over the waves, carrying behind it a giant metal scoop, which miraculously swept us up and carried us to a rescue vessel a few miles away over the horizon."

"As another part of our survival training on land," he went on, "we did escape-and-evasion exercises, replicating the conditions that might be encountered were we ever to be shot down behind enemy lines. It was all good Boy Scout stuff, although treated rather more seriously by those in charge.

Together with a companion, I was blindfolded and driven to some unknown spot, from which we had

48 hours in which to discover where we were, and then make our way home undetected. We had nothing with us apart from sufficient small change to make a phone call in case of emergency, and we were urged to use our wits and initiative to escape the police and military search parties out scouring the countryside looking for us.

The prospect of uncomfortable nights spent hiding in ditches and under haystacks did not particularly appeal, but we had no immediate plans in mind. Not long after being dropped, we found ourselves hiding at the top of a steep bank overlooking a small, winding country road. In the distance I saw approaching a dark blue van bearing naval markings. As it drew near, I saw it contained only a solitary WREN driver. Having been given free rein, I acted on impulse and dropped down onto the road directly in front of her, precipitating a screech of brakes. Outnumbered two-to-one, she had little option but to comply with our request. This was very simple. She was to drive us directly back to the base we had just left, and while we lay concealed in the back, was to enter the main gate, distract the sentry, and deposit us close to our Napoleonic fort. She performed faultlessly.

Like all good forts, it was surrounded by a water-filled moat and approached by a bridge—fortunately no longer a drawbridge. It was a quiet morning, and the base was largely deserted. It would be several hours, so everyone imagined, before anyone on the exercise would attempt to return, and the guards were not yet out in force.

Choosing our moment carefully, we slipped over the edge of the moat and climbed up into the girders supporting the underside of the bridge. Well concealed, we clambered across the moat and gained entry to the fort through an unlocked office window.

When my Commanding Officer returned after a leisurely breakfast, he was startled to find me sitting in his office, my feet on his desk, reading his 'Times' newspaper. Thunderstruck, he was momentarily speechless. Taking the initiative, I started to say that I had but done as he had ordered, returning to base as quickly as possible. A reasonable man—with a sense of humour—he saw that, apart from the contempt shown to his desk and newspaper, my conduct was exemplary, and we remained on good terms for the rest of my training.

Although the training was at this time all pre-flight, we periodically had opportunities to fly for pleasure, sometimes with the gliding club, and also whenever we could bum a ride from the helicopter squadron stationed with us. Flying helicopters, we discovered, was an art. One didn't so much move the stick as just think about it. We were regularly treated to the horror of having the engine cut out, causing the helicopter to drop like a stone. Those who have no previous experience of this see their life pass before them as the bottom literally drops out of their world. Those to whom it had happened before simply experienced the exhilaration of free fall, safe in the knowledge that the pilot will eventually feather the rotor blades and bring his craft down to a landing only a little less gentle than usual. It was on one of these excursions that we flew over a local nudist colony—apparently a favourite destination. Here we were treated to the unforgettable sight of a man clad

only in his chef's hat, rushing out to shake his fist at us."
For reasons that escape me, on one occasion after telling this
story, John's mind suddenly recalled an unconnected event in
Bali.

> "We were driving up in the mountains when we came
> across a fine new restaurant that seemed curiously out of
> place, for it was in an area that saw few, if any, tourists.
> Always on the look-out for new places to take our clients,
> we decided to stop for lunch as the views were striking.
> When someone had to be dispatched to find staff, we
> realised that it would probably be a long meal, but we like
> to support new ventures and so we sat and waited. The
> menu was clearly designed to appeal to western visitors,
> and in due course we chose the curiously named "Chicken
> Gordon Blue". After waiting for over an hour, our meal
> finally appeared. It was not the culinary masterpiece we
> had hoped for, but a wholly new and unrecogniseable dish
> we promptly christened "Shrivel of Chicken". There was
> no surprise when, passing that way again a year later, we
> found the restaurant abandoned and deserted, no longer
> needing to scour the surrounding forests for kitchen and
> dining room staff when guests arrived, for there were none."

## Discursus Nineteen
# Flying High

Perhaps the highlight of John's time at HMS Siskin was the great base defence exercise, when there were simulated attacks by enemy forces to be repelled. His class of potential pilots were given the enviable role of fifth-columnists, their job being to aid the attackers from within. They were told that they could do absolutely anything—except put sugar in the helicopter fuel, as this was both dangerous and costly—it completely and permanently blocks the carburettor.

Entering into the spirit of the game, John engineered to have himself appointed Officer of The Day, thereby giving him access to the nerve centre from which the whole defence operation was coordinated. It was remarkable that nobody in authority thought to question his presence, for at least a few of the more senior officers must have known that the class was working under cover.

"From my position of strength at the very nerve centre of the defending forces, I was able to spread chaos and confusion, misdirecting units to places where there was no threat and likewise leaving key points on the base periphery unguarded when incursions were to be made. Knowing in advance that the HQ building would also be housing any enemy prisoners captured, I laid plans to effect their escape. It had been ordered that everybody was to carry gas masks in case of a poison gas attack, but some of the senior officers felt that they were above such things—no poison gas was actually destined to be released—or so they thought. At the appropriate moment, after a significant number of prisoners had been brought in, I released a quantity of chlorine gas into the building—through the simple addition of hydrochloric acid onto some potassium permanganate crystals.

Chaos reigned for a few minutes, during which time I was able to unlock the cell door and set everyone free. The senior officers who had failed to carry their gas masks as instructed suffered considerably and there were calls for my head on a platter. However, as I had acted entirely within the rules, nothing untoward happened—but another black mark was, I suspect, added to my sagging OLQ rating."

Not all John's time at HMS Siskin was spent in pre-flight training. Through a chance wardroom meeting he was invited to join the crew of the Fleet Air Arm yacht, a 50 metre-square 'borrowed' from the Germans at war's end. They were to participate in the Owers Lightship race. Conditions for the race were appalling and although it ended officially after thirty-six hours, by that time not one competitor had crossed the finishing line.

"It was a traumatic experience for we found that our craft was far from seaworthy and water poured in through the cabin-top. Tossing like a cork, we literally bailed for dear life, quite convinced that we were sinking. Never have I endured such a horrible forty-eight hours, or been more convinced that my life was about to end. I retain a horror of drowning to this day."

For some reason John decided that he would like to go parachuting. In trying to make the arrangements—he had thought one of his helicopter squadron friends might take him up—he discovered that the navy had very inflexible views on the subject. Their argument was clear. If a pilot were to discover just how easy it is to jump out of an ailing aircraft, he might be tempted to abandon his plane in time of crisis before it was really necessary—and aircraft are expensive. Parachuting was a forbidden pastime, and as he has said regretfully on several occasions, he has never taken it up since.

"I did, however, take up hang-gliding for a time. This was a marvellous experience, although somewhat bruising now and then. The first occasion was during a family holiday in South Wales, when I gained my pilot's certificate. Financial considerations had initially limited my planned participation. However, once again Providence intervened on my behalf. Driving to the launch site behind the owner of the school, I suddenly noticed that his Range Rover was on fire. Rushing ahead I managed to stop him, he being completely unaware of the flames. Only because I was carrying a fire-extinguisher was his vehicle saved, in recognition of which I received the gift of a full course of training.

It was during a filming expedition to South Africa many years later that I had my most unusual hang-gliding experience. I had been taken by some local filming friends to a site south of Cape Town and instructed to fly in a particular direction until I came upon a wide beach, which would be a good landing site. What they did not tell me, however, was that this was a nudist beach. Most remarkable, bearing in mind that apartheid had not yet been abolished, was that this was both multi-racial and un-segregated by gender. As the only fully clothed individual present I felt particularly conspicuous, which doubtless contributed to a singularly inelegant landing."

It was the sudden, deafening roar of two low-flying military jets disturbing the peace of a languid lunch on the terrace at Alogny that prompted him to observe:

"It always seemed odd to me that the Navy sent us to the RAF for flight training, while the RAF in turn sent their pilots to be trained by the Canadians. A trip to Canada would have been nice, but we had to make do with RAF Syreston near Nottingham, a strange location indeed for training navy pilots, being about as far from the sea as its possible to get in England.

Apart from learning to fly, which was enjoyable, I found it all a bit boring, for we flew only on predetermined routes at predetermined altitudes, and were really little more than glorified taxi drivers. Moreover, I found I was prone to altitude sickness above ten thousand feet (this was before I became a mountaineer) and would think I was flying on course with wings level while weaving all over the sky. The onset was quite quick and first manifested itself with a tingling of the fingertips—at which point I learned to descend rapidly regardless of my official flight plan.

It was not until I travelled as a cameraman in a light plane, contour flying over the dunes of the Great Salt Desert in Iran at fifty feet in the first light of dawn, that I discovered what a real joy it can be to fly.

Our low-flying area at Syreston was crossed by pylons carrying high-voltage electric cables. Needless to say, there were strict instructions that under no circumstances were we to attempt to fly under them. Knowing that there are old pilots and bold pilots, but no old, bold pilots, I never had any great urge to risk the consequences. One of my class-mates, however, had a narrow escape when he returned with twigs and bits of hedge sticking out of his engine cowling.

I have to admit that my flying career was not very auspicious, and came to a sudden end when posted to RAF Valley in Anglesey to do a conversion course from piston-engined Provosts to jet-powered Vampires. Looking me up and down in disbelief, I was told that were I ever to use my ejector seat, my legs would be cut off halfway up my thighs as I left the aircraft. I was far too tall to fit in their aircraft—something one might have thought the navy would have considered before deciding to send me for months of expensive flight and pre-flight training. I was sent home on leave while my naval future was decided upon. For three months, while drawing full flying pay, I was forgotten about, until one day there was a rather worried call from a girl at the Admiralty, wondering whether I might please come back. It had provided a three-month paid vacation dedicated to natural history."

SUBLIME LUNACY

## Discursus Twenty
# Shoot to Kill

Although the policy was to change shortly afterwards, at that time anyone released from flying duties lost their officer status and had to return to the lower deck, starting once again at the bottom of the heap as a new recruit. "This proved a bit irksome, to be sure, but my earlier passage through the system had alerted me to all the ways in which the usual duties could be avoided, so I had an easy time. Aware of my somewhat unusual situation, the authorities took pity on me, and I soon found myself posted to HMS Hornet, where I joined the crew of a high speed MTB. Except for the time when I was detailed to scrape and paint the inside of a rather narrow torpedo tube, it was a good life. Bearing the unfortunate designation of 'Gay boats'— we were 'Gay Archer'—these small, fast craft could travel at well over 40 knots. In addition to their deck-mounted torpedo tubes, they also carried guns fore and aft, typically a 4.5 inch cannon for'ard and either a 40mm Bofors or a 20mm Oerlikon aft. The Admiralty was considering the introduction of a new twin-barrelled 20mm Hispano Suiza, which had a very rapid rate of fire—something in the region of 3000 rounds a minute. We were called upon to perform a statistically significant weapons evaluation trial at which the performance of all four guns were to be tested under all possible conditions—firing ahead, abeam, astern: in daylight and at night; in calm seas, in medium seas and in rough weather. It kept us busy for many weeks.

Our targets were varied. Sometimes they were empty hulks towed far astern another MTB, but at other times we were firing at fully-functional MTBs under radio control. The Hispano Suiza proved its accuracy when we sliced a towed hulk neatly along her waterline causing her to sink. Despite its superior fire power and accuracy, the Admiralty did not accept it into service because of a small removable component that could easily be dropped overboard in rough weather.

My reputation was greatly enhanced on board by a lucky shot. I was, on that occasion, in command of the 4.5 – a massive weapon for a lightly built plywood vessel. It had an enormous recoil to prevent it ripping out the deck upon which it was mounted. We were to fire at a radio controlled target, the belief being that it could never be hit. Wrong! The very first round of the forty we were to fire scored a direct hit, and naturally we were delighted. However, we had by chance penetrated the compartment containing the boat's electronics, which lay next to the fuel tanks with their huge quantities of high-octane aviation fuel. Almost at once a fire broke out. The Commander of the radio-control unit was furious. The parent vessel, another MTB, was sent in along side, and two unhappy seamen put aboard with fire extinguishers. The whole boat could have exploded in a ball of flame at any moment, and the parent vessel was stood off quarter of a mile away. With only one hope for survival, the two sailors laboured mightily and eventually quelled the flames. We heard later that they been awarded medals, which I felt were well-deserved."

While reminiscing about his naval sojourn, John recalled the unfortunate occasion on which a young, wholly inexperienced officer was ordered to take an MTB into its appointed birth—his first time at the helm. By a cruel twist of fate the mechanical linkage between the engine room and the cockpit had become misaligned. Imagining that he was approaching the birth at "slow ahead", the engine room was running at "half ahead". On ostensibly cutting power, the engines were still running "slow ahead". When, in desperation, the novice helmsman gave the order for an emergency "slow astern", the craft was still gliding inevitably towards the hard, with predictable consequences. John said that he often wondered whether the budding skipper ever had any future as a naval officer.

As one of his guests lit a cigarette at the end of a meal, John could not resist, like so many other ex-smokers, of commenting on his own success in vanquishing the addiction, adding:

> "I am quite surprised that nobody yet appears to have sued the navy for encouraging them to smoke. Cigarettes were not free when I served, but they cost so little they might as well have been. Many an innocent national serviceman became a nicotine addict through the combination of availability and peer pressure. We also received, should we so wish, a daily rum ration—the alternative was three pence a day added to the pay packet if one proclaimed oneself teetotal. Under normal service conditions the rum ration would be diluted 3:1 to prevent it being stored. It should be added that this was not your everyday commercial rum,

but a dark brew of exceptional potency (and wonderful flavour) prepared specially for the Royal Navy.

On board the MTBs, where crews were small and intimate, our rum ration was served by the bosun undiluted. Inevitably some would be bottled for future use, and on weekends the parties could get quite out of hand. It was a rule that there should always be two crew members on board to stand fire watch, but nobody ever checked to make sure they were sober enough to cope in an emergency.

I had learned early on in my naval career that I do not particularly enjoy inebriation. The sensation of the room revolving around me is one I do not wish to encounter again. Fire watch was very tedious if one did not enjoy drinking, but I found that there were ways of making it less so.

HMS Hornet, adjacent to the submarine base, HMS Dolphin in Gosport, was home to the Royal Naval Sailing Club, and I made full use of their facilities. Every weekend when I was on fire watch—and on weekday evenings too—I would leave my partner in control, and sail far and wide up and down the Solent, and out around the Isle of Wight in a sailing club dingy."

Returning to the subject of smoking, John revealed that as an undergraduate he was still in thrall to tobacco in all its forms. However, the pressure to quit became intense after the Royal College of Physicians published their report linking smoking to lung cancer—a report to which his father was a signatory. Withdrawal proved a difficult challenge for the whole family.

"My mother tried to ease the burden by switching to cigars,

which she was forbidden to smoke in the house. For a brief period of time she was forced to sit in her car in the driveway if she wanted to smoke, but the claustrophobic atmosphere and inconvenience combined to cure her quickly of her addiction."

For John, breaking the grip of nicotine proved to be harder and more drawn-out. Although the number of cigarettes was significantly reduced, there long remained the urge for a postprandial indulgence.

"The final break came during a filming expedition to Costa Rica. I consciously took a limited supply of cigarettes with me, knowing that once they were finished there would be no more. Gradually I was reduced to one or two puffs after dinner from a previously ignited butt— until finally there was nothing left to draw on. It was a couple of years later that I was persuaded by my son to have a cigarette with my glass of whiskey. To my delight I found the taste so obnoxious after so long an interval that I have never wanted to try smoking again. Today, even the occasional joint gives little pleasure—although there are more enjoyable ways to sample the delights of THC than smoking."

# SUBLIME LUNACY

## Discursus Twenty-One
# Maggots

After listening for some time as several guests described their distress with slipped discs and similar back problems, John eventually intervened with his own experiences. In attempting to pick up a heavy coil of rope the wrong way, while at HMS Hornet, his back suddenly went out and he was taken to the Naval hospital at Haslar, not far distant.

"A slipped disc was diagnosed and I became trapped in a plaster cast extending from my armpits to my thighs. It was summer, and in the heat and sweat of my plaster jacket I slowly started to rot. Nothing could relieve the itching, and nothing could suppress the smell. When, eventually the cast was removed, my flesh was green and rotted, hanging off me in great sheets. With my back only partially repaired, I now needed treatment for the treatment.

Once mobile, I was allowed to wander out into the gardens, where I could sit and read. In the course of my garden excursions I happened to meet a young medical orderly, who worked in the high-security psychiatric block. He described in some detail the miserable conditions under which the patients there were kept—mostly unhappy young sailors who in desperation had thrown themselves overboard in mid-ocean.

Would I, he asked, come and spend time talking to them. Some, he said were well-educated but dying of boredom in their isolation. It proved to be a sobering experience. Visiting a prison would not have been harder as I passed through a series of gates and courtyards to enter the wards. All means of self-destruction had been removed. The patients had no shoelaces, no underwear. Radiators against which they might have thrown themselves were inset behind grills. People just sat, some talking to themselves. Some were confined in padded cells. It was irredeemably depressing. I quickly became friends with a young national service man who was manifestly unsuited to military life. He was very intelligent, a talented poet and desperately unhappy at his condition. If only for his sake, I made regular daily visits into this hell hole until I was eventually discharged."

Unfitted for sea duty because of his back, John was posted to HMS Diligence, a base on the shores of Southampton Water. Here small craft—mainly wooden inshore minesweepers—were collected from the boat yards all around the country, where they had been built, and brought back with small ferry crews to be worked up into fighting condition. Many would then be handed over to Commonwealth navies.

On one occasion a party of Burmese sailors came to collect a craft, remaining at the base for several weeks. They seemed rather isolated, with nobody caring to mix with them, so curious about Burma, John started to spend time with them and became friends. He would often sit with them at meal times, noticing that they always brought with them a great jar containing some kind of condiment that was mixed liberally with the plain naval fare. Eventually, after expressing curiosity, he tried some and found it rather pleasant—somewhat salty like Marmite, with a vaguely fishy tang.

> "When I enquired what it was made from," he said, "I was not a little surprised to be told that the principal ingredient was "maggots from decayed waterfowl". It never tasted quite as good after that as upon close inspection, one could readily spot the chitinous larval head capsules."

John's job was to put together suitably qualified ferry crews containing the right mix of specialists in various nautical trades—seamen, electricians, engineers and suchlike, and dispatch them to the various boat yards to bring back the new hulls. It had taken his predecessor all day to accomplish this simple task, which he was quickly able to streamline. Devising a punch-card system, John could put a crew together in under ten minutes, leaving him plenty of time to read the newspaper that was delivered to his office each morning. In gathering data for his punch cards, he discovered the joys of creating questionnaires.

> "I would circulate forms with large spaces for single-word replies, but small ones where many words were called for. Trained always to do as instructed, I discovered that people would answer any questions put to them in a service environment. Married? Divorced? Cohabiting? Legitimate children? Illegitimate children? Religious affiliations? Sexual orientation?—The list was endless and comprehensive. I could, had I so wished, send out a ferry crew that were, for example, all gay, teetotal Catholics from Glasgow."

The best part of this posting, John said, was that he could live 'ashore' with some distant relatives who had a house in the wonderfully named village of Dibden Purlieu. They had served in the Far East during the war and their conversation was liberally sprinkled with Malay expressions, of which 'makan angin', literally 'eat air', meaning to take a brisk walk, proved unforgettable.

While visiting the Andaman Islands, at that time a very remote and little known archipelago in the Indian Ocean, they were surprised to see in a headman's hut, a shelf filled with tall silk top hats. Examining them, each was found to bear a label from one of the best hatters in Victorian London, neatly inscribed with its owner's name. These had once belonged to sea captains who had had the misfortune of being blown ashore here, only to be killed—and perhaps eaten?

"Situated on the edge of the New Forest, the Bryers' house was a perfect base from which to head out on my motorcycle to collect spiders. It was in this rich heathland habitat that I encountered for the first time the strange pink crab spider *Thomisus onustus* whose colouring makes it totally invisible as it sits on the heather, front legs extended as it waits to embrace visiting insects. In the same area I also had my first experience of *Atypus affinis*, the purse-web spider, which excavates a nine-inch vertical burrow, which it lines with silk. The silk is continued for another couple of inches above ground, lying horizontal and camouflaged with debris, but with no opening. An insect accidentally touching the exposed bit of tube attracts the attention of the spider, which positions itself to impale the visitor through the silk with long, curved fangs. Once the victim falls quiet, the spider releases one fang and makes a small slit in its tube, through which the prey is dragged inside. A few sweeps of silk with its spinnerets seals the opening, and the spider retires to feast on its prey at leisure underground. In time the indigestible parts of the prey will come to form part of the camouflage on the exposed section of tube."

Having had a casual introduction to the Malay language while in Dibden Purlieu, it seemed not unreasonable to seize upon a volume entitled "Teach yourself Malay" when one was subsequently encountered in a naval library while awaiting discharge. Little did John suspect that this brief indulgence would bear fruit years later, when the island of Bali came to figure prominently in his life, Malay (or Indonesian) being the local *lingua franca*.

# SUBLIME LUNACY

## Discursus Twenty-Two
# Dreaming Spires

The freedom of Oxford, John observed one afternoon, came as a breath of fresh air after life in the Navy, adding that for many it would be the very aura of freedom that would eventually prove their undoing. In some circles an appearance of idleness—of the grasshopper fiddling away while the ants laboured—was almost *de rigueur*, and far too many able minds, suddenly exposed to an environment free from restraint, would come to grief when the grim reaper called for them in the examination schools.

If one wished to present the appearance of grasshoppering through the countless distractions that pressed on one continually at Oxford, there was only one strategy for survival. Only after 1:00am, when peace had finally descended on the college, he explained, could one work unobserved and, more importantly, uninterrupted.

"Of course," he went on, "there were occasional distractions, even as the college slept. My first year at Merton was spent on the top floor above the main college gate. Reached by a spiral stone staircase that also continued on to give access to the roof above, it was generally a tranquil place in which to study.

It was about 2:30 one morning, when my silent world was suddenly interrupted by a horrendous crash somewhere above me—a crash that brought down showers of plaster as the ceiling buckled and jammed the door firmly shut. Moments later there was a loud knocking at the door and sounds on the staircase outside of someone trying to get in. After some exertion the door yielded to our combined efforts, and there, covered in dust and not a little anxious, stood a dishevelled John Newbould in evening dress.

John I already knew, for I had sought him out early on as an active member of the University Exploration Club, an organisation I was anxious to join. An ex-Royal Marine officer, John would become a good friend and travel with me in Africa, but that came later. At this moment we both had other matters on our minds. A keen climber, John had been traversing the rooftops of Front Quad after pioneering a new route into college. In those days the college gate closed at 10:00pm and those who chose to stay out late had to call on generations of undergraduate experience to find a way back in over the wall.

Whilst on the roofs, the sight of the small castellated tower that housed the stairs running past my room had proved an irresistible challenge. As John pulled himself up the final pitch onto the top of the tower, a large piece of masonry forming one of the castellations, came away under his weight and crashed onto the roof beneath, shattering slates and tiles before careening off into space and embedding itself in the unyielding surface of the quadrangle far beneath. As I have observed on numerous occasions since, a single loud noise in the middle of the night attracts little attention. It is only the discharge of, for example, the second barrel of a shotgun that arouses the curiosity of those unknowingly awakened by the first barrel.

A few drinks later John, still in evening dress, set off into the darkness while I returned to my essay on the adaptive radiation of gastropod molluscs. However, John did not retire for the night. Seeing the dislodged battlement, some two feet square and ten inches or more thick lying rather prominently in the open expanse of Front Quad, it seemed prudent to remove it, in the hope that the night's exploits might pass unnoticed by the college authorities— clearly a vain hope in view of the gaping hole in the roof and the fresh crater in the ground. The arrival of Bert Davis, my scout, as he came to wake me next morning, revealed that a search was already underway to find not only the miscreant(s), but more importantly, the whereabouts of the missing battlement."

News travels fast among the underground network of night climbers, and it was soon learnt that the missing piece of stone now resided out of sight on the bottom of the Isis, somewhere along the fringes of Christ Church meadow. To the undergraduate mind a mere piece of dislodged stone will have little monetary value—at least until a demand for its replacement is presented. With rare enlightenment, doubtless born of long experience, a compromise was reached. It was quietly made known by the college that if the missing stone were to be replaced intact on the spot where it had landed, no further disciplinary action would be taken.

It was indeed a fair compromise, but one that presented considerable difficulties to John, and his chosen nocturnal helper, Quentin Macleod. The problems of disposing of the evidence faded into insignificance in comparison to those involved in its recovery. Even for a tough marine like John, searching the river bed in the middle of a cold November night was a challenge, not to mention the engineering expertise needed to bring it to the surface. After that, carrying the massive deadweight of masonry back across the meadow and into college would have seemed relatively simple. Once replaced where it had fallen, the college authorities were as good as their word, and nothing more was said.

This story prompted John to report on another episode involving John Newbould, one in the wake of a Myrmidons dinner. The Myrmidons, a Merton dining society founded by Lord Randolph Churchill, is inevitably a somewhat exclusive body for in addition to being able to pay for the very best food and wine at the termly dinners, the chief requirement for membership is that every member wishes to sit next to you, which inevitably keeps the membership quite small. With eight-course dinners lubricated by an even greater number of wines, it is not unusual for the evening to become somewhat rowdy.

A ban on the Myrmidons dining in college, a periodic inconvenience the members suffer from time to time after a particularly enjoyable evening, had been lifted once again, and John Newbould had dined well. In the postprandial darkness he was prowling around college bearing an old muzzle-loading shotgun filled with wads of toilet paper. Eventually, and not by accident, for he had already discharged it several times, he encountered John Roberts, the Principal of Postmasters—the college disciplinary officer.

The overheard conversation went:

"Mr Newbould, please hand me your weapon."

"Certainly sir…..Would you care for me to discharge it?"

Whereupon, before there was time for a reply, first one barrel, and then the second echoed around the confines of the college quadrangle. As glowing sparks of burning toilet paper descended through the smoke, John Newbold handed over his weapon as requested.

"This episode," said John, "was a ground-breaking event in the history of the college, for it set for the first time ever, a monetary value on a member of the senior common room. John was fined £3, thereby setting the worth of a Principal of Postmasters incontrovertibly at thirty shillings a barrel."

# SUBLIME LUNACY

## Discursus Twenty-Three
## **Ascendens Nocte**

A s a biologist, John did not lack for scientific anecdotes, particularly when they served as an aid to teaching. The conversation had turned one evening to what constitutes a species, something that has prompted much technical debate over the years. Traditionally species were distinguished primarily on morphological features—small but consistent differences in structure. John then paused to say that the great Linnaeus, father of zoological and botanical classification, was perceptive enough even in the mid-seventeen-hundreds, to recognise the importance of non-morphological characters, and he quoted as an example the case of earthworms. Now to the uninitiated one earthworm appears much the same as any other—something that has caused confusion even among professional zoologists. The species to which Linnaeus gave the name *Lumbricus terrestris*—the "common earthworm", could not later be readily distinguished from its close relatives on the grounds of the physical features alone that he had described. However, Linnaeus added *"ascendens nocte"* to his description, thus linking the name indubitably to the worm Linnaeus had before him; *L. terrestris* is the only European earthworm known to emerge at night.

Pausing to take in the effect of this revelation on his listeners, John quietly repeated *"ascendens nocte"* to himself, so setting off a whole new and totally unrelated train of thought. He is the first to admit that in his youth he had been somewhat wild, with a love of risk-taking that included rock-climbing and mountaineering. North Wales provided the nearest cliffs of any merit, apart from the Avon Gorge in Bristol, but to get there entailed a five-hour drive from Oxford—passing en route, he told us, a firm of estate agents in Kidderminster improbably named "Messrs Doolittle & Dalley".

> "In those days, undergraduates were not allowed to travel far from the city without special permission. We had to endure all sorts of paternalistic nonsense like mounting a distinguishing green light on all undergraduate motor vehicles—and we were not allowed to keep an airplane within twenty miles of the city; admittedly a restriction that not many found irksome. One consequence of the restrictions on travel was a need to find local rock faces on which to hone our climbing skills. A railway tunnel next to the Horsepath sewage farm near Littlemore, just outside Oxford, provided some interesting challenges. A traverse across the top of the tunnel opening held some technical points of interest, which could become quite demanding on the rare occasions when a train would pass through. The already tenuous friction holds seemed to become even less supportive when one was suddenly enveloped in noisy clouds of smoke and steam—when a fall might result in one being unwittingly carried to wheresoever the train was bound."

In the absence of natural cliffs, Oxford's stone buildings posed an attractive alternative. To the technical challenges of climbing on them were added two additional factors that served to enhance the experience, not least the special exhilaration of exploring the rooftops under cover of darkness. Such expeditions were viewed most severely by the university authorities, and immediate rustication, if not expulsion, was the penalty if caught.

"Concern for our safety was one legitimate concern of the authorities. The other was for the safety of their buildings. In retrospect", he said, "our elders and betters were quite right in wishing to suppress our nocturnal ascents. It was a dangerous undertaking. Poor Stuart Godfrey, a friend from Shrewsbury was not an experienced climber. One night, after more drinking than was prudent, he attempted to scale the dome of the Radcliffe Camera, a particularly demanding ascent.

No one accustomed to night climbing would commit himself to the uncertain security of a mere lightening conductor. Attempting to negotiate the large overhang at the top of the chimneying pitch between paired columns, Stuart apparently placed his faith in the lightening conductor, which came away and sent him crashing onto the flagstones far below. His body was found next morning."

The builders of Oxford's older structures—those dating from the thirteenth and fourteenth centuries or earlier—clearly understood the relative worth of stone excavated from quarries in the area, and used only the most durable for outside construction. The more easily worked 'freestone' from local quarries such as those at Headington were used only for interior decorative work. With the great building boom that took place in Oxford during the seventeenth and eighteenth centuries, the earlier mediaeval wisdom was forgotten—or more probably suppressed by avaricious quarry owners and builder's merchants—and widespread use was made of the softer, less durable local material that could be supplied more cheaply from nearby quarries. In consequence, many of Oxfords buildings had fallen into scabrous disrepair.

The extensive renovations that took place in Oxford after the Second World War replaced much of the decayed stone with harder material from the Clipsham quarries, which made night climbing safer, but many structures still harboured a residue of dangerously friable material.

A long-standing target for amateur climbers has been the Martyr's Memorial in St. Giles, which commemorates the burning of Ridley, Latimer and Cranmer in 1555. The delicate carvings on the memorial are particularly fragile, and it is impossible to climb without doing significant damage. A quick look early one morning while still a schoolboy convinced John that it was not a climb he should attempt. Waxing eloquent on the joys of night-climbing, he announced:

"Perhaps the finest ascent of an Oxford building was the conquest of the dome of Tom Tower at Christ Church. Several distinguished climbers, including members of the successful Everest expedition, had tried and turned back defeated. It was Jim Murray, a quiet zoology post-graduate from Virginia—later a professor at the university in Charlottesville—who led the climb. The evidence for all to see on Coronation morning was a Confederate flag fluttering from the lightening conductor on the summit.

There were some repercussions later when, among the new climbs described in the OU Mountaineering Club magazine, was one named Tom Tower, ostensibly on a Welsh crag—whose name in translation proved to be Christ Church in Welsh. The anonymous writer warned that "the slabs on the final pitch" (i.e. the dome itself) "are liable to be icy in winter."

## Discursus Twenty-Four
# Wheel of Fortune

Turning once again to a favourite topic, John told how late one night (actually early one morning) during his second year he was hard at work in his rooms in Mob Quad when there was an unexpected knock at the door. Two friends appeared from the darkness, accompanied by a massive brass-bound teak ship's wheel. They had, they said, found it while walking at night down by the river in Christ Church Meadows. The fact that it had, at the time, been attached to one of Mr Salter's river steamers only emerged later. Knowing that he was a keen night climber, they wished, they said, to present it for the embellishment of some suitable Oxford landmark.

The traditional decorative item in Oxford had long been the old ceramic chamber pot, and there are many stories concerning them. One favourite concerned an elderly, cantankerous don whose rooms overlooked the front quad. Hearing a commotion outside, he rushed to his window to remonstrate with those disturbing the peace. At that moment a chamber pot appeared, dangling on a hook just outside the window bars. In a fury he grabbed the chamber pot, which came free of its hook, leaving him holding it, unable to bring it in through the bars, yet unable to let it go lest it hit some unfortunate out of sight beneath. A large crowd soon gathered to watch his discomfort.

A chamber pot suspended in the Fellows Quad at

Merton was soon brought down by a well-aimed rifle shot. The next night the chamber pot was replaced, in the same inaccessible position, by a large target.

Not long afterwards a row of metal chamber pots, all painted in bright Easter colours, appeared suspended across Front Quad, one end attached to the chancel cross on the chapel roof, and the other end to an equally inaccessible spot on the hall roof. John commented that it was somewhat embarrassing to find that the bill for the pots had inadvertently been charged by Coopers, the ironmongers, to his father's account, not least because his father was a fellow of the college.

John, commenting on the ascent, said that the first pitch to the chapel roof had been greatly aided by some conveniently placed scaffolding, but that the original route had to be changed when it was found that the masonry to be climbed was loose, slabs of stone lifting easily to the touch. Instead he climbed up the lead cladding, between the tower and 2-inch-high standing seams up to the ridge, and then shuffled to the end of the chancel roof. Quentin Macleod made a similar ascent of the hall, he and John each dropping a thin line down to assistants below, who then attached the ends of the rope that would span the quad, to which the chamber pots had already been attached.

Pictures duly appeared in the local paper, and the workmen who had been called in to bring the decorations down were interviewed. Proudly they boasted that anything 'them students' chose to put up, they would get down within two hours. Here was a challenge that could not go unanswered.

"It was at this moment that the great brass-bound ship's wheel appeared. I quickly consulted with Quentin Macleod, who had previously joined me on a number of nocturnal adventures. If we were to win the challenge thrown at us, it would be necessary to try something novel, and an earlier climb had suggested a possible location. Rather than place the wheel on top of a roof or spire in the normal way, we decided to suspend it inside, from the apex of the lofty ceiling of Merton hall.

It called for careful planning and meticulous execution, but this would be a climb with purpose. From the gallery in the hall, it was possible to gain access to the first set of beams. Although overhanging, it was possible to clamber up the overhang to the ridge. Just below the ridge ran a series of transverse members spaced about three feet apart, and there was just room to squeeze along on top of them from one to the next – some 70 feet or more above the floor.

Quentin, being slightly smaller, undertook the traverse. I seconded him on the ascent and then climbed back down to ground level to supervise the action there. Carrying only a light line, Quentin made his way out to about the mid-point of the hall—a distance of some 50-60 feet. As the line dropped down I attached first the end of a nylon climbing rope, then some nylon slings and finally a pulley. With the pulley attached to a cross beam by the slings, the climbing rope was threaded through and lowered back down for the wheel to be tied on. The ground party then hoisted the wheel up as far as it would go for Quentin to secure it. A few minutes later Quentin himself abseiled down out of the darkness and we retired to bed well-pleased with the evening's activity.

The following morning the four of us made a highly unusual appearance at breakfast to witness the effect our nocturnal labours might have. Beneath the wheel, a large amount of dust and cobwebs littered the tables, exciting some adverse comment, but if anyone had looked up, they never noticed the wheel, hanging like a sword of Damocles in the shadows far above. Unable to bear the suspense, we started to comment loudly and gesticulate upwards, until eventually the wheel was noticed.

And what of the challenge? Well, it proved to be a resounding victory. It took two full days (rather than hours) to get the wheel down, as scaffolding had to be erected all the way up to the apex of the roof before the workmen could get near. Their comments on whoever had been fool enough to put the wheel there were a joy to overhear—and they never did work out how it was done. Again, they got their pictures in the Oxford Times—this time on the front page."

Another front page in the Oxford Times sported a photograph of an armless tailor's dummy standing proud on top of the dome at The Queen's College. "She looked," John said, "like an attractive Venus de Milo, the pink of her body contrasting most effectively with the blue sky and the green copper of the dome."

More than fifty years later John was visiting Queens, curious to see if he could recall details of the rooftop route taken to position the dummy. An incautious remark about the purpose of his presence in the wrong college alerted the Porter, who suddenly demanded, "You weren't responsible for the dummy, were you, sir?" To so direct a question he felt obliged to make an embarrassed confession of guilt, but expressed surprise that anyone apart from himself still remembered it. "Oh no sir" came the reply, "They're still talking about it. Why only at the last Gaudy, sir, someone came with pictures." Such is fame.

SUBLIME LUNACY

## Discursus Twenty-Five
# Mountain Rescue

Not all climbing while at Oxford was confined to buildings, John explained. From time to time the OU Mountaineering Club would organize weekend expeditions during term to climb in North Wales. Although it was nominally against the rules, the university proctors generally turned a blind eye to such activities—until it was forced on their attention. One spring, 1958 as I recall, there was such a trip.

"It was Hilary Term. We drove through the night in a hired bus on Friday, leaving Saturday and Sunday free to climb, and with the intention of returning to Oxford by Monday morning in time for lectures and tutorials. The weather was fine and the rock faces on the three cliffs in the Llanberis Pass were dry in the early sunshine. On the Sunday, while most of us were enjoying pleasant conditions on the West-facing crags, one party headed for Cyrn Glas, a grim cliff high on the slopes of Snowdon. Being in shadow for virtually the whole day, conditions here had remained unexpectedly wintry.

As we began to gather our gear together for the long haul back to Oxford, word reached us that there had been an accident on Cyrn Glas, and that a member of the club was trapped on a narrow ledge, probably with a broken leg.

A rescue party set out at once, while others mobilised the local mountain rescue team. This was headed by Chris Briggs, landlord of the Pen-y-Gwyrd hotel, the famous mountain inn where the 1953 Everest Expedition had based themselves for training. Chris and I were old friends, having collaborated together on a number of previous rescues. This one would prove to be one of the most challenging either of us had ever experienced.

It was already dark by the time we reached the foot of the cliff, and reports filtering back from the advance party were not encouraging. With gullies still filled with snow and the exposed rocks coated with ice, it became clear that a direct nocturnal ascent up to the injured man would be nigh impossible.

By now the rescue party had swelled in size as word spread among other groups of climbers camping throughout the valley. In moments of crisis everybody joins in, recognising that next time they might be the ones in need. Chris decided that a strong party of experienced climbers should try to find a way to position themselves directly above the injured man and his companions, who by this time were in danger of frostbite as they huddled inadequately clad on a tiny shelf of rock in sub-zero conditions. With no lights to signal their precise position on the cliff, it took several false attempts to locate them.

All through the night the upper party slowly negotiated the frozen rocks, abseiling down and then having to climb back up, each time drawing closer to their quarry. It would be almost daybreak before they reached their destination. Meanwhile, those of us waiting below in the snow also began to suffer, Chris himself getting badly frostbitten toes.

It was 9:00am on Monday morning by the time

the stretcher and its unhappy patient could be lowered down to us, and a further hour or more would pass before we could carry him to the waiting ambulance far down on the road along valley floor. But for us the day had hardly started. The rescue had resulted in large quantities of valuable ropes and other equipment being left dangling over the crags. After a quick breakfast we were all back on the mountain clearing up, and it was late afternoon before we could leave to head south.

For those with Monday morning tutorials it was plain that some creative excuses would have to be dreamed up to account for non-attendance, but for the rest of us we simply hoped to slip quietly back into the woodwork without our absence being noticed. It was not to be. We were greeted on Tuesday morning not by quiet anonymity, but by newspaper headlines, both local and national, describing the rescue in which we had just taken part. This was scarcely surprising, for we had been interviewed by more than one reporter before we were even off the mountain ourselves. We had previously learned the hard way that no matter how much one wished not to talk to reporters, in the long run it was better to give them the facts rather than leave them in ignorance to fabricate a story that was highly misleading.

Those responsible for maintaining discipline, both within the university and within the individual's colleges, could no longer turn a blind eye to our misdeeds in being away from Oxford without permission during term. Each undergraduate club and society has to have a senior member of the university to monitor their activities and give advice where needed. The mountaineering club had as its senior member David Cox, a distinguished alpinist, and fellow of University College, who had become paralysed by polio while climbing in the Alps. Through his intervention, the proctors were persuaded to impose only minimal sanctions, although we were enjoined not to be caught again."

## Discursus Twenty-Six
# Man Trap

D ons in the less mainstream subjects can sometimes enjoy a life free of burdensome teaching, and devote themselves wholly to research in their chosen field. Every Don cherishes a dream—the appearance of his *magnum opus*, the culmination of years of dedicated intellectual effort. For many, death supervenes before the work is completed— and in not a few cases, before it is even begun.

The professor of Celtic Studies, an endowed chair at Jesus College, was one of the fortunate few. Years would pass without the necessity of lecturing, but the time came when a thoughtless postgraduate embarked upon a course of Celtic, and required lecturing to—in solitary state.

Encountering the professor in the street one day, John's father maliciously enquired about his audience, a keen follower of field sports, and received the disdainful reply: "Last week—it went beagling!"

To those outside Oxford it may seem strange that the one quality not demanded of a Don is an ability to teach. While some were brilliant lecturers, who attracted large and enthusiastic audiences, there were others for whom lecturing was nothing more than a painful responsibility, a penance with which they were obligated to acquiesce if they were to continue receiving the bounty of college wining and dining.

Such lectures, even if the lecturer were himself a leading authority in his field, could prove exceedingly dull.

Charles Elton, who virtually invented the science of ecology, was a prime example. With the lecture theatre immersed in total darkness, Elton would sit at the bench, almost invisible, with only a desk lamp illuminating his notes. Here, with his face only inches above the surface, he would murmur to himself for an hour, totally divorced from his audience. John came to know him quite well, and found him to be an inspiring teacher—but only when chatting informally one-to-one.

"When I later became a lecturer myself, I devised a measure of my colleague's ability to hold their listener's attention. This, like the measure of radioactive decay, I termed 'Audience Half Life', and it is painful to record that for some, just three lectures would leave an inert residue of just two or three semi-conscious forms draped over the front bench of the lecture theatre.

There was an embarrassing occasion when I rashly decided to drop in on an entomology course being given by George Varley. George I had known well since long before coming up to Oxford, and I have always admired his encyclopaedic knowledge of the world of insects. However, he was not an inspiring lecturer, particularly for those with no special interest in his subject. My presence had swelled his audience by 33.3 percent and I therefore felt obligated to attend the rest of his course until the end of term as my absence would have been embarrassingly conspicuous."

This episode reminded John of Dr Froude, a rather eccentric Fellow of Corpus Christi College during the reign of Queen Victoria. Irritated by people walking on the grass outside his rooms, he set a man-trap—one of those horrendous toothed implements beloved of gamekeepers to discourage poachers. A few days later in the early morning, as Dr Froude was shaving, he heard loud screams rising from the garden outside his window. Rushing down, he found he had caught the Professor of Moral Philosophy. By way of penance, Dr Froude attended the professor's lectures for the rest of term.

## Discursus Twenty-Seven
# Thespian Interlude

One of the delights of summer in Oxford is the profusion of outdoor dramatic productions, both by OUDS and by less auspicious college dramatic societies. John was never stricken with the acting bug, although he did find himself being volunteered to fill three separate roles in a Merton production of Beaumont & Fletcher's 'Two Noble Kinsmen'. It was, therefore, quite a surprise to find himself unwittingly caste one day in a leading role.

"For zoologists like myself, each day would start with a one hour lecture at 9:00am, followed by lab work for the rest of the morning. I quickly learned which lectures were worth getting out of bed for—and it was not a large number. For the remainder I found it more rewarding to cover the same ground in the library at my own pace and convenience. I also discovered that the practical lab work could be done more expeditiously in the afternoon when there were fewer people about.

Thus it happened that one summer morning I arose late and staggered bleary-eyed to a favourite café on the High for a much-needed fix of caffeine. I was vaguely aware that the place seemed much busier than usual, but failed to understand the significance of the numerous lights and tripods. Before I could find a vacant table at which to greet the day, someone grabbed my arm and a loud voice said: " Ah…beard…come and sit here."

So it was that I found myself unintentionally

playing a prominent role in a film about Oxford being made for the Central Office of Information. Over the next couple of hours I was plied with countless cups of coffee and endless cigarettes. Completely bemused, I did as I was told, and apparently did it moderately well. As filming came to an end I was instructed to present myself the following day at a designated location to continue filming. So it was that I found myself passing much of Trinity term in front of the cameras.

The film, which was to be used by the British Council—that organisation dedicated to bringing Shakespeare to the starving masses—purported to show undergraduate life in all its varied facets. Thus one day I was shown making toast on the end of a fencing foil before a gas fire in someone's college rooms. I remember questioning the veracity of this scene as no undergraduate rooms that I knew enjoyed the luxury of a gas fire. Another day was spent on the river. Unnaturally clad in white flannels, with blue blazer and straw boater, I was filmed propelling exceptionally attractive young ladies in light summer frocks and jolly hats up and down the Cherwell in a punt.

Returning from these exertions through Magdalen College glades I chanced, to my considerable embarrassment, to come face to face with Geoffrey Muir, the Warden of Merton. "My" he said, "You do cut a fine figure!" With an unnatural bravado—undoubtedly brought on by the embarrassment of the moment—I replied offhandedly "My audience expects it!" I still cringe as I recall the scene.

Although there was a farewell party for those who had participated in making the film, term ended without my having seen a single frame of the finished product. Indeed, I would only see it once—some two or three years later, and under curious circumstances."

Membership of various clubs took up a lot of time that should have been used for study, and the demands only increased when simple membership grew into office-holding. A major distraction came when John was elected chairman of the OU Exploration Club. Constructing an interesting program of visiting speakers with the club secretary was somewhat time-consuming, but even more so was the help, both official and unofficial, given to budding expedition leaders.

From the 1920s onward Oxford has had a fine track record of overseas expeditions. Although the majority were to the arctic—for example prospecting possible landing sites for transatlantic seaplanes on lakes in Greenland—there were also major expeditions to Sarawak and other tropical locations.

"The first Greenland expedition had spent an arduous summer taking soundings from a small boat across several lakes that appeared suitable candidates for seaplane landing spots. Transect after transect criss-crossed the lakes, building a mountain of valuable data. When a follow-up expedition came to continue the work the next summer, they found the whole exercise had been in vain as the lakes had dried up and entirely disappeared."

The OU Exploration Club has enjoyed many great talks over the years. One that John has mentioned several times was a Cambridge expedition to the Tibesti Mountains on the southern fringe of the Sahara Desert. He had hoped in vain that the expedition would have brought back specimens of the freshwater jellyfish *Limnocnida*, said to exist there in small rock pools, as it seems a very improbable habitat for such a delicate creature—presumably a relict of the time when the Sahara was still relatively lush. However, the expedition did bring back a detailed photographic record of a trepanning operation, performed the same way it must have been done in Palaeolithic times, evidenced by ancient skulls with neat tell-tale circular openings.

"One day the expedition was approached by an old man complaining of demons battling within his head. Examining him, it was clear that on some previous occasion he had had a two-inch diameter circlet of cranium removed. This, he said, had provided wonderful relief the last time he suffered from demons—could the expedition now repeat the operation on the other side as the demons had returned? Unwilling to risk the possible consequences of such an unfamiliar operation themselves, they agreed to help send a message to someone who could. The audience found it touching that the patient would show such faith in mere Cambridge men.

Three days later the surgeon arrived by donkey, accompanied by his assistant, a little boy of about ten, who quickly built a camel dung fire in which to sterilise the surgical instruments. These consisted of an old kitchen knife and several large nails with their ends hammered flat. The patient sat quietly on an upturned box and removed his turban, allowing the surgeon, without a murmur, to cut the scalp on three sides and fold it back to expose the bone underneath.

Slowly, for more than an hour the surgeon carefully scribed a circle with a sharpened nail, gradually chipping away at the cranium until suddenly the disc of bone lifted out to expose the pulsating brain beneath. As his demons escaped, the patient breathed a sigh of relief and signified his thanks. The scalp was then put back in position, secured with a generous application of camel dung paste, whereupon the patient replaced his turban and disappeared into the desert. Throughout the operation, a large tick had slowly travelled around the patient's scalp without attracting any undue attention."

One lecturer John was particularly happy to lure to Oxford was Colonel F. M Bailey. A member of the 1904 Younghusband expedition to Lhasa, Colonel Bailey had led an extraordinary life, much of it in the Himalayas. In 1912, as an Intelligence Officer, he made an epic journey of some 2700km[8] on foot to determine the route of the Tsangpo river, which follows Tibet's southern border, before vanishing among impenetrable mountain gorges. He was able to confirm that the Tsangpo was indeed a tributary of the Brahamaputra, a major geographical conundrum at the time. He also discovered that it flowed through a gorge both longer and deeper than the Grand Canyon; actually the deepest canyon on earth. On his journey he collected plants and butterflies, including a new species of blue poppy, *Meconopsis baleyi*.

---

8    Roughly the distance from New York to Denver!

"When he came to speak to us in Oxford he was already approaching 80, but very spry and amusing. As British Resident in Sikkim, he was the only member of the colonial administration who was able to converse with the thirteenth Dalai Lama in Tibetan without the help of an interpreter. Over the years he maintained a long and intimate correspondence with His Holiness that carried with it certain unexpected benefits. There were, apparently, many details of formality that had to be scrupulously observed—for example the precise manner in which letter and envelope should be folded. If properly performed, the reply would be accompanied by a small bag of gold dust and a bolt of raw silk. Mrs Bailey was wearing a beautiful silk dress, one of many apparently, and was adorned with truly pharonic quantities of gold jewellery, that provided vivid, if mute, testimony to the volume of the correspondence. Sitting in the front row she would occasionally prompt her husband by asking questions like "What about the currency in Tibet?" for example to keep him on script.

"Oh yes, the currency," he replied, plunging his hand his trouser pocket to bring out a handful of gold coins as he embarked on the next section of his talk.

From Tibet, we moved on to his travels in Turkestan. This was an era in which the "Great Game" was still being played in earnest. The new Bolshevik government were rumoured to be planning incursions into Afghanistan and India to challenge the British and gain access to the Indian Ocean. Col. Bailey was sent on a diplomatic embassy, by way of Kashgar in Chinese Turkestan, to make contact with the Bolsheviks to learn something of their intentions.

It quickly became a challenging assignment. From the outset he was considered a spy, and soon forced to go into hiding. His considerable linguistic skills enabled him to join, undetected, the *cheka,* the local Russian secret Police, while they were searching for him. In this capacity he received a telegram asking for information about his own [Col. Bailey's] location, and urging his elimination.

With wonderful *sang froid* Col. Bailey himself composed a reply (in Russian): "Englishman Bailey reported recently in vicinity. Last seen heading towards......" (a location diametrically opposite to his intended route). The telegram ended with the cryptic comment: "Finglestein knows all!". Apparently the Russians puzzled and fretted over this latter piece of intelligence for weeks. After an epic journey through Samarkand and Bokhara, he finally escaped into NE Iran.

Colonel Bailey introduced us to the real Great Game, and the thrill of true exploration, giving us an evening that none of his audience could ever forget."

## Discursus Twenty-Eight
**Firearms**

In the early years of the last century the undergraduates at Merton petitioned the college to install baths, and received a curt note from Warden Broderick saying: "Gentlemen are reminded that the term is only eight weeks long."

To those outside the university, the fact that formal teaching only occupies three eight-week terms, and hence just 24 weeks of the year, may seem rather strange. In times past, however, the 28 weeks of vacation were traditionally put to good use. Tutors would gather a group of undergraduates and take them on prolonged reading parties in North Wales, the Lake District, the Highlands or the Alps. Here extensive reading and deep philosophical discussions would be interspersed with valuable physical exertion.

To a large extent the tradition of the vacation reading party was already in serious decline when John was an undergraduate, and the long weeks of summer given over to either pleasure or money-making activities. He recalled, as an example, a friend at Christ Church, grandson of the Lord Chief Justice, who had worked one summer as a sleeping-car attendant on the trans-Canadian railroad. It was also the time when expeditions could be mounted to foreign parts.

"George and I started planning an expedition during our first term at Oxford, its purpose to collect spiders in some remote and interesting region. We debated a number of suitable destinations, and eventually settled on Eastern

Turkey. Its arachnid fauna was essentially unknown; it was an area where several major faunal regions came together; and it was not so remote as to be prohibitively expensive to reach. We also debated the pros and cons of applying to become an official university expedition, which carried with it certain obligations, but also provided access to particular sources of funding. We decided to go it alone, and called ourselves simply the 'Oxford Expedition to South-Eastern Turkey', without reference to the university.

There followed a spate of letter-writing as we approached firms for support and applied for grants from every fund we could find. The generosity of firms was remarkable. We received free supplies of toilet paper, sugar, margarine, tobacco, petrol and much more. The offer of petrol would prove particularly welcome. Our truck was a thirsty brute, particularly under rough conditions, getting a mere 5 miles to the gallon. Fortunately BP had generously arranged for the expedition to receive free petrol at any BP service station—and even more generously donated a significant sum of money with which to buy it when out of range of a BP station.

The Ministry of Agriculture, Fisheries and Food provided us with huge quantities of dehydrated meat, vegetables and fruit as part of a program to test proposed new military rations. We were required to maintain detailed diaries with notes recording the relative taste and digestibility of the various products. The dried carrots passed through the human digestive tract seemingly undamaged, while the dried meats—steaks and minced beef—were extremely tasty straight out of the can, requiring no re-hydration. Likewise the dried blackcurrants and raspberries. The slabs of compressed cabbage, however, swelled to ten times their packed size when wetted, and would have been lethal if not properly cooked."

Geoffrey Muir, Warden of Merton, and Hegelian philosopher, was a dedicated rowing man. John has never determined whether his acceptance at Merton was the result of being an oarsman at school, or simple nepotism. If the former, he proved to be a disappointment as his back injury during National Service precluded any further rowing. Geoffrey Muir and his colourfully eccentric wife Molly were old friends of John's parents, who would often be invited to the parties and dinners that the heads of houses at Oxford would be expected to host periodically. They reported that Molly, a member of the Wills tobacco family and hence sufficiently well-off to behave exactly as she wished without censure, would often leave the events she was nominally hosting at the first hint of boredom.

"At a party for freshman undergraduates Molly spotted me in the throng just as she was about to go home, and swept over. "Daaarling boy! I hear you are going to Turkey. I must give you the warden's pistol."

Thus I acquired the first weapon in the expedition armoury. It was an immaculate 9mm Luger that Geoffrey had brought back as a souvenir from the First World War. For some thirty-five years it had lain unused and unlicensed in the bottom of his chest-of-drawers. It should be remembered that in the 1950s very few people in Britain owned firearms (other than shotguns) and the maze of red tape involved in obtaining a firearms certificate was deliberately discouraging. To obtain a certificate for a hitherto unregistered weapon was well-nigh impossible—at least in the law-abiding circles in which I moved.

Through contacts at the Cobra, my favourite Indian restaurant (of which more anon) I learned of a gunsmith of questionable antecedents who might be able to help. The name of Robin Braid-Taylor was not wholly unknown to me. As a boy at the Dragon School a few years ahead of me, he had acquired some notoriety after accidentally shooting himself in the head with an automatic pistol—a mishap that resulted in his expulsion. I recalled encountering him briefly at some social function, which I felt was sufficient grounds to engineer a meeting."

Robin had a shop deep in the, at that time un-renovated, St. Ebbes slums but was rarely there. Consequently it took some determination and time to track him down and arrange a meeting. He proved to be warm and affable—and happy to help. He expressed only mild interest in the collection of nominally unrelated pistol parts John had brought in (despite the fact that each part bore an identical serial number).

"He told me to return a few days later, when I received a complete Luger pistol in perfect condition, together with a bill of sale that would enable the Police to issue the necessary certificate.

This meeting with Robin was my first contact with the shadowy world of international arms dealers, but would not be my last. It was after Robin's name had figured prominently in press reports of arms dealings in Algeria, and Central Africa, that our paths crossed again."

George Halcrow, owner of the afore-mentioned Cobra restaurant, had become a good friend, and owned several houses in Oxford, most of which were rented out as inexpensive student lodgings. After some of his tenants had become concerned over a large collection mysterious crates they had discovered in an attic, George and John went to investigate.

> "Our suspicions aroused, we pried a lid off the first crate and found ourselves staring at rows of neatly packed machine guns. The next crate was filled with hand grenades and a third with ammunition. There was no question as to whom this cache belonged, for Robin had not long before rented rooms in the house. George may well have recognised the danger of retribution if the police were to be called in, and in any case they would be bound to ask potentially embarrassing questions. So much simpler to call Robin and ask him quietly to move his crates elsewhere."

SUBLIME LUNACY

## Discursus Twenty-Nine
# Byzantium Bound

During his first long vacation at Oxford, John and his friend George Lampel organised a zoological and botanical expedition to eastern Turkey, an area that had been closed to foreigners for many years. For transportation they purchased a one-ton Ford truck that had survived the WWII desert campaigns in North Africa, before being purchased by the Marquis of Bath to work on his Longleat estate. Retired from aristocratic employment, it then passed to an Oxford undergraduate expedition to Morocco.

"It came well-equipped with a huge inventory of spare parts, including starter-motor, alternator, bearings, brakes, springs etc. Before taking delivery, it had, we were assured, been thoroughly overhauled and serviced by one of Oxford's best-known garages. Consequently I felt confident it would not let us down.

The Oxford Times sent several reporters and photographers to cover our departure, with supplies and equipment neatly packed in old champagne crates—relics of recent college Commemoration Balls. But it was not an auspicious start. After spluttering briefly, the engine died before the truck had even left my parent's driveway. Diagnosing a fuel problem, the carburettor was dismantled and as night fell the float chamber was found choked with red dust from Morocco. Clearly the vehicle had not received the level of servicing for which the garage had been paid."

One member of the five-man team considered himself well-informed on international currency dealings, and had plotted a route that would facilitate an increase in funds through carefully thought-out currency deals in successive countries across Europe. As traveller's cheques were cashed and bank notes exchanged, the accumulated funds were hidden inside the massive front bumper of the truck, which was skilfully dismantled and reassembled in successive bank parking lots. It is unlikely that more than a few pounds, if any, were gained through these transactions.

Crossing from Trieste into Yugoslavia, they were preparing to make camp one evening in the forests of Bosnia-Herzegovina when they noticed a truck full of people slowing down to look. "We thought nothing of it," John said, "after all; we certainly looked a bit unusual." A few minutes later the truck and its passengers returned; but without the uniformed policemen they had noticed earlier.

"We were immediately encircled by a group of some fifteen men, who looked extremely menacing. One of them addressed us in German, and unfortunately George was able to reply. Clearly we were mistaken for Germans—and not at all welcome. It was with some difficulty that we persuaded them that we were all British—our passports at first did little to convince them—but eventually they believed us.

At that point their attitude towards us changed wonderfully. They later took us to the remains of their village and showed us the pock-marked wall against which the inhabitants had been lined up and machine-gunned by the Germans during the war. Had we not successfully proved our nationality, I have no doubt but that we should at best have been severely beaten up.

A few days later we were near Pristina, in Kosovo—an area now familiar for its Serbian-Albanian ethnic unrest. When we broke down there on a remote country road in 1956 it was almost off the map. Suspecting that a bearing might have blown, we dropped the crankcase, and discovered metal fragments that indicated serious engine damage. With unwarranted confidence, and in conditions far from ideal, we started to dismantle the engine by the roadside. We found a little-end bearing had shattered, seriously damaging a piston. We next discovered that the crankshaft had at some point been re-ground, but to a non-standard size, so none of our spare bearings would fit. Somewhere along the way we had also broken a key component of the oil circulation system, which may actually have been the prime reason for the bearing failure. There was no alternative but to try and make a replacement from scratch. With infinite patience we sawed and filed and hand-drilled for several days, even cutting a screw thread with a triangular file, until we had created a piece that fitted and worked—just. I consider it an improvisational *tour-de-force*."

After much discussion it was decided that the least strain would be put on the engine if it were re-assembled, but without a spark plug in the cylinder with the damaged piston. It was reasoned that at least the crankshaft would be evenly balanced by doing this, but the damaged piston would be spared the force of detonation.

Inserting a length of garden hose into the spark-plug opening to carry away the petrol vapour, they set off for Istanbul sounding like a rather elderly tractor. In Istanbul they figured they would be able to find a garage that could effect a proper repair; but there would be several adventures before they reached Turkey.

## Discursus Thirty
# Gaol Birds

Arriving at the Yugoslav frontier post at Gevgalia, ready to cross into Greece, the expedition found themselves in unexpected trouble. Because of the delay caused by their breakdown they had unwittingly overstayed their ten-day transit visa through Yugoslavia. It was, said John, his first experience of arrest and imprisonment.

"Our 'cell' was the barracks toilet, a large wooden shed with a low barricade at one end, beyond which the floor was missing to reveal a huge stinking open cesspit. The temperature being around 105°F, it was not a nice place. There being little chance that we might escape, we were occasionally allowed outside to walk around the compound in the sunshine and escape the flies and smell."

On one such excursion they found at ground level a small window leading to an underground dungeon. Inside were two Turkish engineers, who had been held there for over a year because of some irregularity in their papers as they were passing through on their way home from Germany, where they had been working. It turned out that nobody knew where they had vanished to, and they begged that information on their whereabouts be transmitted to the Turkish authorities. Surreptitiously their passport information was written down, and in due course passed on. Whether these efforts were successful in effecting their release is unknown.

Meanwhile the expedition had its own problems to

sort out. After several days it was decided by their captors that two members of the party should return to Tito Veles, the Macedonian regional capital, to obtain exit visas. Not allowed to take their own ailing vehicle, they were obliged to hitchhike.

"It was hot when John Keylock and I set off. We had had little to eat, and carried neither food nor water. There was almost no traffic. The outlook was depressingly bleak, when suddenly a big black limousine appears. The young party official inside is very friendly and subsequently we stop at every bar along the way as he insists that we join him in downing glass after glass of slivovitz—dangerously strong plum brandy. In our weakened state we have little resistance to alcohol, and soon become totally, uncontrollably drunk.

I retain relatively few memories of subsequent events, but certain details stand out vividly. We found ourselves perched on high bar-type stools with spotlights shining on us. In a tight circle around us stood menacing figures with Tommy-guns pointed in our direction, and from somewhere beyond the lights we vaguely heard questions being fired at us. That we were being interrogated was clear enough, but the questions themselves remained incomprehensible. We had no knowledge of Serbo-Croat, assuming that to be their language, and they had no knowledge of English. Through the haze of alcohol and tobacco smoke we could also vaguely distinguish some questions in broken German, but again, neither of us had any idea what they might actually mean.

John Keylock had been raised in South Africa, and through his nanny had heard a few nursery rhymes in Afrikaans. When one is very inebriated, Afrikaans and German sound not dissimilar to the untrained ear. As the German questioning became more insistent, John, with a seraphic smile on his face, would respond with his limited repertoire of Afrikaans nursery rhymes.

I found this to be unbearably hilarious and kept falling off my seat with laughter. I have faint recollections of laboriously trying to climb back up—before all goes blank. I have no idea what happened afterwards. All I know is that when I regained consciousness next morning we were back at the frontier, the only evidence of the previous night's activities being a magnificent Macedonian visa, valid for just twenty-four hours, that still graces a whole page of my old passport."

Armed with the necessary exit visas, the expedition members were released to make their way across the frontier and into Greece. When reunited with their truck, they found that their captors' children had decked it in wreaths of marigolds and filled it high with watermelons. "As we departed," reported John, "we were treated to a send-off better suited to victorious allies than erstwhile prisoners."

The route to Greece lay across an elderly wooden bridge, high above the Vardar, the river that marked the border between the two nations. A large sign announced that there was a weight limit on the bridge—a limit that was roughly half the weight of their truck. Leaving John alone to drive, the others all crossed ahead on foot. The best strategy for getting across seemed to be driving steadily, but not too fast—despite the urge to complete the perilous crossing as quickly as possible. As he drove, he could hear wooden planks cracking under the weight, and when he eventually reached safety on the Greek side, he looked back to see several large gaping holes in the bridge. "I have often wondered," he mused, "what happened to subsequent vehicles that tried to cross".

## Discursus Thirty-One
### Tuz Gölü

The expedition's guardian angels continued to accompany them, and came to their aid again when they finally reached Istanbul. On the advice of the British Embassy, they were directed to a large garage where they might hope to get the truck repaired. Miraculously, it turned out that the owner was a Turkish graduate of Merton College, who was overjoyed to welcome them. In a short time they saw the truck being dismantled by teams of small boys, none of whom could have been older than twelve. Like victims engulfed by a column of army ants, the truck was quickly broken down into its constituent parts and soon lay scattered across the floor of the large, hangar-like garage building.

Unable to bear further the sight of their beloved truck being torn apart, and anxious not to waste precious collecting time, they set off for a few days to visit the Tuz Gölü, Anatolia's great salt lake. Travelling by bus—actually an old American school bus with tiny cramped seats designed for young children—they were deposited close to the lake shore, leaving instructions for the bus to stop and pick them up on its return journey three days later. It proved to be a valuable, albeit uncomfortable, learning experience. They badly miscalculated the amount of water needed. Also their rations, which included pemmican and oatmeal blocks, were better suited to arctic conditions, and proved almost unbearable in the desert heat. They had also failed to appreciate just how cold the nights could be in the high deserts of central Anatolia.

"My memory of the long night hours," John reported, "is of sitting upright in a small cave wrapped not only in my thin sleeping bag, but also in my inflatable 'lilo' mattress. We laboured nobly in our collecting, and despite the heat, lack of water and lack of sleep, marched far out across the ice-like salt surface of the lake. From time to time we would dig down to reach the damp ground underneath, and it was here that we collected several large earwigs. It was disappointing to learn after our return that these specimens, collected at such personal cost, were exactly the same species that could have been found in any English garden!"

Once back in the welcome civilization of Istanbul, the expedition waited impatiently for their transportation to be ready for the next stage of the journey. They were quick to recognise that the earlier mishap in Yugoslavia had been a blessing—albeit very well disguised. Once reassembled under the watchful eye of the old Mertonian garage proprietor, the truck would now doubtless be better able to withstand the rigours ahead.

"Our time of enforced idleness in Istanbul was not, of course, wasted. We took the opportunity to study Turkish (not to any great effect, I should add) and visited Hagia Sophia, the great Blue Mosque of Sultan Ahmed and other notable sights. We also began our exploration of Turkish cuisine. We were particularly taken by the way, in small restaurants when there was no written menu, we would be ushered into the kitchen to choose those dishes that appeared most attractive or interesting."

Once mobile again, the expedition headed East across the Anatolian plateau bound by a roundabout route towards Lake Van and the mountains of Hakkiari. At frequent intervals, particularly when there were large numbers of rocks lying about, a stop would be called for collecting spiders. While John and George were turning over stones to see what was hiding beneath, John McNeil would go botanising, seeking out plants to press, while Noel tended to the truck and domestic arrangements. Each evening camp would be established off the road and concealed from passing traffic—mostly aged trucks with patched tires, the patches made from tire fragments bolted on.

"Each morning, special attention would be paid to the animals that had gathered beneath our groundsheets during the night. These would usually include a few scorpions and the occasional solifuge or wind-scorpion. About 3 inches in length, these fast-moving remarkable creatures were not venomous, but compensated for this omission by possessing the most ferocious mouthparts in the animal kingdom. The most heavily armoured tenebrionid beetle could be crushed easily—the splintering sound audible from some distance away. These are beetles that can withstand being stepped on by a person. Solifuges, also called jerrymunglums, are only active after dark and normally only glimpsed briefly as they run into the circle of illumination surrounding a pressure lamp on the ground to grab and carry off moths and beetle attracted by the light. They proved to be extremely difficult to keep for long in captivity as they required not only a desert climate, but an ample food supply and plenty of space in which to run and forage. George eventually discovered what was necessary and kept them alive in his rooms back in Oxford for several months."

# Discursus Thirty-Two
## Diplomacy

J ohn, as OU Exploration Club chairman, later sat on the
committee, mostly composed of senior members of the
university, that examined all the proposed undergraduate
expeditions that sought official recognition and possible
funding. It was a profitable experience, shedding valuable
light on logistics, funding, medical planning and much else.
Through his own travels in Eastern Turkey he was familiar
with some of these problems, but learned much much more
through the experience of others. It had, for example, never
crossed his mind to check the sexual preferences of expedition
members. Others had made the same mistake, and paid dearly
for the oversight when one of their group was discovered
making overtures to small boys along the way. In many parts
of the world this can result in swift and painful retribution.

"Although I had never experienced this particular problem
myself, we did encounter an unusual situation in Turkey.
Noel Marshall had joined us from Cambridge. He was
not a scientist, but as President of the Cambridge Union,
added a veneer of culture and respectability to an otherwise
scientific enterprise. Less active than the rest of us because
of his artificial leg, Noel opted to stay in camp while we
climbed Artos Dagh, a nearby mountain. On our return
he proudly announced that he had recorded a young
shepherd boy playing his Pan pipes. The tape recorder was
new and quite complicated to use, but un-technical Noel
was confident. With a group of curious villagers gathered

around Noel, playing to the gallery, switched on the machine. To his consternation, and our boundless delight, it was not the sound of the shepherd boy's pipes that floated out under trees, but an earlier, un-erased recording of Bach's sixth Brandenburg Concerto."

But this was not to be the worst of Noel's problems. A day or two later John and the others returned to find the camp in uproar.

"A large crowd had gathered, and at its centre, being held down on his back by several determined men, lay a loudly protesting Noel. It was undoubtedly the volume of our combined shouts, rather than our fluent command of Turkish invective that attracted the crowd's attention. As the dust settled—and Noel assumed a more dignified posture—we gradually worked out what had been happening.

Observing Noel's artificial leg, the village had become very animated. It turned out that they had in their community a man with no legs. Suddenly Allah had sent to them a man who had a detachable leg. Clearly, they argued, it would be just if the man with the removable leg were to give it to the man with no legs. It was a sound, completely logical argument in which I could detect no flaw. Noel seemed far less convinced.

It was a fraught situation for hospitality, both given and received, is a major element in the *mores* of these tough mountain communities, and we had been forewarned about inadvertently failing in our honouring of these traditions. Long discussions, only partially understood on either side, ensued. Back and forth the arguments raged, until we eventually reached a compromise.

If Noel were to share his leg, that would be a wonderful gift, would it not? Over Noel's protests, we suggested that he take up residence in the village, so that they could both use the leg on alternate days. Perhaps Noel might even agree, we said, that their legless neighbour be permitted to use the leg four days out of seven in return for their hospitality. This won high praise.

At the psychological moment, just as this idea was catching on, a potential problem was quietly introduced. Of course, it was pointed out, if Noel were to live amongst them in order to share the leg, the village would have an on-going obligation to feed and care for him. What, we began to enquire, might it cost to maintain Noel for one, two, three....who knows how many years? As the implications of this began to sink in, a compromise was artfully suggested. How about, we said, if we were to provide the necessary money to enable the legless man to purchase his own—perhaps even two? This would be, we suggested, an all together more mutually beneficial solution. We were fortunate that this line of argument held a certain appeal, and before fresh counter-arguments could surface, we hurriedly packed camp and moved on after leaving a suitably generous donation for leg purchases."

They say that fortune favours the bold, and John would be the first to agree. It was again in eastern Turkey, very shortly after the problems with Noel's leg. They had become, they believed, the first to drive a motor vehicle into the crater of Nemrut Dagh, a dormant volcano to the North of Lake Van.

"We had heard that the crater lake contained hot springs, and we were curious to see whether these had any local effects on the insects and spiders of the area. It was an audacious drive and not without incident. We eventually pitched camp on a nice patch of grassy level ground within the crater, revelling in the apparent solitude. The next morning we realised that we were not the only inhabitants of this remote spot. When George woke up he found that the edge of his tent had been lifted in the darkness, and his kit bag containing all his belongings stolen. Three of us set out to discover the whereabouts of the thief, deducing that there must be some sort of habitation not far away. Sure enough, we had not gone far when we walked into the encampment of some Kurdish nomads. There were probably about two hundred of them, all armed to the teeth with knives and firearms. We could not fail to recognise that they formed a militarily superior force, but we knew that we had right on our side.

Taking a note from the diaries of Burton and Meinertzhagen, we bluffed it out. With three pathetic pieces of armament—a 12-bore shotgun, the Warden's 9mm pistol and a .32 Mauser pistol—we marched boldly into the centre of the camp and were instantly ringed by a crowd of, if not hostile, at least overly curious faces. After using our few Kurdish words of greeting, we demanded (in our infantile Turkish) to speak with the leader, who eventually emerged from his tent and came over to us. He was, I think in retrospect, highly amused by the brash effrontery of these three young strangers. With some difficulty—for it is hard to retain diplomatic face when only able to speak like a dyslexic two-year-old—we explained our mission. Playing the hospitality card, we said that some member of his clan had apparently grossly abused our unspoken status as guests within his domain. The shot found its mark, and immediately the word went out. The thief was to give back our property—immediately—and with suitable apologies. We all parted on the best of terms and we remained guests in their crater for several days longer until George sustained a nasty injury that necessitated his immediate removal to the nearest hospital."

George had been chasing an errant spider beside the crater lake when he impaled himself on a viciously sharp reed, which penetrated the cornea of one eye, but fortunately did not reach as far as the retina. The pain was extremely severe but as always in those days, John carried several self-injecting ampoules of morphine in case of serious injury. Semi comatose, George was laid in the back of the truck and they set off down the mountain. As the effects of the morphine started to wear off, each bump in the track would trigger stabbing pain.

"I recall," added John, being interested to note that although only one eye had been injured, the resulting trauma triggered complementary neurological effects in the other eye as well, presumably a reflection of the fact that signals from the optic nerves are processed centrally in the brain's visual cortex."

They had, of course, no idea where they ought to go. The few peasants encountered in the countryside, assuming they understood the questions, had no suggestions to offer. Eventually they passed a rustic police outpost, where they learned of a military hospital a few hours drive away. When they finally reached it they were well received, although nothing about the place was in any way reassuring. They even considered leaving to let George to take his chance of recovering at the next campsite. Deciding that any medical support was better than none, George was abandoned to his fate and the reduced expedition set off for further travels, with the assurance that they would be back in a week or two. Suspecting, quite rightly as it turned out, that few if any drugs would be available, they left a supply of dried penicillin ampoules, together with the necessary distilled water to be mixed with them.

Returning some nine days later George was overjoyed to see us—indeed overjoyed to be able to see anything. His eye had healed without any apparent lasting damage, and they set off once more. As they drove through the wild and barren landscape, George gave dramatic accounts of his experiences in a Turkish military hospital. Administering injections to a foreign visitor, even one as unprepossessing as George, clearly carried with it considerable *kudos,* and competition among the orderlies for the privilege was intense. To his considerable dismay, on more than one occasion the competing medical orderlies actually came to blows over who would wield the syringe.

Even more alarming was the discovery, towards the end of his confinement, that none of the distilled water had been used. The obvious assumption had to be that ordinary, unsterilized well water had been used to make the injectable solution. For days George was scrutinised for any manifestations of incipient septicaemia.

Driving along the shore of Lake Van, the expedition came one evening to the village of Ahlat—today a thriving town. The weather was bad, and so they decided to seek accommodation in a hotel or rest house. Enquiries revealed that the best—perhaps even the only—hotel and restaurant belonged to the mayor. Here they received a warm, nay a royal welcome.

> "While the wind and rain could be heard rattling against the windows outside, we dined well, as only the Turks can. Course followed delicious course, and drink followed drink. The conversation was lively, but somewhat impeded by linguistic hurdles. The only medium for our exchanges was fractured French, but it was sufficient to provide a hilarious night. I forget the details, which is not surprising, for raki is a very potent drink, but vividly recall we and the mayor discussing the chief characteristics of the Turkish and English senses of humour; each side giving examples in execrable French."

The roads in eastern Turkey were, at least in 1956, unpaved, rough and indescribably dusty—when they weren't a quagmire after rain. There was no way in which those travelling in the back of the truck could avoid being coated in thick layers of grime, and so inevitably the expedition presented a pretty grubby appearance most of the time. They worked long hours under difficult conditions, and sartorial elegance was not one of their priorities. If the truth were known, they probably resembled more a band of rather disreputable brigands than aspiring scientists.

For almost twenty years foreigners had been banned from this part of the country, and not surprisingly the expedition believed they were the only visitors in the region.

"Parked by the roadside in a remote village, imagine our surprise, our total disbelief, when a clean pale face, surmounted by immaculately brushed hair, appeared at the window and addressed us in unmistakably Oxford tones. It was, we soon learned, an archaeologist clad in freshly laundered and pressed bush jacket and shorts, who was bicycling through the eastern provinces on his own collecting shards. It was a wholly improbable Livingstone and Stanley scene."

## Discursus Thirty-Three
## **Under Cover**

Word of the proposed Turkish expedition had caught the attention of the news media in England, and for several weeks before departure the members were interviewed and photographed several times. All this publicity had not escaped the notice of the security mandarins in Whitehall, and one day John received an invitation—quite firmly worded—to come and have lunch at one of the better London clubs. It turned out that he was being recruited to gather information on behalf of the Ministry of Defence.

> "As no foreigners had, for many years, been permitted to travel in the areas we planned to visit, and the British military felt singularly ill-informed about road conditions—and in particular about the construction and strength of the bridges. Would I…, would we……? I was not really given much option, and besides the pill was considerably sweetened by an offer of maps. Maps of eastern Turkey were hard to come by, and generally quite inadequate. The maps on offer were irresistible. Based on American aerial surveys (of which the Turkish authorities had no knowledge) they provided wonderful details totally unobtainable elsewhere. It was made clear that under no circumstances should knowledge of these maps be disclosed to anyone. Indeed, they were clearly stamped in red Top Secret."

The summer was over and the expedition was heading for home, westward across the desert regions bordering Syria. At Harran the daytime temperature had dropped to 120°F, and so work had resumed at the archaeological site that David Storm Rice was excavating. Harran, despite its remote and inhospitable location, has a long and varied history stretching back over three thousand years. The site of Jacob's Well, it was here that Jacob toiled twenty years for Leban. It was hard to appreciate that in Umayyad times this was the capital of an empire that stretched from the Iberian peninsula to Central Asia. There being no trees in the area to provide roof beams, the houses in Harran are constructed with tall conical roofs that also create cooling air currents. Whatever its archaeological attractions, everyone was glad to leave Harran after two nights.

"It was a wild area, and soon after leaving we were very surprised to come across a major hard-surfaced highway. It was not shown on any of our regular maps, but as it appeared to be going in the same direction that we were headed, we decided to use it. After driving for some time we began to wonder where we were and where the road might be taking us. Puzzled, we broke out our large-scale secret maps to see if they could help us establish our location. I was driving, while George and Noel started to study the map beside me. However, before our whereabouts could be determined there was a distraction. A sudden rattle of musketry some distance away caught my attention, and turning to the others I apparently said: "Good lord! I think we're being shot at."

Recalling Churchill's observation during the Boer War, that "there is nothing more exhilarating than to be shot at—ineffectually", I pressed down on the accelerator and kept driving.

A few moments later there was another burst of fire and a bullet entered the cab just two or three inches behind my head. The hole would remain a powerful reminder of how lucky I had been. My companions left me in no doubt that they wished me to stop.

Before we even had had time to get out, we were surrounded by a large group of very animated and distinctly unfriendly Turkish soldiers. Our previous experiences with the Turkish military in Hakkiari, the mountainous villayet lying to the South of Lake Van, suggested that it would be prudent to do as they told us.

"We had not been held captive for long before a group of officers arrived, very smart in neatly pressed uniforms. It was quickly discovered that they had all trained at the Sandhurst Royal Military Academy, spoke faultless English, and seemed quite delighted to meet us. In a moment our status was transformed from being suspected Syrian smugglers into honoured guests. Indeed, they were quite apologetic that we had been subjected to detention by their men, but explained that the road we were driving on was a secret military one and that had we been using it legitimately, we would have known to stop at a secret check point that we had unwittingly passed by. Even so, it was hard to accept that we really looked like Syrian smugglers, particularly as we were driving on English license plates—I still remember the number in Turkish—alt'yuz seksen beş, 685. On second thoughts, perhaps it wasn't so surprising considering our shaggy, unwashed appearance.

The affair ended with a riotous evening at the officer's mess that lasted into the small hours and would have been awarded high marks for hospitality in the mess of any British regiment. The evening was also memorable for a personally embarrassing incident. My love of Indian cooking meant that I was fully familiar with hot, spicy food. However, one dish served that evening was of a ferocity that was beyond anything I had previously encountered. We each had our own small table on which the food was served, and unable to stand the pain, I "accidentally" knocked my table over, consigning the offending dish onto the floor, amid protestations of apology and embarrassment. The shame was a small price to pay for such blessed relief. It might easily have turned out differently had our hosts noticed the 'Top Secret' maps still lying unfolded in the cab of the truck!"

On reaching Istanbul again, the expedition finally regained contact with the outside world. The prolonged silence, exacerbated by a complete lack of letter writing by everyone had, we discovered, generated considerable parental anxiety. John still has the worried correspondence between his mother, the British Embassy, The British Council and the British School of Archaeology. Odd rumours of their presence in the eastern vilayets had filtered back, suggesting that they were still alive, but only their reappearance, bearded, dirty and unkempt, stilled speculation as to their possible fate.

The return journey to England apparently passed uneventfully—but only after they had left Bulgaria. Anxious to avoid crossing into Yugoslavia again at Gevgalia and risk a return across the dilapidated frontier bridge, they had chosen to take a more northerly route through Bulgaria—still a Soviet satellite—thinking it would be quicker.

> "Our arrival at the Bulgarian frontier seemed to generate undue curiosity—perhaps not unsurprising in view of our still decidedly piratical appearance. We were instructed to remove a number of our trusty champagne boxes for examination. It was unfortunate that on the very top was the crate holding our current spider collecting gear. I should, perhaps, explain that after collecting at a particular location, the pickled specimens would then be sorted and labelled in the evening. To hold the large numbers of small open glass vials filled with alcohol during sorting, we used plastic racks that held fifty vials each. It so happened that these plastic racks were originally designed to hold fifty rounds of 9mm ammunition."

The customs inspector immediately recognised their provenance, and demanded to see the weapon concerned. It quickly became obvious that the truck would be stripped if they didn't comply, and so with great reluctance John burrowed down to produce Geoffrey Muir's Luger, complete with its official British firearms certificate. Encouraged by his success, the chief officer, now supported by a growing force of soldiers who stood around glaring, Tommy-guns at the ready, demanded to know if there were other weapons. John humbly presented a 12-bore shotgun, which elicited further excitement. By the time a little Mauser .32 pistol had been unearthed, it seemed their fate was sealed.

SUBLIME LUNACY

## Discursus Thirty-Four
# Nemesis Approaches

Knowing of the many distractions that occupied so much of his time at Oxford, John's father generously enquired whether a fourth undergraduate year might not be good idea. Indeed, it was an excellent idea—and probably originated with Prof Sir Alister Hardy, head of the zoology department and an old family friend.

> "My tutors seemed to have deluded themselves with an exaggerated opinion of my capabilities, and suggested that I compete for a Christopher Welch scholarship. One, and occasionally two, of these prestigious scholarships are offered each year, and in my mind seemingly belonged to an academic firmament far beyond my horizon. My protestations fell on deaf ears, and I found myself put forward as a reluctant candidate.
>
> The scholarships are awarded, I learned, not on the candidate's demonstrable abilities or proven track record, but rather on a hypothetical research proposal he (or she) submits. The written exam is designed with a choice of questions tailored to the specific interests of the candidates, which can be drawn from any branch of the biological sciences.
>
> By good fortune I already had in hand a small spider research project concerning the taxonomy and functional morphology of the two British species of *Dysdera*. These relatively large, and rather beautiful spiders, are specialist feeders on woodlice, and both

occur around Oxford. For many spiders the ultimate distinguishing characters that serve to separate species are found in the male and female genitalia, which can often be extremely complex. In *Dysdera,* however, the genitalia are relatively simple—and in the females wholly internal. I felt that a better understanding of the structure, and particularly the function, of these organs was an obvious prerequisite to assessing their taxonomic value.

There is no question that I had a double advantage—unbounded enthusiasm and already a pretty broad familiarity with spiders and their biology going back to my early teenage years—and the examination questions, skilfully drafted, played right into my court. Nevertheless, once finished, I dismissed all memory of the examination from my mind and turned to other distractions, convinced I had no hope of success.

Through my association with the OU Exploration Club, I had been asked by Arthur Cain, my tutor and later my supervisor, to join and help organise the university expedition to Guyana, and I quickly immersed myself once more in South American biology.

The news that I had been awarded a Christopher Welch scholarship came as a total and wonderful surprise—a surprise that would shape the course of my future career. Perhaps the most significant short-term consequence was psychological. No longer was I haunted by the spectre of finals looming ever closer. The scholarship effectively rendered unimportant the outcome of finals. Regardless of what class I might be awarded in the final examination, I was secure to pursue my spider research for the next three years. The sense of relief at knowing my life would not depend on how I performed during three hot summer weeks was boundless, and I returned to my studies as a pleasure rather than an obligation.

But academic work was not my sole occupation. Through my friendship with David Eccles, a post-graduate student working on fresh-water gammarid shrimp ecology in nearby Wytham Woods with Charles Elton at the Bureau of Animal Population, I had assumed an advisory position in the planning of an expedition to the Kungwe-Mahali Mountains on the shores of Lake Tanganyika. David had been raised and educated in southern Africa and was a graduate of both Witwatersrand and Cape Town universities. His encyclopaedic knowledge of African biology, combined with his grounding in geology, made him a fascinating companion, and I found myself spending more and more time in his company.

Planning was already well advanced when a key member of the Kungwe-Mahali expedition was suddenly obliged to drop out. This placed me in a difficult quandary when I was invited to replace him. Should I go to central Africa with David Eccles, or to South America with my future supervisor and George Lampel?

In the end Africa won. One factor that swayed the decision was the possibility of remaining in Africa after the expedition officially ended and undertaking a more ambitious program of fieldwork related to my *Dysdera* studies. Specifically, I wanted to search for Dysderidae in the Sudan and along the Mediterranean coast, extending if possible all the way into Morocco.

In order to fund this extended fieldwork it would
be essential to seek financial aid. Although my Christopher
Welch scholarship was wholly inadequate for this purpose,
it proved a particularly valuable asset in loosening purse
strings. An application to the Royal Society for a grant-
in-aid quickly produced a positive response, and another
piece of the puzzle dropped easily into place."

The examination process at Oxford is, by any measure,
arduous. In the sweltering heat of summer, renowned for its
particularly somnolent properties in the Thames Valley, the
candidates are required to sit, for perhaps six hours a day,
writing complex answers to challenging questions that will
directly impact the rest of their lives. Not surprisingly some
undergraduates break under the strain. The fortunate ones are
allowed to take their examinations from the sanctuary of the
Warnford, one of Oxford's local mental hospitals.

As doctor Johnson observed, nothing so focuses a
man's mind as when he is shortly to be hanged[9] So it is with
the final examination. In the misguided belief that three years
of neglected learning can be rectified by last minute studying,
many candidates damage their chances of success by overwork
and failure to care properly for themselves at this crucial time.

"I had the good fortune to count among my friends
Eric Korn, who had obtained a first in zoology the year
before me. His research was centred on the effects of LSD
(Lysergic acid diethylamide) on the molluscan nervous

9       Actually "Depend upon it, sir, when a man knows
he is to be hanged in a fortnight, it concentrates his mind
wonderfully."

system—this was just before LSD entered popular culture as a recreational pharmaceutical, and Eric's room contained enough LSD to send the whole of Oxford on a six-month trip. Sadly we were, at the time, unaware of its potential for pleasure.

Instead of urging me on to ever-greater feats of memorisation, Eric bluntly announced that we were to spend the days before the final exams in hill walking through the wilderness of North Wales. I could have received no better advice, and returned relaxed and refreshed to face the examiners.

I have long urged an overhaul of the examination system at Oxford—and indeed elsewhere. The existing system not only places enormous strain on the candidates, but equally makes miserable the lives of those called upon to read all their papers.

After three years of weekly one-on-one tutorials, tutors are well able to judge the academic potential of their students. It would lift a terrible burden if tutors were empowered to recommend an appropriate class. If the student were in agreement, that class would be awarded. However, should the student feel hard done by, and worthy of a higher class, then he can opt to be examined in the normal way."

John went on to say that the iniquities of the traditional examination system were brought home to him most strongly when an undergraduate, who shall remain nameless, fell foul of the examiners. Everyone who had tutored this man had no hesitation in pronouncing him first class material. To everyone's surprise and dismay he failed to get any class at all—

not even a pass degree. That might well have been the end of this individual's career, but the Oxford system is not wholly harsh. Although a class, once awarded, cannot be changed, if the candidate ploughs completely he is allowed to come back for a second bite. In this particular case the candidate came back, took a first class honours degree in biochemistry and went on to a distinguished research career.

"Sometimes those closest to a candidate, however, are unable to form a just opinion. I encountered a dramatic example of this when I had the pleasure of tutoring John (now Lord) Krebs as an undergraduate. His ability far outshone everyone else's (with perhaps one exception) but his father remained plagued by doubts. On several occasions Sir Hans Krebs, the distinguished biochemist, came to me in considerable agitation, anxious for me to give him an honest assessment of his son. Did John really, he wondered, have the ability to get a good degree—or were people just being nice? There were, of course, no doubts in anybody's mind that had had the pleasure of tutoring him, and John went on to a first class degree followed by a distinguished career in science, ultimately returning to Oxford as Principal of Jesus College. He was also among the first of my students to become a Fellow of the Royal Society, perhaps the ultimate accolade for a scientist—after a Nobel Prize."

## Discursus Thirty-Five
# Kungwe's Domain

John's African adventures, which gave rise to many stories, began a few days after he had finished his final exams at Oxford—and before he even knew what degree he might have gained. Leaving by Comet from Heathrow and bound for Dar-es-Salaam, it was the first time he had ever flown in a commercial airliner, and more significantly, it was the first time that he had flown with a stranger at the controls and without either inflatable dingy or parachute.

One of the flight attendants became particularly solicitous for his well-being. As they chatted over generously large drinks, she explained that there were three categories of passenger. The first, she said, were those who flew frequently and are totally relaxed. Those who have never flown not unnaturally exhibit a certain level of anxiety. However, in the third category are those who are used to piloting themselves. His discomposure ill concealed, she immediately identified him as belonging to this last group. However, as he was quick to point out, he did not remain in it for long.

From Dar-es-Salaam he took a light plane to Mbeya and thence overland to Abercorn, a small town at the southernmost tip of Lake Tanganyika. Here he heard for the first time about C.P. Ionides, the distinguished herpetologist, who after only a few days of reaching the Dark Continent, had taken off his wristwatch and flung it into the bush, saying that time had no meaning in Africa. It was on the dockside at nearby Mpulungu that he had later attracted no small attention as with long tongs, he collected water cobras while comfortably seated in his wheelchair.

After a few days to recover from the strain of his 'finals', John went down to the dockside to board the MV Liemba. This remarkable vessel shuttles back and forth between Mpulungu and Kigoma, the railhead towards the lake's northern end.

The Liemba had been built in Germany in 1913, and carried piecemeal from the coast. At Kigoma she was reassembled and briefly served the Kaiser's colony in German East Africa, plying the length of the lake.

As Tanganyika became a British protectorate after the First World War, the Germans scuttled the Liemba and for several years she lay on the lake bed. Eventually the British raised her and restored her to service.

In 1959 she still exuded a wonderful old-world elegance, a loving vignette of an era long passed. Although today she is showing her age and is far from elegant, she remains the oldest working boat in Africa. Pausing briefly at villages along the eastern shore, the Liemba would bring mail and supplies, always surrounded by small boys in little dugout canoes, endevouring to trade goods with the passengers.

The first members of the expedition had already arrived some days earlier as the Liemba cruised south. The chosen site for the base camp was on the lake shore some 100 miles south of Kigoma, at the foot of the Kungwe-Mahali Mountains. The basic elements of the camp were already in place by the time John arrived as the Liemba returned on the northern leg of her fortnightly journey.

With the Liemba anchored for an hour or two some two hundred yards off shore, he was ferried in aboard the expedition's small outboard-powered skiff. Several newly constructed thatched huts clustered under a huge spreading mango tree some yards inland from the beach. Behind there rose up the bulk of Mount Kungwe, the streams running down its slopes clearly visible as green strands of gallery forest. High above, a circlet of cloud concealed the summit, where a constant rumbling of thunder was known to be the voice of Kungwe himself, the resident deity. This was to be home for the next three months, and nothing could have delighted him more.

With David Eccles he supervised the construction of a shared zoological laboratory, behind which they built sleeping quarters. Next door David Harley reigned in "The Darlington Memorial Herbarium"—an in-joke for Prof Darlington, head of the Botany School at Oxford, was a geneticist with no interest in plant taxonomy.

The Kungwe-Mahali mountains and their fauna & flora were, at that time, little known. Subject to much higher rainfall than the surrounding regions, the mountains support a relict community much more characteristic of West rather than East Africa.

An expedition from Oxford had visited the northern part of the range the previous year, but had concentrated mainly on geology and the shoreline ecology. This second expedition was to explore the higher levels. Attention had first been drawn to the mountains after Reg Moreau, an English ornithologist, had briefly sent in African collectors, who returned after only a few days with seven endemic bird species—birds found nowhere else. The most striking was a beautiful sunbird—the African counterpart to the New World hummingbirds. *Cyneris regius anderseni* is jet black, with a brilliant scarlet triangle on its breast. John would find it not uncommon on the edge of clearings in the high forest.

It was the extraordinary richness of the spider fauna that provided him the greatest delight, for it was his first experience of the tropics. *Cladomelia*, for example, is a bolas spider and bears three great rhinoceros horns on its carapace, and with a pair of shiny, bright orange globes like light bulbs projecting from the shoulders of its abdomen. Its habits are no less remarkable than its appearance. The female, much larger than the male, sits exposed on a branch and pays out a single fishing line. On the end she secretes a sticky globule that includes a component that mimics the assembly pheromone of certain moths. Swinging the thread and its globule like a bolas, male moths lured in by the spider's chemical subterfuge become entangled and are then drawn in and consumed.

Quite common were the large tarantula-like spiders belonging to the genus *Pterinochilus*, who live in silk-lined burrows. Lured out of their home with a grass stem jiggled to mimic a passing beetle, they will raise themselves almost vertical and emit a loud hissing sound. Even more alarming is their aggressive behaviour. With fangs open to reveal a mass of red hairs, they lunge repeatedly at their putative attacker.

It was here also that he witnessed his first *Dinopis* or ogre-faced spider. These are large-eyed nocturnal spiders who emerge to spin a web the size of a postage stamp, that they hold by the corners as they hang inverted an inch or two above the ground. As an insect walks past within range the spider expands its web, and like the *retiarius* at Roman gladiatorial contests, throws its net over the victim.

Amongst the profusion of exotic spiders, the many species of Salticidae or jumping spiders provided a special treat. Brightly coloured and patterned, these would constantly drop onto the dining table underneath the great mango tree. Some were convincing ant mimics, others sought to persuade they were coccinellid (ladybird) beetles. The richness, the diversity, the sheer beauty of the fauna that dropped daily from the mango branches overhead never ceased to amaze.

A popular addition to the expedition diet, were the large freshwater mussels living in the lake at a depth of about 20 feet. Domenico, the *pishi* or cook, would serve them up in white sauce on toast as a savoury to finish off the meal, for the Oxford tradition of fine dining was not easily abandoned. John Newbould even changed into dinner jacket and black tie periodically.

Of encounters with larger animals, John gave several accounts. One of the most memorable occurred while snorkelling for mussels.

"Out of the clouded waters, there suddenly loomed the unmistakable bulk of a hippo. Allan Root had not yet introduced the television public to hippos under water, so the experience was entirely novel and unexpected.

I knew, of course, that hippos are herbivores, but in that moment I recognised that the zoological training I had received at Oxford provided no practical information on the aggressive propensities of hippos or their likely reaction to being confronted by a swimmer beneath the surface. My immediate reaction was to turn and head for shore, but two things held me back. First, I was unsure whether the hippo had even detected my presence, in which case it might be imprudent to attract its attention by sudden flight. Second, I was completely entranced by the beauty of the scene. Here was an animal that on land could well be labelled by many as grotesque, and yet here in its natural aquatic habitat it was a *prima ballerina* moving with exquisite grace through a slow-motion underwater ballet. Time and time again I would swim to the surface for air, only to return at once for another glimpse, becoming bolder each time until we were swimming close together. I later felt almost offended that I had been so completely ignored."

Many years later, when he himself had become a wildlife filmmaker, John and his colleagues received a letter from Allan Root, written from his hospital bed in Nairobi. In it Allan described how he and Joan had returned to Mzima Springs to shoot additional hippo footage for an up-coming TV program. Although they had extensive experience filming hippos here, by some oversight they positioned themselves between a mother and her calf. Joan suffered only shock and lacerations as a tusk grazed her cheek and ripped off her face mask. Allan was less fortunate. The mother hippo seized him in her mouth and flung him into the air. In the process a tusk sank deep into his thigh, opening a hole into which a coke bottle could easily fit. As Allan observed, "she demonstrated a profound knowledge of human anatomy, for although she penetrated to the bone, she skilfully avoided damaging any major nerves or blood vessels." In conclusion he remarked that he was at last symmetrical, the hippo wound neatly balancing the one on his other cheek, where a cheetah had bitten him.

It was some weeks after watching the hippo ballet that John said he learned that the lake was also inhabited by crocodiles, which could easily attack and kill a lone swimmer. The discovery was made when the expedition was approached by a deputation from a small fishing village some distance to the north along the lake shore, asking if someone would come and shoot a crocodile that had already killed several people in their community, and taken many domestic animals.

David and John went up the lake together, arriving after dark at the village. It was thought best to try and shoot the croc at night, when its eyes would reflect brightly in the light of a head torch. With considerable misgivings John was persuaded into a small dugout and was paddled out into the lagoon, feeling decidedly unsafe. It was not long before a pair of gleaming eyes was spotted peering out of the darkness. It was a far from ideal situation from which to try and shoot, but he felt committed. Movement of the canoe made aiming more than usually difficult, but judging when the sights would align with the space between the eyes, he touched the hair-trigger and fired. The recoil from his 8mm Mauser rifle almost tipped them backwards into the water, but somehow the canoe remained upright, thanks to the skill of his boatman.

A violent thrashing, soon followed by silence, suggested that they had been successful, but it would not be until daylight that the corpse would be recovered to confirm the kill. With a gratifying, if childlike, faith in his marksmanship, the village had no doubt that their nemesis was dead. Fêted as heroes, the celebrations continued long and wild until dawn.

His mind still firmly lodged in Africa, John started to talk about Col. Richard Meinertzhagen, whose 'Kenya Diary, 1903-1906' he had recently re-read. At first attracted by his exciting life, he also voiced the suspicion that some of the entries had seemingly benefitted from the wisdom of hindsight—in particular his supposed pronouncements about the probability of a Kikuyu revolt in response to European sequestration of their land.

> "Much as I enjoyed it, I could not but wonder about the validity of Meinertzhagen's diary. The Mau Mau uprising was already well underway when the diaries were published and his observations seemed too good to be true. Also, I wondered how he had kept tabs on the huge numbers of animals he recorded as having shot—how did he manage to count and record over a thousand sightings of a single species in one day while marching huge distances? It seemed improbable, if not impossible"

It is always hard when one's heroes are revealed to have feet of clay, and Meinertzhagen's remarkable life has now been exposed as at best a gross exaggeration, and more probably fraudulent. A distinguished ornithologist in later life, many of the specimens in his collection have subsequently been found to have been stolen from museums, and accompanied by spurious collecting data—a gross and very unscientific deception.

John, however, tells of an encounter with a species that legitimately bears Meinertzhagen's name—while his halo was still intact.

"It was high in the forests on Kungwe, and I had paused to answer a call of nature. With my rifle propped against a nearby tree, I was squatting down semi-dressed, when a Giant Forest Hog, *Hylochoerus meinertzhageni,* emerged on the other side of the clearing, its crest of black hairs clearly visible. It showed no sign of seeing me—and I was fortunately down wind—so I decided it would probably be best to remain quietly where I was, utterly immobilized, and wait for it to stroll slowly back into the forest. After that I made sure my rifle was always within easy reach, particularly when alone in the bush."

## Discursus Thirty-Six
# Buffalo Beans

Conspicuous among the trees along the lake shore were the large sleeping nests made by chimpanzees. The population was clearly large, but the chimps themselves were seldom seen. No doubt they preferred to keep away from the busy camp area. It was interesting long afterwards to learn that the following year Jane Goodall began her research on wild chimpanzees just north of Kigoma at the Gombe Stream reserve—now the Gombe National Park.

A year or two after returning from Africa, John was invited to stay at the Lake District estate belonging to David Eccles' godfather, who had been DC Kigoma just before the war. It was he who first observed the chimps at Gombe and ordered the area be declared a wildlife reserve. Had he ever visited the Mahali range, Jane Goodall might well have worked there rather than Gombe, for the chimp population is much larger. The Kungwe-Mahali mountains have today become a National Park, renowned (among other things) for its primate populations. The original remote and primitive campsite now supports a host of expensive tourist lodges advertising encounters with wild chimpanzees.

John readily admits that he was not familiar with buffalo beans (*Mucuna pruriens*) on his first arrival in Tanganyika, but he did not remain in ignorance for long. Ten or twelve inches in length and clothed in a rich reddish-brown velvety pubescence, buffalo beans shed their pharmacologically active urticating hairs everywhere as they dry. As he was making his way up a stretch of gallery forest, through which ran a fast-moving cooling stream, punctuated by small limpid pools, he became suddenly aware of a burning itching on his arms and legs. Numbed by discomfort, and following instinct, he stripped off and sank thankfully into the nearest pool, never noticing that the surface was covered by a thin film of hairs. Within moments the hitherto localised urticaria became universal, no part of his body escaping. He reports having only the memory of running down the mountain in twenty-foot strides, his one desire to reach camp and break open tubes of numbing Cortisone cream. He much later wondered whether the otters that were common in such streams, ever suffered from the Buffalo Beans—or had they learned how to avoid swimming in such waters?

Witnessing the discomfort, Ray Harley wondered about the mechanism whereby the buffalo bean effects its fiendish magic, unaware that it had already been widely studied. Imagining it to be a worthwhile research project, he gave instructions, from a distance, for a parcel of beans to be prepared, packed within several layers of carefully-sealed plastic bags. These were then dispatched to Oxford when the Liemba next passed. Despite dire warnings about their contents, and the need for special care when opening the bags, they reached the Oxford Botany department in disarray. Irritant hairs were everywhere, inside and outside the parcel. Before the entire parcel was incinerated, it is reported that the language of the lab technicians was quite spectacular. It could only be assumed that HM Customs had not only misguidedly opened the parcel en route but sent it on its way in haste without bothering to re-seal it. There was a certain malicious pleasure in pondering the customs officials' discomfort resulting from failure to heed the conspicuous warning labels.

***

Loath to leave the subject of Africa, John told of setting out late in the day to join David and Ray at the high camp they had established in the Elfin Forest not far beneath Kungwe's summit. Fearing the vengeance of the great god Kungwe if they were to enter his kingdom, the porters resolutely refused to go higher up the mountain. Out of respect for their sensibilities they were assured that no one would sully the summit by stepping on it, a promise that was scrupulously observed. However the expedition did climb to a lesser peak somewhat below the summit and there drank a toast to Kungwe with bottles of Guinness. These had been supplied to the expedition as a gift by Guinness & Co. Pictures of the toast to Kungwe were later published in the company's in-house magazine.

Darkness in the tropics falls with disarming rapidity, the long twilight of more northerly latitudes being quite unknown. It therefore came as no surprise when John found himself still far from camp as the light failed. It would have been foolish to struggle on in darkness alone as he had only the vaguest notion of where he was headed, and was relying on the insignificant blazes left by a passing panga slash on tree trunks along the way.

The situation was not entirely unpremeditated. Ever since his first unplanned bivouac while climbing in the Alps, he claimed to enjoy the challenge of confronting nature in solitary hand-to-hand combat, as it were. Clearing a small patch of level ground, he laid out his sleeping bag and ate a light supper. All around the forest was alive with a thousand mysterious sounds—nocturnal bird and insect calls, faint and not-so-faint rustlings of unknown origin in the undergrowth, and cries that might be bush babies going about their business. After the hard march, it was not long before he fell into a deep sleep.

It was a dark night, with little moonlight filtering through the canopy. Something large but unrecognisable was snuffling around the bottom of his sleeping bag when he awoke suddenly. The immediate thought was "Wart Hog", and so he lay still waiting for it to go away. As the mysterious visitor moved off he caught a glimpse of the unmistakable silhouette of a leopard. Could he, he wondered afterwards, have reached successfully for his rifle lying nearby—and could he have discharged it to effect in the dark at such close quarters?

Still fresh in his mind was the graphic story of Hammadi, the skinner who had been attached to the expedition from the Game Department. Quiet, with an engaging smile, Hammadi could transform a mangled, shot-ridden corpse of a small bird into a work of art that would have competed well against the work of the best museum taxidermists—and all in about twenty minutes.

Rarely seen without the cap that bore his badge of office, Hammadi's scalp and body bore terrifying scars, which had prompted John to enquire after their cause. Self-effacing, it was left to others to describe Hammadi's story.

A party of Game Guards had been sent to a remote village that had suffered several deaths from a pride of lions that had taken up residence nearby. Sleeping in a hut with the other guards, Hammadi was wakened by the terrified cries of his companions as they were being mauled in the blackness by a visiting lion.

Feeling for his shotgun, Hammadi had reached out until he felt the lion's fur, and then explored its body until he could find its head. As he was about to fire, the lion had clutched him, digging its claws deep into the flesh of his back and tearing at his head with its teeth. As the frightened villages ran towards the commotion they heard a shot, and when they entered the hut their kerosene lanterns revealed the remains of two dead game guards, the lion, and a severely wounded Hammadi. Replacing the tattered remnants of his scalp back on his head, and securing them with a poultice of fresh manure, they stemmed the flow of blood from the gashes on his back and chest and waited. The arrival of a departmental jeep some days later enabled Hammadi to be taken to hospital where he made a remarkable recovery and soon returned to his duties.

Not long after John reached the high camp, David and Ray set off on a safari of exploration, leaving him to pursue his studies in splendid isolation. It was a magical spot that he described; a forest clearing close by a spring, which proved a magnet to lure in surrounding forest dwellers. The water issuing from this spring in Kungwe's high forest was sweet and pure.

Yet in this realm of perfect water, there was one spring that stood out above all others. The only European to visit Kungwe's slopes previously had been the then District Commissioner in Kigoma, making a safari sometime in the early1930s. In the course of this journey he had drunk from a spring of exceptional quality, and for the rest of his posting he would send runners each week 100 miles in each direction, to bring him Kungwe water to put in his whiskey. Such were the excesses of colonialism.

It was in Kungwe's magical forests that John found himself immobilised with the recurrence of a back injury sustained during his naval service. For several days he lay unable to move, wholly dependent on his porter companions for food. Far from despondent, he said he welcomed the opportunity to observe undisturbed the comings and going of the local wildlife, not least the black & white colobus monkeys gliding among the branches high above.

It was on the third day of immobility that a runner suddenly appeared, bearing a package. Apparently the villagers at a settlement some distance north along the coast had killed a wild pig that had been uprooting their crops. Being a Moslem village, the meat was considered inedible and so they decided to sell it to the strangers camping nearby. There being more than could be readily consumed by the party at base camp, they had thoughtfully sent some up to the high camp. Apparently the grilled kidneys were truly memorable. Not only did he feast well while immobile, but he also enjoyed the opportunity to read uninterrupted. It was a rare pleasure indeed, he said, to read Dostoyevsky's 'The Idiot' from cover to cover without a break—and in such exotic surroundings.

SUBLIME LUNACY

# Discursus Thirty-Seven
## Foot Safari

Every couple of weeks the Liemba would stop by to deliver mail and supplies, taking away in return live specimens and film for processing. On one such trip the expedition discovered that the District Commissioner in Kigoma had decided to pay them an unexpected visit. A party was quickly organised, and drummers were soon assembled to provide a suitable greeting. However, there was little in the way of festive European drinks with which to welcome their august guest.

The local African *pombe*, a beer made from maize or millet, was considered pretty undrinkable. However, once distilled into *pombe ya moshi* it becomes a potent and highly acceptable alcoholic beverage. It was also highly illegal. It therefore gave particular illicit pleasure to serve it to the DC, who drank it with gusto and was polite enough not to enquire from whence it had been obtained.

The distillation process was simple yet elegant. A large earthenware pot containing the raw beer was placed over a fire. On top was placed a smaller pot containing cold water that blocked the opening, and on the bottom of which the alcohol vapour would condense. The condensed alcohol would then drip down into a small pot placed inside the big one. It worked well, and could be disassembled in a moment should any officials appear. The three pots would attract no attention being everyday cooking items.

One day John described for us an *ngoma*—an all night party of drumming and dancing—to be held at a village some distance up the lake.

"It was a pitch black moonless night", he said, "when we went down to the lake shore and boarded several dugout canoes. Navigating solely by the distant sounds of surf breaking on invisible beaches as we passed bay after bay, our fishermen-guides eventually turned to the shore and we ran gently aground on the shingle. We had landed just a few feet from a narrow track leading inland through the undergrowth. This ability to come ashore at exactly the right spot was yet another dramatic example of the villager's symbiotic relationship with their natural environment and their finely tuned senses.

We marched in single file in utter blackness for almost an hour before we heard, far off in the distance, the magical sound of steady, pulsating drums beckoning us towards the village. In the village centre was an open expanse thronged with people dancing, dimly illuminated by a large bonfire. Drums seemed to sound from every direction, the complex rhythms forming intricate patterns of exhilarating music that continued without cease for hour after hour. One indelible image is of a small boy sitting astride a huge, horizontal bass drum, leaning far out over the end to beat out his elaborate rhythmic sequences."

\*\*\*

"All too soon the expedition drew to a close. Specimens were packed for shipment back to England, and the expedition members dispersed to their various destinations. We had become close to many of the men who worked for us, and it would be hard to bid them farewell. One, rather more elderly than the others, had become a particular favourite. Soon after my arrival I was playing my trumpet perched on a rock looking out across the lake one evening. Gradually he drew closer, until at last he could contain himself no longer. Would it be possible, he asked, if I might allow him to play my trumpet? I was happy to hand it to him, and he then explained that years before he had served in the King's African Rifles and had been a bugler.

His lip had gone, but with a little practice his earlier skills returned. From that time on the whole routine of the camp was mediated by military bugle calls. On my departure, I felt I had no option but to give him my instrument, but I have often wondered what retaliatory action his neighbours might subsequently have taken to dampen his strident playing."

It would be at least a couple of months before John was due to embark on another solitary expedition to further his own spider researches, so he and David Eccles decided to remain behind and undertake a safari on foot, circumnavigating the Kungwe-Mahali mountain range, and on to Kigoma.

It was a journey right out of a 'Boy's Own' magazine of the previous century—a return to the Africa that Meinertzhagen had experienced when he first went to Kenya in 1903. With seventeen porters bearing loads on their heads, the two of them set off to explore, having only the vaguest plans of where they might go, or how long they might stay.

Although they had maps that hinted at the major physical features of the terrain through which they were travelling, the details were somewhat speculative. In particular, the location of villages proved exceptionally fanciful. In time they came to understand the reason, but initially they found it somewhat disconcerting. The villages were named for the headman at the time data was being collected. However, from time to time headmen would decide to move on to a new location, taking, of course, the village name with them.

Sometimes the porters would have information as to the whereabouts of the planned destination for the night. An advance party that included the cook would set off ahead, subtly marking the route as they went. By the time the rest arrived, camp would be established and a meal prepared. Common courtesy required that John and David negotiate with the headman to stay in his village, and to lubricate the transaction they carried supplies of canned cigarettes and ropes of tobacco. On other occasions, arriving at the chosen destination, they would find that the site had been long abandoned, and would have to make their own arrangements, not the least of which was to locate the nearest spring from which to get fresh water.

"It was in the course of this safari," John enthused, "that I came to marvel at the knowledge and resourcefulness of our companions. If a load began to slip or loosen, a quick excursion into the surrounding bush would result in finding a piece of bark, from inside which could be stripped off lengths of strong fibre that served as first class string.

David and I trained ourselves to drink very little while on the march, re-hydrating ourselves with countless mugs of tea once we reached camp. However, it would sometimes happen that the route was long, rough and hot. The landscape would suggest, to our eyes at least, a total absence of available water, and we would begin to wonder whether we could last the day until camp appeared. Several times when thirst was beginning to dominate our thoughts, our safari headman, Jacobo, who looked exactly like the bog-bound Tolund Man, even down to his hat, would disappear off the trail. Returning a little later, he would lead us to a spot that appeared no better than that which we had just left. Searching among the undergrowth he would locate some hollow stems, and then, using them as drinking straws, he would thrust them through an insignificant patch of moss on the ground—and low, there was clear, cool drinking water in abundance hidden beneath. We could have been at death's door and would never found such a place on our own.

One purpose of our journey, and one reason for the train of porters, was the collecting of specimens. Our principal non-arthropod quarry was birds, although I regularly shot for the pot as well. Each evening, as we gathered around our campfire, Hammadi the skinner, would prepare the day's trophies as museum skins.

I think it true to say that I have never experienced such a sense of absolute freedom, tranquillity and peace of mind as I did on that safari, apart from camping alone in the vastness of the Great Salt Desert of central Iran many years later."

SUBLIME LUNACY

# Discursus Thirty-Eight
## Royal Welcome

The European club in Kigoma catered to the twenty or thirty white families living in the area in 1959, and was the centre of social life. Each month the club held a film show, and this happened to coincide with David and John's arrival. Naturally the DC invited them along, and after a convivial meal and a few drinks, everyone settled down to watch the film.

> "The film started, and I was interested to see that it was about Oxford. Then it gradually dawned on me that the film we were starting to watch was none other than the film about Oxford in which I had taken part a couple of years earlier. Never having seen the film, it took a little while before I could be certain, and in growing horror I slumped down further into my chair hoping nobody would notice. Vain hope, indeed! My presence was sufficient to ignite a party that lasted until dawn. Despite much searching, I have never seen the film again since."

After parting company in Kigoma, David to return to a teaching post in South Africa, John headed slowly north, with the intention of travelling down the Nile to Egypt. His first stop was Usumbura (Bujumbura) at the tip of the lake in Burundi, and then on to Bukavu in Rwanda. It was here that he was pleasantly surprised to find far less racial segregation than in British East Africa, in particular being favourably struck by seeing European waitresses serving a largely black clientele in a bar.

Because his baggage was somewhat bulky, containing collecting equipment and specimens in addition to the usual traveller's necessities, he would often send it on ahead for convenience. He soon discovered, however, that baggage shipped in this way seldom arrives intact at the intended destination. In self-defence he developed s strategy of waiting to find where it had gone, and then travelling there himself to collect it and send it off on the next leg. It made for interesting, unplanned journeys.

From Bukavu he made his way to the IRSAC research station at Lwiro, in what was then still the Belgian Congo—just. It seemed an idyllic spot. Strawberries were, he was told, in season fifty weeks of the year, while the waters of Lake Kivu were free of schistosomiasis (bilharzia) and safe to swim in. He had only been there a short time before being offered a job. It would have been a great spot to return to once his doctoral thesis had been finished, and he was seriously considering accepting. At that time the idea of Congolese independence was something being talked about as a possibility in the far distant future. Yet by the time he had returned to Britain some six months later it had happened—with tragic consequences.

The Belgians ran a very paternalistic regime (following earlier atrocities, it should be added) and all administration was carried out by expatriates. No Congolese had been trained for administrative posts, let alone national politics. When the Belgians simply walked away, the result was mayhem.

"When I left Lwiro, hitchhiking proved difficult because of reports that the streets of Goma, whence I was headed, were running with blood following another outbreak of violence between the Bahutu and their traditional overlords, the Watutsi. As a result I found myself stranded by the roadside one evening as dusk was falling. I was preparing for a rather uncomfortable bivouac when a lone European drove by. Seeing me, he stopped and we got into conversation, both speaking French. It was several minutes before it emerged that we were both British. Darkness had already fallen when he suddenly said: "This is ridiculous! You can't stay here. Come and spend the night at my place."

As the evening wore on, I discovered that he had been up at Christ Church in Oxford, and was most anxious to catch up on all the university gossip. I was repeatedly urged to stay "just one more night" only to find that a full day's activities and more had been planned for the morrow. On one day we went by boat to a private island on Lake Kivu to visit the Prince de Ligne in his magnificent mansion, where we received a royal welcome.

After a week of wonderful hospitality, it was only with great difficulty that I was able to tear myself away and continue my journey. I am sorry to say that not long after my return to England I saw a newspaper report that in the violence following independence, my host had been attacked and badly beaten.

John had long cherished a desire to follow in his Aunt Dorothy's footsteps and climb the fabled 'Mountains of the Moon', the snow-covered peaks of the Ruwenzori range. Hoping that he might find like-minded companions in Fort Portal to mount a small expedition, he continued North, passing the Virunga volcanoes, and marvelling at the luminous red coronet of cloud hovering at night over the summit of Nyiragongo, lit from deep within the glowing crater.

> "The Queen Elizabeth National Park stands out in my memory, but sadly not for its wildlife. I had hitched a lift with two Italians in their elderly Mercedes, which finally died on a particularly remote stretch of dirt road. We tried pushing, but Mercedes are heavily built and stubbornly resisted our efforts. We had no option but to attempt a roadside repair—this time in circumstances far more demanding than our breakdown in Kosovo. Not the least of our problems was a striking absence of food, water or spare parts.
>
> The problem proved to lie with the radiator fan, which had flown apart and disintegrated. Without a fan to cool the engine we could barely move—and we figured some 200 miles lay between us and civilisation. My companions were beside themselves with anxiety and seemed utterly at a loss. To me it appeared essential that we create a makeshift fan, and I set too with my Swiss Army knife to carve one. It was a long job, but in the end we had an inelegant but effective fan that survived long enough to reach a settlement—at which point I gladly left to hitch a ride on a passing truck"

When it became obvious that an ascent of the Ruwenzoris would not materialise—a combination of persistent bad weather and no companions—John headed for Kampala, where a distant relative was teaching at Makerere College, the premier university in East Africa at that time.

"I arrived on November 22nd, just in time to attend a memorable Saint Cecilia Day concert. The other highlight of my visit to Kampala was the discovery of a milk bar, where I was able to compensate for months of deprivation in a veritable orgy of milkshakes that left me feeling decidedly unwell."

***

The story of John's travels through Africa, and previously across Turkey, would be incomplete without some mention of the scientific results—although it is something he would prefer to forget.

"Our extensive collections, once sorted and prepared, were consigned to appropriate institutions for safe-keeping and eventual publication. What remained of our hard-won bird collection after the DC Kigoma's cat had attacked it was duly written up by ornithologists at Lund University in Sweden. The Harvestmen (Opiliones) were sent to Prof Roewer in Bremen. Also known as 'Daddy-long-legs', it was particularly appropriate in view of my considerable height, that one new species should be named in my honour – the new generic name, Lukundamila, commemorating the village in which it was captured Whether David Eccles ever published an account of the fishes, or Ray Harley the plants, I know not. I hope they fared better than my prized arachnid collections."

Detailed arrangements had been made with the Entomology Department at the University Museum in Oxford to receive and care for the extensive collections John had sent, and later would bring back. Unlike insects, which can be preserved dry, spiders and their relatives are soft-bodied and need to be pickled in alcohol. Collections in alcohol require on-going curatorial care to ensure that the alcohol does not dry out. It was unfortunate that the Turkish material was stored in jars with lids that gradually rusted, and because nobody made regular checks, after several years the alcohol evaporated and the specimens were destroyed.

The fate of the Tanganyika collection was equally lamentable. Every two weeks the SS Liemba would pick up another consignment to be shipped to Oxford. These contained not only preserved material, but live specimens as well, the intention being that immature (and hence largely unidentifiable) spiders would moult to maturity on the journey or soon after arrival. It was only after John returned many months later that he learned that the young technician who had volunteered to care for the material had suffered a nervous breakdown before even the first consignment had arrived,and was sent to a local mental hospital. The boxes that arrived in Oxford consequently remained unopened, the contents being left to die or evaporate unseen. Today little remains of the collection. It was a tragic end to so much labour—but not an uncommon fate for expedition material consigned to an institution.

# Discursus Thirty-Nine
## White Father

After a brief sojourn amid the fleshpots of Kampala, John set off on his descent of the Nile. His first destination was the Murchison Falls, where water flowing out of Lake Victoria passes through a gorge only seven metres wide. It is an area particularly rich in wildlife.

"I set out on foot to explore, looking forward to photographing the local wildlife at close quarters. Hippos, crocodiles, lions and much else were plentiful, but I felt safe for I was in the company of an experienced local guide, armed with a large-calibre rifle. Only when we parted company at the end of the day did I discover that my erstwhile protector carried no ammunition, and the all the security he provided was purely psychological.

It was at Murchison that I discovered how silently elephants could move, despite their size. I had been searching on my own for small game—insects, spiders and the like—and for about half an hour, had been creeping about on hands and knees. Lost in my own world, I had become largely oblivious to my surroundings. I suddenly became aware of the rumbling of distant thunder—except it wasn't thunder and it wasn't distant. I did not immediately recognise the gurgling sounds of an elephant digestive system, and was more than a little startled on looking up, to see the unmistakable bulk of a large cow-elephant looming just a few yards away—although its gender was not instantly apparent from my viewpoint.

I had to assume that she had seen me. Not wishing to alarm her, I did not stand up and run, but crawled slowly with all the deliberation I could muster to the far side of the nearest thorn tree. There was no dramatic end, no hasty ascent into the upper branches—although the possibility certainly crossed my mind. To my great relief the elephant wandered off without bothering to investigate further, but I couldn't help wondering how many others were foraging silently nearby."

Boarding a paddle steamer at Juba, John travelled at a leisurely pace through the interminable papyrus swamps of the Sudd, one of the largest wetland regions on earth. The boat would continually brush against the walls of vegetation bordering the navigable waterway, and whenever anything came within reach he would pull it on board and search for resident spiders. It was a long journey, but the time passed quickly.

"Travelling through East Africa I had acquired a passable smattering of up-country Swahili, the universal *lingua franca*. Many Swahili words are derived from Arabic—a legacy of the slave trade—but with the addition of a terminal vowel. Hence maj (water) becomes maji in Swahili and samak (fish) becomes samaki in Swahili. Thus I found myself with the basis of a ready-made Arabic vocabulary as I passed into the Arab world. On board the boat was a charming Egyptian, who spoke faultless English. On learning of my intended itinerary, he promptly took me in hand and insisted that he teach me some basic Arabic. It was hard work for both of us, for I am a congenital non-linguist."

On arrival in Khartoum John visited the British Embassy, paid his respects to the memory of General Gordon and signed the visitor's book—then promptly departed by train for the Red Sea Hills, where he hoped he might find some dysderid spiders for his coming research—although admittedly there was nothing but intuition to suggest they might be found there.

> "On the journey I found myself sharing the compartment with one of the White Fathers, a Roman Catholic missionary order active in Africa. I exchanged little but courtesies, holding as I do a very negative opinion of his line of business, but we had not been long out of Atbara when he fell ill. By the time we reached my intended, somewhat remote destination it had become clear that I had little option but to accompany my patient on to Port Sudan and get him into hospital."

This simple act of charity would bring in its wake rich rewards. In seeking advice on how best to transport his patient to hospital, John chanced to meet an Australian fisheries expert working in the area. They became friends and made several long camel rides together through the surrounding desert. He also arranged an introduction to Goffredo Lombardo, the distinguished Italian film director, who had chartered a local yacht to go SCUBA diving.

> "Outgoing and generous, Goffredo insisted that I join him on board for Christmas. Accompanied by an admiring entourage of young and extremely attractive aspiring starlets, it developed into one of my best Christmases ever. The clear waters of the Red Sea were filled with huge

populations of brightly coloured fish, the likes of which I had never seen before. I also encountered for the first time giant Manta Rays. Twenty feet and more across the wing tips, they are magnificent creatures. I was cruising along a reef when I became aware of a great dark shadow above me. Looking up, my first sensation was one of acute embarrassment. A recent graduate in zoology, and I was unable to recall immediately what Manta Rays fed on as I looked at close range into the cavernous mouth. As plankton feeders, they are, of course, completely harmless to swimmers, although they can accidentally strike you with a wing. The waters also swarmed with sharks and barracuda.

The boat was based at Suakin, with its beautiful old balconied waterfront buildings. It was hot, humid and filled with flies. I once bought some freshly roasted fish from a dockside vendor, and the flies clustered on it in such numbers that it was impossible to shoo them all away before putting a piece in my mouth. It was not the taste of flies—or the thought of where they might last have alighted—so much as the frantic buzzing as they tried to get out of my mouth, that proved most upsetting."

One of the favourite dive sites was on the Wingate Reef off Port Sudan, now recognised as one of the best SCUBA locations in the world. A major attraction was the wreck of the Umbria, an Italian munitions ship that had been scuttled in 1940. Fearing that it might explode at any moment and engulf the town, the authorities forbade any diving in the vicinity, but there was never any come-back from the numerous times Goffredo and his friends visited the wreck and it remains a favourite destination even now, more than fifty years later.

> "Entering through the missing cargo hatches, we found the holds filled with mountains of loose ammunition, grenades and torpedoes. Their boxes long since broken and rotted, the cargo had cascaded like scree down a mountainside, into the shadowy depths, everything clothed in all manner of encrusting marine organisms. Delight at the diversity of reef life surrounding me was tempered by an underlying concern that accidentally dislodging anything in that hold could trigger a cataclysmic explosion".

Reluctantly bidding farewell to Goffredo and his delightful companions, John finally reached his original destination, a small railway halt in the Red Sea Hills. This was the home territory of the Hadendowa, one of the Beja tribes, immortalised by Kipling for their bravery, and whose proudest boast was their breaking of the British Square—a traditional military defensive formation. They were imposing, indeed frightening hosts, but generous as is the way of desert nomads

> "It was a secret hope that I might have found a new *Dysdera* species in this wild and forbidding land, naming it in their honour *D. hadendowensis,* but the species still awaits discovery
>
> My hosts were extremely camera-shy, but I found an underhand means to capture images of their faces. I removed the pentaprism through which I normally viewed my subject, and exposed the ground-glass screen beneath. As the tribesmen gathered around to see what I was doing (clearly not pointing the camera directly at anybody) I encouraged them to look at the screen. As they directed the camera at their companions I would then periodically

press the button and grab an exposure.

Sadly the rolls of film were destined never to make it home to England—and likewise a magnificent Beja dagger in a silver sheath, the purchase of which had almost bankrupted me. Posted a while later in Egypt, the parcel vanished en route—almost certainly, I now believe, before it had even left the post office. Oh the gullibility of youth, untempered in the bitter hearth of experience."

## Discursus Forty
# Ozymandias

Stopping along the Nile to visit various archaeological sites in the expectation that they would have interesting spiders beneath their abundant fallen stones, John travelled on to Cairo. He passed a long and uncomfortable train journey cramped with two locals in the toilet—a journey, he reports best forgotten. Thence to Alexandria, where he turned west along the North African coast.

"El Alamein, Sidi Barrani, Mersa Matruh—powerfully evocative names of major conflicts during the North African desert campaigns in World War II. Now no longer just names on a map, they became powerful symbols that brought the war to life for me, vivid reminders of so much hardship and sacrifice. In Egypt, and later in Libya, it was impossible to escape the ever-present evidence of war. Rows of crosses in remote desert cemeteries, abandoned rolls of barbed wire, empty shell cases lying in the sand and exposed by the wind. So much sorrow in such beautiful surroundings!

Walking through the desert some five miles inland from the coastal plain—somewhere above Mersa Matruh—I felt like Shelley's traveller from an antique land when I came across a huge unexploded shell lying, like his vast and trunkless legs of stone, half-covered in the wind-blown sand. Sixteen inches in diameter, it must have been fired from a British warship from far out to sea and I couldn't help wondering whether there was ever an HMS Ozymandias."

The desert appeared at first sight a bleak and lifeless wasteland. John was, therefore, intrigued to find innumerable snail shells lying on the surface. Curious to learn more, he collected a number in the hope they might be identified on return to Oxford. It was only some years later, as the shells were being washed in preparation for study, that the snails within were found to be still alive, emerging in response to the sudden moisture in the expectation of browsing again on fresh green shoots. Adapted to survive the long intervals between desert storms and the resulting brief and infrequent blooms of plant life, the snails had continued their aestivation unconcerned on the museum shelves. How long they might have survived in this alien environment can only be guessed at.

"I eventually reached Solloum, close to Egypt's border with Libya. The sight of a new, gleaming white hotel on the beach was tempting—the prospect of a hot bath and laundry service were hard to resist. Moreover, it appeared to be the only accommodation available. Upon enquiry I discovered that I could stay for the princely sum of just two shillings a night, all found—approximately fifty cents. I was surprised to find that I was the only guest, but figured it was a combination of being newly opened and the wrong season for tourists.

The nearby sand dunes proved to be a profitable hunting ground, and I spent three happy days searching for spiders without interruption or even observation. It was only on the last day, as I was preparing to leave, that I learned why my highly desirable hotel was deserted. It was, the concierge confided to me, built in the middle of

an un-cleared minefield. Why only the previous week two German tourists—the hotel's only guests—had been killed by a mine in the very area in which I had been working."
John's departure coincided, not by accident, with the weekly bus service to Libya. Checking with the Libyan embassy in London before leaving for Africa many months before, he had been told that as he held a British passport, no visa was necessary. This was, of course, well before Libya acquired its later, rather sinister international reputation.

"A cold wind, carrying with it stinging grains of sand, swept across the desolate landscape as we arrived at the frontier. A sagging barrier across the road marked the border, where we were instructed to dismount from the bus and enter the frontier post for processing. A small, brown mud building, it stood bleak and alone, apart from a couple of nearby shacks. It was hard to imagine that people might actually live here.

"Passport!" barked a bored-looking official in a rumpled kaki uniform, holding out his hand. Flicking through the pages, he said "No visa". It was hard to tell whether this was a statement or a question, but the consequences were unambiguous. I could not enter Libya. In vain did I protest that the embassy in London had assured me no visa was necessary. That, I learned, would only have been true had I arrived by air direct from London. As I was trying to slip in from Egypt, I would have to be detained while enquiries were made.

A small knot of dishevelled gendarmes had gathered round to watch my discomfort. In desperation I claimed that my family owned Thomas Cook, the travel company, and that by detaining me they were jeopardising the future of Libya's nascent tourist industry. I was still waxing eloquent on the point when the bus departed, leaving me stranded—probably at best until the next bus a week hence.

Recognising that Libyan officialdom would not yield, I reluctantly offered to return to Egypt and obtain a visa from the embassy in Cairo. This, I next learned would be impossible, for I had no exit visa to leave Libya.

By now night was falling, and the officials suddenly announced that our discussions would have to be adjourned until tomorrow.......and unfortunately there was nowhere I could get a meal, although I might sleep in one of the adjacent sheds. The sleeping platform was about five feet in length, for the Libyans are not tall, and consisted of wooden planks covered by a thin layer of old straw. Moreover, it was already filled with some ten slumbering Arabs. It was not my best night's sleep—indeed it was the only time in a long life of travel in which I would be attacked simultaneously by fleas, lice and bedbugs.

When negotiations resumed the following morning, my first question was how I might obtain the necessary exit visa that would allow me to return to Egypt. That could only be issued in Benghazi, they said—but as I had no entry visa I could not possibly be permitted to proceed thence. Gradually it dawned on me that I was being blackmailed, and that some form of financial inducement might reveal a solution. I carried little cash with me, but still had some traveller's cheques, which were useless without access to a bank. Herein might lie salvation.

If permission were to be granted for me to travel on to Benghazi, I would return with more money, and hopefully the necessary exit visa to return to Egypt. Meanwhile I could offer whatever money I had with me at the moment to cover the cost of the phone call they would doubtless have to make to get the necessary permission. It worked, and I hitched a ride on a crowded and ill-maintained truck to freedom."

Benghazi, Libya's second city, and home to the Senussi royal family, was something of a boom town. Libya's nascent oil industry was attracting a growing number of westerners, and through a few casual coffee-house encounters John soon gained entry to this expatriate circle. A valuable introduction was to Hamilton Browne, who had first come to Libya during the war as a navigator with the Long Range Desert Group, with whom he had won a Military Cross for valour.

The exploits of the LRDG became legendary as they harassed the German forces without warning from desert bases in regions believed to be impenetrable. Under cover of darkness they would blow up fuel and ammunition dumps, attack convoys and liberate allied prisoners, before vanishing back to their desert sanctuaries.

After serving as mayor of Benghazi, Hamilton Browne, now ran a consultancy service much in demand by the oil exploration companies. One wall of his office was covered with a huge map of the desert on which were recorded landmarks, tracks, minefields and emergency caches of food and water.

"Hamilton Browne introduced me to the local operations manager of BP Oil Exploration, who it transpired, had read zoology at Oxford a year or two ahead of me. Through this happy coincidence I was offered the use of a Land Rover and with Hamilton Browne's geographical guidance, freedom to travel wheresoever I wished through the Sahara.

My first destination was a British encampment on the edge of the Kalansho Sand Sea, a region of challenging white dunes. With the British penchant for mortifying the flesh, the team was camped in diminutive pup tents that provided little protection from the elements. Dressed in shorts, they endured constant pain from the unceasing blast of wind-driven sand against the skin. Upper lip stiffness was taxed to the full.

From the challenging Boy Scout British camp, I headed off again into the wild beauty of the desert, bound for a putative American camp, whose location was uncertain. With a confidence that in hindsight was undoubtedly misplaced, I drove through a landscape that the more experienced would consider dangerously challenging. Secure in my understanding of the principles of navigation by sun compass, and well supplied with jerry-cans of water, I revelled in the experience of solitude. Here every ripple on the sand surface, every protruding rock and pebble, assumes disproportionate significance. One's senses and perception become heightened through the absence of distracting detail. It is a pristine world.

Navigating through this fascinating wilderness, I came upon some protruding rocks that called for attention. A limestone outcrop, it consisted of layer upon layer of thin lamellae, like the exposed pages of a giant book, polished smooth by the wind and sand.

Much of my spider collecting involves searching beneath stones, and here were stones waiting invitingly to be turned over. Although it was still early in the year, heat from the sun made the rocks almost too hot to touch, yet at night temperatures would plunge below freezing. On some mornings, dew would have fallen, becoming frozen to form an icy crust across the desert, only to vanish as the first rays of the dawn sun grazed the surface.

I was not convinced that anything could live in such an exposed and extreme environment, but the urge to look was intense. What, I wondered, could possibly survive here? Close examination revealed that between the limestone lamellae had accumulated small fragments of wind-blown vegetable debris. This provided sustenance for the first rung of the food chain, a population of silverfish, primitive insects that can survive in very dry habitats. The silverfish in turn provided food for prodidomid spiders, an obscure family associated particularly with extremely arid locations. It proved to be a new species, which I was later happy to name *Zimirina vastitatis* in recognition of the great open wasteland it called home."

In contrast to the rugged conditions of the British exploration team, the Americans, once John found them, were enjoying unparalleled luxury. Gleaming aluminium Airstream caravans, fully air-conditioned and luxuriously appointed, provided complete isolation from the desert outside. Here, in a fleet of mobile oases, he feasted on massive hamburgers, accompanied by twelve different sauces and pickles available at each table.

"The real revelation was to come a few days later when I arrived at the camp of a French oil exploration team. Oh, what contrast! After generations of colonial experience in Algeria, the French understood how to live well in the desert. Their camp could easily have served as a set for another re-make of Beau Geste. The lofty marquee that served as the dining hall was lined with festoons of pale blue silk, and pictures hung on the walls. Everyone was dressed in immaculate khaki uniforms, and exuded an air of professional competence, overlain with an easy, welcoming manner—not at all the typical British image of their Gallic neighbours. The French were clearly at home here in the desert. Wine flowed in abundance, and live pigs provided fresh pork and limitless sausages."

Finally back in Benghazi, John reluctantly returned his Land Rover to BP and planned his next move. He had been taken in by a young English couple, who were expatriate schoolteachers. For their hospitality he later named another new spider species, *Prodidomus rollasoni,* in their honour.

Through the Rollasons and his network of new friends he chanced to meet a somewhat disordered Welshman who was Professor of English at the local university. With him they visited the nearby oasis considered by the ancient Greeks to be the fabled Garden of the Hesperides, where Hercules sought the three golden apples.

A few years later this brief excursion would bring unwelcome repercussions. A geologist friend at Oxford, returning from a field trip to Libya reported that he has seen John's name on a list of prohibited immigrants, for evermore banned from visiting the country again. His first reaction was that reports of his encounter at the Egyptian border had somehow filtered through the bureaucracy and was even now recorded in the government archives.

Further research, however, revealed a different explanation. The Welsh professor had apparently published a book describing his Libyan experiences, in which he made a number of observations that were held to be anti-Libyan. One day, for example, whilst urging his students to work harder, he reported that their response was: "What need have we to work? We have oil instead."

Not only was the author himself banned from ever returning to Libya, but so too were all the people mentioned in his book, deemed to be his friends and hence holding similar, imprudent opinions.

With limited funds, John often relied on hitchhiking for travel. Enquiring about possible rides among friends in Benghazi, he met a family who were bound for Tunis to take up a new appointment. They were delighted at the prospect of being able to fly while someone else drove their car the six hundred-odd desert miles, and so he found himself with a perfect means of transport that would allow collecting along the way.

"There was just one hitch, however. Would I also take their cat? In preparation for the flight, the cat had apparently been given tranquillisers and disappeared. Many hours later it was found asleep in a rolled up carpet, by which time the flying party had already left. I was happy to have a companion on my journey, but unexpectedly found the cat to be also a valuable, albeit unwitting, research assistant. It so happened that the cat was unaccustomed to long journeys, and was a very poor traveller. At ten-mile intervals the car would become filled with piteous mewing that I soon learned meant that I should immediately stop for the cat to be carsick. Pulling to the roadside and opening the door, the cat would take off like a bullet, vanishing from view over the distant horizon. The first few times this happened I was overcome with anxiety lest my charge should be lost. How was I to break the news to her owners? Fortunately the cat, doubtless recognising the hazards of abandoning the journey in such inhospitable surroundings, would come padding back after some thirty minutes.

Once the routine had been established, I was able to take advantage of the cat's rest stops to do some collecting, sampling spiders at regular intervals all along the route."

John had barely reached Tunis, when he was stopped by a policeman outside the royal palace. He demanded to see 'papers'. It was an awkward moment, as he had no idea where such documents, if indeed they existed, might be found. In addition, he once again did not have a visa.

"Expressing my profound apologies for the oversight, I said that everything was in my hotel room—"Just wait here", I assured him, "and I'll be back in a few minutes." There was just time to hand the car and cat over to their owners before I left to stay with friends in Carthage. For all I know my obliging policeman is still there outside the palace, patiently awaiting my return."

## Discursus Forty-One
# Mortal Remains

As a young graduate student starting work on his doctoral thesis, John lived for nothing but his research. "At that time," he said, "I did not realize that 'research' actually meant 're-search—on the grounds that it has usually already been done before."

Although technically in the zoology department, he had been offered accommodation by Prof George Varley in his entomology department. He was given an attic room high up in the roof of the University Museum, not far from the hall in which T.H. Huxley had so effectively silenced the Bishop of Oxford, 'Soapy Sam' Wilberforce in their famous debate on Darwin's theory of evolution in June 1860. Wilberforce had provocatively asked Huxley whether he was descended from an ape on his mother's or his father's side. Huxley witheringly replied that he "would rather be descended from an ape than from a divine who uses authority to stifle truth", a response that has since passed into history.

"The glorious museum", Tuckwell wrote in his Reminiscences, "rose before us like an exhalation." Designed by Woodward, it is a masterpiece of Victorian self-confidence, every decorative detail a bold, dogmatic statement. The museum became John's home, and on some nights he would even sleep in his laboratory.

"There was a special pleasure in wandering the building alone in the middle of a moon-lit night, conjuring up in my mind's eye the individuals responsible for its creation. Dr Acland of Christ Church, the moving spirit in persuading the university that such a structure was needed, and the alcoholic Shea brothers from Ireland, masons whose fancy created the exuberant, still-unfinished carvings. I also recalled the great Dr Kidd, whose attitude was typical of the minds that Acland was determined to convert. Long before the museum opened its doors, Dr Acland would hold soirées at Christ Church to which senior members of the university were invited to view Acland's growing collection and demonstration of natural history specimens. Invited to observe some miniscule animaculae down Dr Acland's microscope, Dr Kidd is reported to have said: "In the first place, I don't believe it. And even if it were true, I don't believe the Almighty meant us to know it", whereupon he pointedly departed.

In my wanderings I reserved a special place for the memory of poor Giles Covington. The last man to be publicly hanged in Oxford, he was almost certainly innocent of the murder for which he was indicted, having the misfortune to be in the wrong place at the wrong time. I first met him, still hanging, in an obscure attic storage space. His reasembled skeleton dangled from a high beam, and a shaft of sunlight shining through the dusty atmosphere from a skylight above, illuminated it dramatically from behind. It was a powerful, evocative image, and I would sometimes come to pay homage in the night when the moon was full, its beams eerily highlighting poor mister Covington's mortal remains."

As a dedicated researcher, John would sometimes go to hear interesting lectures in other departments. His attention had been drawn to a research talk being given in the Forestry Department, at which a film was to be shown. Gerald Thompson, a lecturer in forest entomology, was to describe his work on certain hymenopteran parasites and hyper-parasites. It proved to be a ground-breaking film unlike anything John had ever seen, filled with highly detailed close-ups of extraordinary behaviours.

> "I was entranced, and couldn't refrain from approaching Gerald afterwards to express my admiration—I was but one among many. With the brash effrontery of youth, I ended my brief discussion with this senior academic with the words: "It was quite wonderful—but what a pity that your insects aren't as interesting as my spiders." Imagine my surprise when, two days later, there was a knock at my door, and there stood Gerald Thompson. "I was thinking about what you said, and went to the library to find out more about spiders. You could be right." He then invited me to join him in making a ten-minute film about spider behaviour. My immediate concern was whether spiders could be persuaded to perform reliably in front of the camera, bearing in mind that exceptionally bright lights would be needed to film in colour at high magnifications. However, the pay-off for me was that I would receive footage of the spiders I was studying that could be used to untangle the details of their mating behaviour."

So it was that John unwittingly entered into a wholly new world, and one that would later come to occupy much of his professional life. Spiders, they discovered performed perfectly before the camera, and made wonderful subjects. The original plans for a single ten-minute film gradually grew into a series of fifteen such films, plus two television programs, one thirty minutes in length, and the other an hour. Even then there was much footage that has remained unused.

With his thesis nearing completion, John was beginning to contemplate what his next move might be. His Christopher Welch scholarship, worth £400 per year, was coming to an end and regrettably he would soon need some form of gainful employment. His habitual cavalier dismissal of, and contempt for money, which he considered mere lubrication for the machinery of society was once again threatened by the forces of reality. However, fate was once more preparing to intercede on his behalf.

Sir Alister Hardy had retired as Linacre Professor of Zoology in 1961, to be succeeded by John Pringle. Pringle was an insect physiologist from Cambridge. A distinguished academic, he was also extremely shy. The first lecture he gave after arriving at Oxford was almost inaudible, drowned out by the rattle of keys and coins in his pocket being nervously shaken. Pringle's shyness made him appear cold and remote. It was said that once one had broken the ice with him … there was only cold water remaining beneath.

The Linacre chair is attached to Merton College, and I have no doubt that John's father, who dined regularly in college and was of a gregarious nature, would have gone out of his way to make the new member of common room feel at ease.

John was surprised, and not a little flattered, when he and his family were invited to tea with the Pringles one Sunday afternoon. Tea was followed by croquet, a game that brings out the demonic nature concealed within even the mildest of bishops. It was a demanding game, for it was played on the Pringle's own, idiosyncratic lawn, and at a distinct psychological disadvantage. Nevertheless John succeeded in beating the august professor on his own turf. It was to this refusal to yield in the face of overwhelming odds that John attributes the offer he received shortly afterwards to become Vertebrate Demonstrator—this, and a little nepotism.

In those days the undergraduate zoology course spent one year on vertebrates and one year on invertebrates—in addition to much else besides. By a happy stroke of luck, John was appointed Vertebrate Demonstrator in an invertebrate year, leaving him with little teaching apart from undergraduate tutorials. This allowed him to devote considerable time to the problems of close-up filming and photography. Towards the end of the year he became conscious that nemesis was fast approaching, for in truth he had little interest in the finer details of vertebrate anatomy, and recognised that he was quite ignorant on the subject.

Just as he was preparing to rectify this vacuum by intensive last-minute study to avoid the inescapable blemish to his professional reputation, another miracle occurred.

David Nichols, the invertebrate demonstrator, accepted an appointment at Exeter University. Just in the nick of time John was offered David's position—one to which he was far better suited—finding himself once again taking up a teaching position in an 'off' year. This time, however, he seized the opportunity to re-design completely the invertebrate practical classes and spent long, rewarding hours working with Peggy Varley to create a wholly new program.

Peggy Varley, wife of George Varley, the Hope Professor of Entomology, had taught the distinguished TV presenter David Attenborough when he was an undergraduate at Cambridge. When David's acclaimed 'Life on Earth' series first appeared, Peggy claimed to recognise in the commentary, substantial passages taken verbatim from her teaching notes.

"All my spare time was, by now, taken up either working with Gerald Thompson on filming projects, which were beginning to encompass more than just spiders, or in developing new photographic techniques and building equipment in the departmental workshops. However, this would carry little weight in the eyes of Professor Pringle. I had endeared myself to him by deciding to investigate the electrophysiology of certain spider sense organs, for this was not far removed from some of his own interests. Positioning myself thus in his favour went some way to mitigate the embarrassment I had maliciously caused at a faculty meeting. Pringle was extolling the virtues of a large influx of complex and expensive new equipment to the department. I could not suppress the desire to remind the meeting of Lord Rutherford's famous observation: that when one did not have a lot of expensive apparatus, one had to think instead. I do not believe I was ever wholly forgiven.

To be honest, I never really took to electrophysiology. Technical difficulties forced me to wonder in time whether the arachnid nervous system might not operate on some new, hitherto unsuspected principle, a system in which electrical impulses played no role. Although researchers in Germany finally developed techniques that worked, I became discouraged and sought consolation in continuing field studies. In truth, I was far happier searching for new spider species on mountaintops in Scotland than staring at an unresponsive oscilloscope screen. Nevertheless, my brief sortie into electrophysiology did result in a close friendship. The room next to mine was occupied by Chris Rees, an improbable graduate student. His research involved recording nerve impulses from within tiny hairs on the feet of small beetles. This unlikely task was to demonstrate the presence of taste organs that responded to the presence of a specific chemical, hypericin, found only on the beetle's preferred foodplant, *Hypericum*. As the beetle's tarsi felt around the edge of a leaf, the presence of hypericin would initiate feeding.

This investigation involved incredibly delicate control in positioning the electrodes, and yet Chris would appear the last person to undertake such work. Often covered in grease from working on his motorbike, he seemed incapable of drinking a glass of beer without spilling half of it down his shirt. It was no great surprise when he set his room on fire—more than once. He was a speleologist and enjoyed the challenge of squirming through tight potholes, and acquired some notoriety among his companions in making the first nocturnal descent of Magdalen College tower, leaving a trail of pitons down the stonework. Of his intellect there could be no doubt. When awarded a scholarship to spend a year in Japan, he decided to take the trans-Siberian railway in order to have time to learn Japanese. When he returned to Oxford he saw a Japanese scientific journal on my desk and had no difficulty in translating it on sight. It was tragic when he had a serious motorcycle accident and sustained head injuries from which he never fully recovered."

While John was spending time with Gerald in the Forestry Department, there were others exploring the uses of film closer to home. Peter Parks, a talented artist whom John had first met as a young zoology undergraduate at meetings of the OU Entomological Society, had been given a job in the museum as an illustrator. One of his particular interests was filming and photographing microscopic aquatic organisms using a system of dark field illumination that he had developed. Peter had joined forces with John Paling, who was interested in fish parasites, and with Sean Morris, a recent graduate, and one of John's brighter students.

With two groups of highly innovative filmmakers now working in close proximity, it was inevitable that they would often meet over coffee and share ideas. They were also drawn more closely together through Chris Parsons, who headed the BBC's natural history unit, and was calling on both groups for special filming projects.

It was Gerald's idea that both groups might work successfully together as a single unit. He had visualised the possibility that the university might be persuaded to establish a scientific film unit, run as a commercial enterprise along the lines of the university press, whose profits would go to swell the university coffers. It was a bold idea, but before it could even be discussed it was necessary to discover whether everyone could, in fact, work amicably together. Experience with the Exploration Club had made John acutely aware that all too often groups of friends might easily fall out when obliged to work in close proximity.

They all decided that a joint overseas filming expedition would be an appropriate way in which to test mutual compatibility. Casting about for suitable locations, they settled on Jamaica, not least because Gerald had an old friend there, Ivan Goodbody, who was professor of zoology at the University of the West Indies.

Ivan proved more than happy to sponsor the project, making available not only his department at the Mona campus, but also the Port Royal marine laboratory. Moreover, as he himself would be in England on leave, he was glad to have his house occupied and used as a base.

Of course, the whole scheme rested on an ability to raise the substantial amount of money that would be needed. Instinctively they turned to Chris Parsons and the BBC. It would be a gamble, for they really had very little experience of filming beyond their own very restricted specialities, but Chris felt confident and managed to sell the idea. As a safeguard, the plans called for Chris himself to join the team for several weeks to supervise them filming themselves at work, and to ensure that suitable sound tracks were recorded.

The hours were long, but the work was rewarding. It was challenging but infinitely enjoyable work. Some days John would spend on the water making plankton hauls or searching for the one particular species of sea cucumber in which the pearl fish, *Carapus,* passed its life. Other days were spent exploring Jamaica's poorly known high forests for bromeliad frogs and velvet worms or onycophorans—the enigmatic *Peripatus* so beloved by evolutionary biologists because of their combination of anatomical features that hints at them being intermediates between annelid worms and insects.

It was while searching for velvet worms high in the John Crow Mountains of eastern Jamaica that he chanced upon a new species of *Sesarma*, a fresh water grapsid crab, and had the satisfaction of learning some time later that it had been named in his honour. Having a new species named after him was of infinitely less importance to John than being able to film and photograph the endemic *Macroperipatus insularis* giving birth to live young—a striking exception to most onycophorans, who produce eggs.

Looking today at the three programs they made in Jamaica, they seem terribly dated and technically naïve, but at the time they were first shown, they were hailed as ground-breaking and remarkable—and the BBC was happy at getting three good programs at relatively modest expense.

# Discursus Forty-Two
## Orchids

It was during a slight lull in the conversation one evening that John suddenly asked how one should define success. After the usual round of responses, which included happiness, wealth, fame and fulfilment (for I had witnessed this opening gambit on past occasions) John elaborated on his question. He was, he said, thinking purely in terms of biological success. Everybody present was happy to attempt a definition, and John listened intently. Some people felt that success could be measured in terms of population size—those species that were the most abundant were clearly, in their eyes, the most successful. This view was countered by those who felt that those species that had the greatest geographical distribution were the winners. A popular contender for the title was the cockroach, on the grounds of number, diversity of habitat and worldwide distribution—on top of having survived virtually unchanged for millions of years.

As so often happens, the question had been posed by John to provide an opening for some anecdote or other, although the true direction of the conversation did not immediately become apparent, for his mind often follows a convoluted course.

"Would you not say," John finally interjected, "that an animals that has managed to invade a habitat that no other creatures inhabits, where there is no competition for food or shelter, where there are no predators—would you not say that such an animal has achieved a remarkably high level of success?" A murmur of agreement ran through his listeners.

Recognising the cue from past experience, I asked with seeming innocence, for some examples of what he meant. "Ah....," he began, "I'm glad you asked...... How about *Psilopa petrolei?*" The blank expressions around the table provided the opening he was seeking.

"*Psilopa* is a small fly that illustrates exactly what I mean. It is unique in having evolved the ability to breed in the pools of crude oil that accumulate around oil wells. This is a remarkable achievement—something that no other animal has managed to do. In this curious and hostile environment *Psilopa* is king, the conqueror of a domain devoid of competitors." When the expressions of amazement had died down, John continued: "Of course surface pools of crude oil are not very common, so *Psilopa* is neither abundant nor widespread, but it provides a valuable example of how important it is to define the precise sense in which a word is used."

Before the conversation had wandered off in other directions, John once again seized the opportunity to embark on a new anecdote.

"Talking of rarity, have I ever told you about the extraordinary Australian underground orchid?" "*Rhizanthella* is a genus of orchid found only in Australia. It not only grows underground, but even blooms underground. First discovered in the 1920s, it long remained tantalisingly elusive, acquiring the status of a botanical Holy Grail. Just a few individual specimens had been found by accident, and nothing was known of its biology. We became interested in it through a film we were making at Oxford Scientific about pollination—about the strategies and deceits that plants have adopted to ensure their pollination. Several of the stories followed in the film occur in Australia, and we had become friendly with several leading botanists there.

Imagine our delight when we get a phone call from the Herbarium in Perth to say that for the first time ever, a colony of *Rhizanthella* had been found near Esperance on the south coast of Western Australia. I was about to leave on a filming trip to South Africa, and quickly altered my route to take in Australia first.

I won't bore you with details, but *Rhizanthella* is saprophytic, feeding through an association with a specific fungus that attacks the roots of the shrub boombrush (*Melaleuca uncinata*). As it grows, it causes a slight heave in the soil, similar to that of an emerging toadstool, but invisible beneath a thick layer of fallen leaves.

By the time I arrived the local orchid society had already cleared a sizable patch of ground and by examining every bump and crack, had discovered about a dozen orchids. Anxious to learn something of the plant's pollination strategy, I had brought a collection of little silk tepees, which I erected over each patch of ground that concealed an orchid. In the next couple of days I discovered what I was seeking. Several tepees contained little black phorid flies—common inhabitants of litter—but these were distinctive, for each carried on its back a pair of little yellow pollen sacs. These had been attached by the flowers, which had then released their little go-betweens to transport pollen to another orchid."

The story ended on an unlikely note. Further colonies of *Rhizanthella* had subsequently been discovered when satellite images revealed areas of appropriate vegetation. However, before yielding the floor to others, John had one further point to make on the connection between success and rarity. He chose to talk about *Coryanthes,* another orchid, this time from Trinidad and Costa Rica. It has what is probably the most complex and improbable pollination story. The details were first recorded by Darwin, and when OSF came to film it, they found that Darwin had been a meticulously thorough observer, missing nothing. The point that John wished to make was that *Coryanthes* depends on luring in the males of one species of small, iridescent green euglossine bee. With its continued existence wholly dependent on the presence and correct behaviour of its sole pollinator, *Coryanthes* is taking a huge risk and is actually facing eventual extinction when changes in climate or habitat cause the bees to move elsewhere. In evolutionary terms, such extreme specialisation is a recipe for eventual disaster, so success must also include plasticity—the ability to change in synchrony with fluctuating environments. One can only hope that *Coryanthes* will survive—it would be a terrible loss if such a beautiful plant, with such an amazing pollination story were to disappear—but the long term outlook is bleak indeed. As an afterthought, he added:

> "I wonder how many society matrons proudly sporting orchid blooms on their ample bosoms realize that the Greek word ὄρχις, from which the plant gets its name, means 'testicle'?"

# Discursus Forty-Three
## Autoproctoscopy

On his way home from the Jamaica Expedition, John broke his journey in New York to visit his now-aging American foster parents from the war years. He also took the opportunity to call on Willis Gertsch, the doyen of American arachnologists, who was curator of spiders at the American Museum of Natural History. They had corresponded frequently for several years, but never met. Here again another small miracle was being set in motion.

"The expedition was in every way a success, and plans went ahead to try and persuade the university to create a niche for us. Ultimately it was our good fortune that the university turned down the idea, although at the time it seemed a disaster. My appointment at Oxford was coming to an end, and I was, somewhat casually, wondering where I might go next. Sue, my wife at the time hankered after being a housemaster's wife at a reputable public school, and was most anxious that I accept the offer from Charterhouse to join them as senior science master. With memories of my own schooldays still painfully fresh, the prospect of joining a community so monastic and self-absorbed held little appeal. Even knowing the school's generous attitude towards outside activities—Wilfred Noyce, a master there, was part of the original Everest team and a regular participant in mountaineering expeditions—I remained unenthusiastic.

Moreover, at the same time I was being approached

to become professor of Zoology at Ibadan University in Nigeria. This held considerably more appeal for me. But then, out of the blue came an invitation to move to New York as Willis Gertsch's successor. This was undoubtedly the top position in the field of Arachnology, and it was an honour hard to resist.

I debated briefly whether it would be better to be well-paid in America and visit Nigeria whenever I wished, or accept a post in Africa that was unlikely ever to pay sufficiently well to allow visits to America. The decision was easy, particularly after visiting medical friends in New York when invited to the museum for an interview. Protesting that they lived hand-to-mouth, I could not help noticing that the steaks they served at dinner hung off the edge of the plate on every side. If that be poverty, I thought, give me more!"

Not long after moving the family to America John realised that he had seriously misjudged the cost of living in New York. The salary that had appeared so generous in England, proved grossly inadequate across the Atlantic, and he soon understood how a successful anaesthesiologist with a salary vastly greater than his own could feel hard up in the city.

The job itself also lost much of its appeal on closer inspection. As a field naturalist, and particularly as a filmmaker, working with the corpses of spiders pickled in alcohol soon lost its appeal. The promises made of graduate students and affiliations with New York academic institutions proved to be nothing more than wishful thinking by the museum authorities, without any foundation in fact.

Added to this, the museum itself proved something of a broken reed. Riddled with internal political intrigue, the science departments held little love for the exhibition department, whom they regarded as a distracting nuisance when approached for help with new displays. Even at the highest level, the Board of Trustees was schizophrenic. Its members had been chosen for the depths of their pockets, and none were scientists. On the one hand, the museum was known to the public for the richness of its displays, and yet its reputation as a scientific institution was based upon the research of the academic departments hidden away on the fifth floor.

In consequence, the trustees were continually consumed by an almost psychotic, schizophrenic anxiety worrying about the museum's image. To describe their attitude, John coined the term 'autoproctoscopic', in recognition of the inelegant posture assumed while their vision was permanently focused on self-examination.

On the other hand, the museum was extremely generous to the curators in the time off given for vacations and in the resulting opportunities for fieldwork. New York becomes particularly trying in the heat of summer, and when he was approached to undertake a survey of the spiders and insects on an island off the coast of S. Carolina recently donated to the museum, John leapt at the chance. He also proposed visiting the museum's southwestern field station at Portal in the Chiricahua Mountains on the border between New Mexico and Arizona. An added bonus was that his predecessor, Willis Gertsch, had retired to Portal.

"So it was that in our first summer the family drove some 12,000 miles on a circuitous journey across the continent, collecting spiders along the way. However, as a photographer, it was inevitable that I should also take pictures—something I did continually in my spare time at home as well. Prompted by the need to enhance my income, when I returned home I began contacting the picture editors of New York publishing houses. It was a time when there was a boom in illustrated natural history books, and I found my material to be in considerable demand.

I had been approached by Grolier Encyclopaedias to read critically a volume they were producing on arachnids—one of a 30-volume series. Translated into English by a non-biologist, from an original Italian text riddled with errors, it was a disaster. So numerous were the mistakes that there was no room in the page margins to comment on them.

Despite my vehement objections, the Grolier editors had not left sufficient time to incorporate any significant changes and the volume was sent to subscribers virtually un-emended. So bad was it that the normally docile recipients started sending books back in droves.

At the time, Grolier encyclopaedias formed, a staple of the much-maligned door-to-door salesmen, who stop at nothing to collect their commission. It was just after I had passed my comments on their arachnid volume to the Grolier editors that my wife inadvertently opened the front door of our Connecticut home one of their salesmen. It proved a valuable learning experience—a brilliant demonstration of the sales techniques I had already described to her

On him introducing his wares, Sue remarked: "Oh yes. My husband writes your encyclopaedias." She could have been talking to a lump of mud. There was no reaction, not a flutter of surprise or acknowledgement. Like a badly programmed computer, once the sales routine had been started, nothing could stop it—there was no "Escape" key. Only pulling his plug, or stabbing him, could have interrupted the flow of honeyed words.

"We would like to put a bookcase filled with this encyclopaedia into your living room. Think of the benefits, the advantages, your children will enjoy." It sounded a great idea. "All we ask is that from time to time you will allow us to bring neighbours in to see how much you are enjoying it." Again, it did not sound unreasonable.

This was the sugar coating to a cleverly concealed trap into which the unwary might easily be led.

"In appreciation for our generosity in placing this valuable encyclopaedia in your home, we ask that you make a small contribution towards the cost—just a few cents only, each week, for each volume.

Like a squid enveloping its enemy in a cloud of ink, the salesman distracts his victim in a cloud of words, never allowing time for the significance of this request to sink in. Forewarned and quick with numbers, Sue was immediately able to point out that when this "small" contribution was translated into real money, the ultimate cost of each volume would be roughly double what one might reasonably have expected to pay in a bookstore.

Even when his program had finished running and he was being shown the door, the significance of what had just been said to him failed to register. He still left the forms for us to fill in to seal the deal should we change our minds. Doubtless he was already mentally spending his commission."

With the return of unprecedented numbers of encyclopaedias, Grolier leaned heavily on the packaging house that produced the series for them, and in desperation they, in turn, approached John as the only professional zoologist they knew. Not only was he to read and suggest corrections to several other volumes, but more importantly, would he totally re-write the arachnid volume? It was a pretty horrendous assignment, given the tight schedule to which publication had been committed, but fate once again intervened.

"I was in quarantine for chickenpox, one of my children having brought the disease back from school. My secretary, Julia, was pregnant and implored me not to come in to work lest she too became infected. It was at this moment that the packagers offered to put me up at a good hotel in mid-town, fully provided with any reference books I might require—plus a high-end Dictaphone. I was to have complete freedom to order whatever I wanted from room service—just write the volume.

So for three or four days I sat in solitary state, dictating furiously and consuming the best that room service could offer. I had, of course, been given certain parameters such as word count and number of pictures, and these I adhered to meticulously. For many pictures there was no time to call in a researcher to scour the city's

4AUTOPROCTOSCOPY

4263

picture agencies, and I was free to supply whatever was needed from my own archives—and charge standard agency fees.

The work completed, I returned home to Connecticut exhausted—and showing the first signs of chickenpox. But the fates were not yet through working on my behalf. Somewhere along the line, the editors had screwed up and given me a word count that was significantly too small. There was no time to write any more—would I please make up the difference by adding more of my pictures?

It must have been about two weeks later, when I was well on the road to recovery, that I got a call from the encyclopaedia makers. The volumes had been put together in record time—and would I just read through them for spelling and other minor errors—and would I accept $500 per volume for doing this. As one of the volumes was the one I had written, read (and already corrected). It seemed a reasonable deal."

# SUBLIME LUNACY

# Discursus Forty-Four
## Sacrificial Lamb

It would be remiss not to make passing reference to John's spider researches, as this was, after all, the prime reason for his being in New York. Much of the curatorial work at the museum was rather dull, for there is little excitement to be had by meticulously describing new species, particularly if they have been found by somebody else and have lain for years preserved in alcohol. However, life became much more interesting when he began to study the urticating hairs found on certain mygalomorph ("bird-eating" or "tarantula") spiders.

The presence of such irritant hairs was already well known, but most accounts were purely anecdotal. However, nobody had apparently thought to examine the hairs themselves, or investigate how they caused irritation. Equally significant, nobody appeared to have studied which families and genera possessed them. It proved to be a fertile field of research. The original paper, co-authored with two colleagues, reported four major types of urticating hair, illustrated with scanning electron micrographs, and gave a summary of their distribution among different taxonomic groups.

"I was curious to discover whether the hairs possessed any chemical irritants, as occur in some caterpillars, or whether the effect was purely due to localised physical trauma. Clearly it would be useful to examine the nature of the inflammation at the histological level, so I offered myself as both high priest and sacrificial lamb on the alter of science, and arranged with a surgeon friend to cut out a piece of tissue from my arm after it had been treated with hairs from a species known to be particularly irritating (*Brachypelma smithi*). We concluded that there was no evidence to suggest spider hairs carried any chemical irritants, and that the effect was purely physical."

The identification of mygalomorph spiders is an arcane study, made more difficult by the apparent absence of reliable characters upon which to base a classification. The discovery of four major types of urticating hair, and the observation that within these four types there appeared to be different sub-categories, prompted John to undertake a more detailed and extensive study. Several immediate questions presented themselves. What variation occurred in the hairs of a particular individual on different parts of the abdomen, and did they change with age? What variation occurred between different individuals of the same species—and was there variation in different parts of the species range? Once these questions could be answered, one would have a better measure of how useful the hairs might be in aiding the determination of genera or even species.

"At the same time as gathering the mass of data needed to answer these questions, I also started to gather hair samples from as many type specimens as I could. These are the single specimens to which a particular name is tied. The starting points would be the major spider collections held in museums in Paris and London, in addition to the ones in our own collection in New York.

It was a major undertaking that promised valuable results. Unfortunately it would also collide with my eventual decision to leave New York, which was fuelled in part by the Museum's displeasure at the expense I had quite unwittingly incurred through using their computer facility.

It turned out that the museum rented time— and very expensive time—on some distant mainframe computer. The multivariate statistical program I was using had been written by a colleague in the museum's geology department, but it still contained many bugs. My requirements apparently taxed it to the limit and we spent many costly hours on line. The bill duly came in to the entomology department, consuming much of its annual budget, and my access to the computer was promptly, and pointedly, curtailed.

Sadly all the data so carefully gathered and only partially analysed, remains unpublished to this day. Although my magnum opus on urticating hairs in theraphosid systematics was doomed to oblivion, the sojourn in New York nevertheless had its highlights.

***

One day I received in the mail a letter, postmarked 'New Jersey', in which the writer asked whether the spider, of which she enclosed a photograph, might be attacking her *Bougainvillia*. It was typical of the queries that landed on my desk, and without further thought I dictated a brief, courteous response explaining that as spiders were wholly carnivorous, they were unlikely to be the culprits in her plant's ill-health, suggesting that perhaps some sap-sucking insect might be responsible. The reply was startling. Would I come with my family for the weekend to discuss the problem in more detail.

So it was that John entered the rarified world of America's super-rich. Corinne Chubb and her husband, doyen of an insurance empire, lived in style on a large New Jersey estate that included its own pack of beagles. The indoor pool was surrounded by *Bougainvillia* and other tropical vegetation, although the problem lay not in New Jersey, but on Peter Island, their Caribbean vacation hide-away.

Corinne, who had at one point apparently given serious consideration to buying the Chase Manhattan Bank, was a wonderful combination of generosity and frugality. She wore old, well-outworn informal shorts, and would, on principle, drive many many miles out of her way to avoid paying freeway tolls, yet had no hesitation in inviting John and his wife to come and examine her *Bougainvillea* problem at first hand in the British Virgin Islands.

"We flew first on a commercial flight to St. Thomas in the American Virgin Islands. From there we were flown in a 7-seat private plane to Tortola, where we were met by Landrover, which took us to the dockside, where a launch was waiting to carry us on the final leg to Peter Island, of which the Chubbs owned about half. There were two sailboats, the larger with captain and crew available to take us out whenever we wished, although I much preferred to take the smaller, 35-foot boat out on my own. For two weeks we swam and snorkelled, before reluctantly returning to Connecticut, carefully refraining from giving a full analysis of the *Bougainvillia* problem in the hope there might someday be a second visit needed. Sadly we returned to England before this happened, which might have been just as well as I have no idea how to treat nematode worm attacks on the roots of *Bougainvillia*; or any other plant, for that matter.

While John was curator in New York, the University of Utah wished to donate the very important R.V. Chamberlin spider collection to the Natural History Museum—mainly because they themselves did not possess the staff and facilities for its proper upkeep. Preserved in alcohol, such collections require constant curatorial care. So it was that John and his staff had spent several weeks in Salt Lake City preparing the material for shipment to New York, ensuring that all the vials of specimens were full, free of air bubbles, and securely packed. When the work was finally completed, they prepared to head home.

"On the way to the airport I chanced to spot a male 'tarantula' crossing the road, and naturally stopped to collect it. I thought nothing further about it after luring it into a glass vial and putting it in my briefcase.

Passing through airport security a short while later, my case was opened and the woman agent threw a fit when she saw the spider. More than being simply scared, she was convinced that I planned to intimidate the pilot and highjack the plane. Had she not been in deadly earnest, it would have been delightfully comical. Nothing that I said would placate her, and the problem was soon passed up the line of command to a senior supervisor.

It counted for nothing that I repeated many times that,

although large and furry, this was a totally harmless spider with no venom of significance. It was made clear that I would not be allowed to fly and that dire, but unspecified, penalties awaited me."

In a moment of inspiration John then asked whether, if they were to consult with the Curator of Spiders at the American Museum of Natural History, they would accept his ruling on the matter. After a brief consultation they grudgingly agreed that they would abide by his verdict.

"Well, I am the Curator of Spiders at the American Museum of Natural History, and I am telling you that this spider is completely harmless."

John made his flight! Almost inevitably this anecdote led on to a broader discussion about 'tarantulas' and John unconsciously lapsed once again into academic mode.

"The term 'tarantula' is most misleading and essentially meaningless as it has been applied to many unrelated animals, not all of them even arachnids. The classical tarantula of antiquity was something that attacked peasants at harvest time, particularly around Taranto in southern Italy, and produced a host of unpleasant symptoms that included fainting, vomiting, abdominal cramps and chest pains. Because it was the most conspicuous creature in the area, blame came to be laid at the door of a large, but actually relatively harmless, wolf-spider common in the region. To this spider was assigned the name "Tarantula".

In the Middle Ages, when the church frowned on anything bordering on pleasure, the peasants were convinced that the only cure for 'tarantula' bites was to have a wild party at which the dancing continued until dawn.

Historians have long considered that dancing a *tarantella* was simply a stratagem to get around the strictures of the church, but I am happy to report that science has at last proved the peasants correct. The true culprit lurking among the wheat and barley stems was indeed a spider, but a relatively small and inconspicuous one. It is none other than the European cousin of the North American Black Widow. It is now well known that the best thing to do when bitten by a *Latrodectus* is to take violent exercise. If you have to bicycle twenty miles in haste to see a doctor, your symptoms will soon dissipate. Thus the peasants of yore were doing absolutely the right thing.

In more recent times, with a lamentable display of ignorance, the term 'tarantula' has come to be used to refer to the large, furry mygalomorph spiders of the American southwest, which are totally harmless, and unrelated to the European wolf spider that was the original tarantula."

John continued with a few further observations on Black Widow bites, noting that they have occurred in all forty eight contiguous states. In the modern world, death from Black Widow bite is extremely rare, and confined to the very young or the very old. Not only is antivenin now readily available, but the real cause of mortality in earlier times was largely a consequence of misdiagnosis rather than envenomation.

"One of the components of Black Widow venom causes uncontrolled release of the neurotransmitter acetylcholine at the neuro-muscular junction, and one effect of this is to cause violent spasms in the abdominal muscles. In times past these violent abdominal cramps were misdiagnosed as acute appendicitis and the patient, already suffering, was tied down on the kitchen table while his appendix was removed, often without anaesthesia. The additional stress, combined with a high incidence of sepsis, led to many unnecessary deaths."

"But how do you know that the big tarantulas you see crossing he road in southwest are not poisonous?" someone asked. It seemed a reasonable question, and John was happy to respond.

"There is no question but that the bite of a good-sized tarantula is painful. It resembles closely the discomfort experienced when one carelessly drives a sewing machine needle through one's finger. The similarity is not an illusion, for the tarantula fangs, like the sewing machine needle, can penetrate until impeded by the bones of the finger—and both wounds take the same length of time to heal. Of course tarantulas do have venom, as do most spiders, but it is only effective against the spider's normal prey and has no perceptible impact on the human nervous system. Of course, the effect on humans of the relatively few poisonous spiders is nothing more than a coincidence, a reflection of their venom's impact on underlying physiological processes shared by all mammalian species"

To a question about how he had had the misfortune to be bitten by a tarantula, John replied by describing some research he had done in Arizona. There appeared to be several *Aphonopelma* species living in the area, but little was known about the In particular it was unclear which males went with which females—unless one could actually observe their courtship and mating.

"Following tarantulas at night, particularly when they choose to wander through dense clumps of desert undergrowth, is not easy. I thought that by tying a fine nylon monofilament fishing line around the spider's waist, I might more easily discover where they went, and which female burrows they attempted to enter. Tying the monofilament on was relatively easy, but removing it at the end of the experiment was another matter unless one had surgical instruments to hand. Several times, while attempting to free my obliging subject, I was repaid by a fiercely unsympathetic bite—the fang scraping along the bone. The trauma was purely physical, and although excruciating, did not appear to be augmented by any venom."

## Discursus Forty-Five
# Happy Birthday

J ohn had been cajoled into serving as scientific consultant
to the museum's exhibition department in their creation
of a new hall devoted to cave biology. Through this work
he crossed paths with Bob Mitchell, a cave biologist at Texas
Tech in Lubbock. It turned out that the two of them were
probably the only people in the world interested in ricinuleids.
At that time the Ricinulei were the most enigmatic and
obscure order of arachnids, with only about thirty specimens
known worldwide. Confined to West Africa and Central
America, nothing was known of their biology.

"My interest, hitherto purely academic, had crystallised
after George Lampel was killed in a car crash in Iran.
During the Oxford University Guyana expedition, while I
was in Africa, George had discovered significant numbers
of ricinuleids inhabiting litter on the forest floor. Bringing
them back to Oxford, he successfully maintained them
in culture and became the first person to witness their
extraordinary mating behaviour, a discovery he shared
with me. After his death it fell to me to continue his work
and we published a joint account of his observations in
the Journal of the Zoological Society of London, together
with descriptions of several new species he had discovered.
Bob Mitchell, I learned, had also found sizeable populations
of ricinuleids, this time in Mexico, and was also studying
their biology. We quickly became friends through our
shared interest in arachnids, and Bob invited me to join an

expedition studying cave arachnids in the Sierra del Abra in the Mexican states of San Luis Potosí and Tamaulipas. In time these trips with Bob's graduate students became regular engagements.

I had done very little caving when I joined Bob on this first expedition, and certainly nothing as demanding. Fortunately my mountaineering experience would prove valuable in this new environment. The entrance to the Sotanó de Yerbaniz is a narrow slit in the rock just a few feet across. Dropping into the darkness on a nylon climbing rope was awe-inspiring. The initial entrance drop is some 300 feet, followed by several more of similar length. Once underground the cave expands into a network of narrow passages and giant cathedral-like chambers. Overcome by the scale, by the beauty and by the excitement of collecting, time passed unnoticed in the darkness. We had been underground, exerting ourselves to the limit, for twenty-four non-stop hours when the time came to return to the surface. Climbing several hundred feet up a rope by 'prusiking' or 'jumaring' is tiring, even when one is experienced. In my inexperienced and exhausted state it proved impossible. I had not climbed far before I developed unbearable cramps in both arms. Stretched out as if crucified, I dangled helpless in the darkness. My chief concern was not to be a burden on the party, and so I returned to the bottom insisting that they go on ahead, leaving me alone. I had no doubt that after some rest I would have little difficulty making the ascent.

Wrapped in a space blanket and sustained by a bar of chocolate, I prepared to sleep in a smooth fold of limestone that enveloped me as though in a hammock. I did not remain awake long—just long enough to visualize some possible mishaps. What, I pondered, would the end be like if the van crashed and nobody was left to report my location, or come back and lower the ropes to me......? What might happen if a passing shepherd stumbled across the great pile of ropes left at the cave entrance, and decide to take them....? Within seconds I was asleep, probably more soundly than at any time before or since.

I was suddenly awakened by a hand on my shoulder. Opening a bleary eye, I saw that the whole party had returned and were ranged all around me. Suddenly they burst into a strangely reverberating rendition of 'Happy Birthday'. Next they produced a celebratory birthday Texan steak breakfast, leaving me quite overcome by this demonstration of friendship. Rested, I found the ascent easy as anticipated, and have never since had a problem climbing a rope. The training would prove invaluable some years later when I found myself climbing to film in the jungle canopy in Costa Rica.

We went on to explore many more caves, but passed on one, the Cueva de las Golondrinas. With the world's second longest entrance drop, it takes twenty minutes to abseil down and an eternity to prusik out. This immense pit opens through a small hole on the surface, expanding 512m below to a floor 305m by 135M

For an arachnologist, the most interesting cave by far proved to be the Cueva del Nascimiento del Rio Frio. Within fifty feet of the cave entrance we were able to find representatives of all eleven arachnid orders—the first time this had ever happened, and perhaps the only place in the world where such a feat is possible."

When John found himself obliged to write up George Lampel's observations on Ricinuleid biology for publication after his death, he was fortunate to find that the notes had been written in English. George's colleagues in the Physics Department were not so lucky.

Raised in a polyglot family, visitors could be forgiven for feeling confused. His parents switched casually, almost unconsciously, between English, Russian and Magyar, speaking German to the maid and often practicing their French and Italian in preparation for forthcoming holiday travel.

It was, therefore, not surprising that George too was something of a polyglot. It was his practice to immerse himself in the languages of the region he next planned to visit in search of spiders. Following his death, the valuable data accumulated for his thesis was found by his perplexed co-workers to be a *mélange* of bad Arabic, bad Farsi and questionable Amharic, all confusingly recorded in their unfamiliar, inexpertly written scripts. At least his Portuguese—the legacy of a collecting trip to the Azores—presented few problems.

## Discursus Forty-Six
# Only in New York

The conversation at dinner one evening had moved on to the subject of improbable experiences. John waited patiently until an appropriate opportunity arose for him to contribute to the conversation.

"We were just leaving my New York friend's apartment on the Upper West Side to drive to the airport when a diminutive black kid out on the street began shouting and screaming at us. I have no idea what might have initiated this stream of invective, which included threats to carve his initials all over my face—he was wielding a carton-cutter with a vicious blade. I believe it was the realisation that he was too small to reach up that far that caused me to laugh, thereby triggering even greater fury. Anxious to catch my flight and not wanting to become involved in a street brawl, I indicated that we should get into the car and drive away. As my friend was climbing into the car, she was hit over the head with a broken bottle, fortunately without experiencing any serious damage. The attacker then tried to shatter the windscreen of the car—again without success. Just as we were starting to drive away a passer-by came rushing to our aid, and I became very concerned that he might sustain serious injuries on our behalf.

Everyone who knows me will testify that I am a benign and gentle being, not given to outbursts of physical violence. Indeed, it was my reluctance to hurt people that long prevented my appearance in the boxing ring at school until severely peer-pressured into it. Nevertheless,

I have always felt capable of defending myself in times of emergency. As Senior Member of the OU Judo Club, my father had taught me the elements of this valuable art. Part of my National Service training involved unarmed combat, and as an undergraduate, I had a good friend who wrestled for the RAF, and happily threw me wheresoever he wished.

As I went to the aid of my erstwhile salvation, this night in New York became the first and only time that my dormant defensive skills have ever been put to the test. After some ineffectual skirmishing, I managed to get a hold with which I was able to disarm the kid and then apply pressure to the carotid arteries – a 'sleeper' in wrestling jargon—and my assailant slithered unconscious onto the tarmac.

Only then did I become aware that a crowd had started to gather, divided I'm sorry to say on strictly racial lines, with one half saying "Kill him" and the other, "Let him go". By this time I was happy to merge back into the darkness and allow six sturdy onlookers to hold the kid down. High on 'angel dust', I later learned, he possessed prodigious strength.

Someone muttered into my ear "watch out, here comes his mother". Sure enough, striding rapidly toward us, knuckles dragging on the sidewalk, this giant gorilla of a woman swept into view. By good fortune, the Police arrived at the same moment. After giving a brief statement I was finally allowed to leave for the airport, where I arrived as the gate was closing, evidently somewhat shaken and with blood still showing on my knuckles. Visibly impressed, and extremely sympathetic, the flight attendants provided admirable service all the way to Heathrow."

The point of the story, John went on to explain, was that his departure was not the end of the story. In a bizarre twist, as could only happen in New York City, John found himself being sued for assault by his mugger's mother.

> "I can only assume that the kid, justifiably afraid of his imposing mother, had spun some tale that we had attacked him violently and without provocation. I was filming in Costa Rica, and could not attend any of the four court hearings. I did, however, have to prepare a sworn affidavit, duly translated from the required Spanish into English—a story in its own right."

The upshot of all this was that John, his friend and their assailant were bound over for twelve months not to molest one another. For John it was no problem, but for his friend it was a different matter. The kid lived in the neighbourhood, and she saw him frequently, during which time he grew markedly and instilled by his very presence fear of walking the dog alone or even going alone to the nearby parking garage to collect her car.

> "About a year and a half later, when I was visiting New York, we came across him with an imposing group of buddies lounging on a street corner. The innate apprehension on seeing him quickly gave way to relief as he waved cheerfully at us and called out "Hi John; Hi Nancy."
>
> Age had wrought a change—and perhaps he realized that he had had a fortunate escape. He might easily have received a prison sentence and thereby be effectively condemned to a life of crime."

# SUBLIME LUNACY

# Discursus Forty-Seven
## Such is Fame

One day while working at the museum in New York John was approached by two local doctors who sought his help in a research project upon which they were embarking. Specialists in pancreatic cancer, they had stumbled upon a report saying that the venom of certain scorpions in Trinidad induced acute pancreatitis in mice.

The doctor's patients were always in terminal stages of the disease by the time they were seen. They wondered whether, by studying the progression of the disease in mice, they might be better able to recognise earlier symptoms and treat it sooner in human subjects. John was more than happy to collaborate—a visit to tropical Trinidad was an irresistible temptation. So it was that he was commissioned to fly to Trinidad and collect the required scorpions.

"Just before leaving New York, I received a furious phone call from Trinidad. It was the doctor who had published the original observation linking scorpion venom and pancreatitis some years previously. He was, he said, "calling from the office of the Trinidadian Minister of Health." "It was outrageous," he spluttered, "that scientists from America should come and steal the research of developing nations." Indignant to the point of incoherence, he said that at his urging, the government had just passed legislation prohibiting the exportation of scorpions, and that I would certainly be searched on leaving the island should I be foolish enough to come. I did not believe him.

I had called several contacts at the University of the West Indies in St. Augustine in preparation for my visit, and somehow word of my impending arrival had eventually reached the ears of the good Dr Bartholomew, who it transpired, had received a substantial grant from the Welcome Trust to pursue the same line of enquiry as planned by the doctors in New York. According to my informant, little if any research had been done and much of the grant had been squandered on brandy, although some years later this assessment was somewhat undermined by the appearance of a short paper by Dr Bartholomew on "The aetiology of acute scorpion pancreatitis" in dogs.

Undeterred, I flew to Trinidad anyway and bearded Dr Bartholomew in his den. My presence almost brought on a fit of apoplexy and was highly entertaining. I did not for one moment believe his threats and happily continued my collecting. It was soon agreed with friends at the university that they would mail to New York any scorpions that I collected. In the event this proved a wise precaution for I was thoroughly searched by Trinidadian customs on departure—something quite unprecedented and a clear indication that Dr Bartholomew did indeed carry the political clout of which he boasted. Whether my scorpions ever contributed to the advance of medical knowledge I never discovered."

Although scorpions had provided the means of getting to Trinidad, the real rewards from the trip would only become apparent later after John had returned to England and joined Oxford Scientific Films.

"One day at the museum I was approached by New Yorker magazine, seeking to conduct an interview. Flattered, I accepted. Following publication, I received quite a number of similar requests—there is something about spiders that seems to capture popular imagination.

One of the local newspapers sent a photographer. He was the archetypal press photographer of popular imagination, unkempt and dirty, with the regulation grimy old raincoat. I was pleased to see we both used the same Nikon equipment, but somewhat horrified to see how his was treated. While my cameras travel pristine in sealed cases, every lens with a cap fore and aft, his lived unprotected in his raincoat pockets. Before putting on a lens, I noticed him removing a large ball of fluff from inside the open camera. It was further testimony to the reliability of Nikon equipment.

I can only assume that it was the New Yorker article that triggered a flood of requests for me to appear on TV talk shows and quiz programs. For the most part it was all a bit tedious once the novelty had worn off— apart from the pleasure of flying First Class to Hollywood and staying in the best hotels. But there was one notable exception to the general rule, and that was the Dick Cavett Show. A lively and entertaining TV host, Dick Cavett was a great conversationalist, who put his guests completely at ease and treated them with respect. Unlike many other hosts, he did not try to score points and showed genuine interest in their replies to his questions.

The show, in July 1970, proved to be a huge success, thanks to a spontaneous response I made to Dick Cavett's question: "How often do people die from spider bites". Without thinking I replied "Only once".

On the strength of that I was invited back, on

which occasion I shared the Green Room with one of my boyhood heroines, the great blues singer Mahalia Jackson. As I later discovered, she had a real phobia about spiders and was not happy to find I carried several large tarantulas with me. Also on the show was Victor Borge. As we were sitting side by side being made up, an assistant came in and announced that the planned program format had been changed. Instead of an interview and film clips, Victor Borge would be invited to perform live. The reaction left no one present in any doubt. He was, he pointed out, a professional who had agreed to come and be interviewed. He had not come prepared to perform—and as a performer he needed to rehearse. The answer was a resounding "No!"

I can only assume that word of this had not reached Dick Cavett, who was met by an unequivocal refusal on camera when he invited his guest to the piano. The audience, and doubtless Dick Cavett too, assumed this to be a joke, but it quickly became clear that Victor Borge was in earnest—and genuinely displeased. To overcome the hiatus I was quickly ushered on stage well ahead of schedule. My only memory of the interview is of Victor Borge sitting next to me on my right, burrowing in my pockets off camera on the pretext of searching for tarantulas. The studio audience's reaction brought back good humour all round."

Some weeks after I had last appeared on TV I was startled to be accosted in the museum elevator by a woman who announced, "I know you. I saw you on television!" As one who prefers to remain anonymous, this outburst was unsettling. It brought home to me just how difficult life must be for people in the public eye, their every move scrutinised and commented on.

This downside to popularity was reinforced many

years later when my stepdaughter, Ilana, graduated from Wesleyan University in Connecticut. The address was given by Oprah Winfry, who warned the graduating class to think twice before choosing a high-profile career. She told of the time she had gone to the bathroom at some public function and overheard a woman whispering to her friend outside the stall. "It's Oprah in there—I heard her peeing!"

While my fifteen minutes of TV fame never reached such heights, it did bring some unexpected consequences. A knock on my office door at the museum was followed by the appearance of a strikingly attractive young woman. She was, she said, interested in spiders and hoped she might be able to volunteer in my department. It was easy to say yes. Only later did I discover that her real goal was seduction, at which she excelled. In order to reach the spider's lair, she had already seduced the museum's deputy director, and later disclosed many hitherto unknown details of his sexual inadequacies. I often wonder what might have happened had I taken up a career in front of the cameras. Was this just the tip of the iceberg of fame?"

High on John's list of famous people, Roman Vishniac is recalled with particular affection. Best known for his haunting black & white images of impoverished Jewish communities in the *shtetls* of Eastern Europe, Vishniac was a remarkable man, holding doctorates in five different disciplines, including biology, photography and oriental languages.

"I first met him by accident at the AMNH in New York. Looking for one of my curatorial colleagues with a question about termites, he inadvertently knocked on my door. As spiders were one of his many interests, we soon found ourselves in deep conversation, and once he learned of my connection with Oxford Scientific and wildlife filming and photography, our friendship was sealed, for he was an early pioneer of filming down the microscope.

In time we found that we lived in adjacent buildings on West 81st. Street, and I became a frequent visitor to his apartment, where our conversations were brisk and wide-ranging. At the time he was working on a follow-up volume to *A Vanished World*, trying to trace what had become of the people he had photographed just before the Holocaust. He was thrilled to find that the subject of one of his most iconic images, a wide-eyed little girl, was a grandmother living in Brooklyn.

One evening stands out in my memory. I had unknowingly phoned him moments after he had arrived home from a lecture tour in Korea. I was greeted with "Ah, a voice from the world of biology! Come round at once." The tour had been particularly difficult and stressful. There were, he said, no Jews in Korea, and no one there had even heard of the Holocaust. In his late eighties, he was required to sit cross-legged interminably, on the floor which he found extremely difficult. In addition, he said, he nearly starved as he had to eat with stainless steel chopsticks, from which little food ever reached his mouth.

## Discursus Forty-Eight
## **Beneficial Divorce**

J ohn's decision to move from Oxford across the Atlantic to the Natural History Museum in New York was a reflection of the hold that spiders exerted over him. However, the choice was not an easy one. The bonds of friendship that he had developed in Oxford with Gerald Thompson through filming ran deep, and now extended to the other members of the Jamaica expedition as well.

"We had clearly demonstrated our ability to work together, and now sought an appropriate vehicle to capitalise on the foundations we had laid. Our dream was to establish ourselves as a scientific film unit within the university. John Pringle wanted us to be an entity within his department, but that idea fell victim to university politics. His plans for a huge new zoology building were already creating widespread tensions, and opening another battle front—the establishment of a potentially successful commercial venture within a university department—was understandably considered imprudent.

The next approach was to persuade the university itself to undertake the venture, citing as a precedent the Oxford University Press, an autonomous organisation whose profits went to benefit the university. This was no idle fantasy. Gerald produced a formal 40-page prospectus, which was duly considered by the Hebdomadal Council, but his appeal fell on largely deaf ears, victim of the petty jealousies that permeate a donnish environment whenever the possibility of financial gain is perceived. It was uncertainty about the future that finally tipped the balance in favour of New York for me."

Meanwhile, Gerald and the others continued developing contacts elsewhere. The Ealing Corporation in Boston were marketing single-concept educational film loops as the latest advance in teaching, and they needed a source of biological subject matter. Paul Grindle, the wealthy founder of the company, who had contacted Gerald after seeing some of the Jamaica expedition footage, made him a generous offer. Ealing would fund the creation of the dreamed-of film unit. In time this would become Oxford Scientific Films.

The birth of OSF was not pain free, and the convoluted story has been well-documented in Paul Crowson's book 'Animals in Focus - the creation of a natural history film unit'. Riding the crest of a wave of optimism, Grindle had offered to set OSF up in business, buying land and building a studio with all necessary equipment. Ealing would guarantee to purchase at market value any and all footage that OSF might produce and share in the revenues generated. It all sounded too good to be true—as in time it proved to be.

When Grindle's business minions came to England to work out details of the contract, Gerald quickly noticed that many of the original terms that had been so attractive when discussed and agreed verbally, were subsequently being pared down and undermined by the lawyers. A canny Scotsman, Gerald turned for help to Messrs. Allen & Overy, high-end solicitors in the City of London with whom he chanced to have some slight connection.

The infectious enthusiasm, technical ability and obvious lack of business acumen resonated with Guy Wilson, one of the senior partners. Suddenly nascent OSF was being represented by one of London's leading legal firms—and at no cost. Under Guy Wilson's watchful eye, OSF's interests were spectacularly safeguarded in the resulting contract with Ealing.

Ealing's new educational film-loop technology was hailed as the way of the future, and projected to bring in huge financial returns, in which OSF would now share. It was not to be. The Ealing Corporation made some very foolish business decisions and successfully alienated most of the educational institutions with whom they needed to do business. Basically they kept changing the physical parameters of their film loops, so requiring the repeated purchase of new viewing devices. Although their market had effectively dried up, Ealing were still contractually obligated to keep paying OSF's annual salaries and expenses and eventually they asked for a divorce. Under the terms of Allen & Overy's contract, OSF was to end up owning the studios and equipment outright, while Ealing retained all rights in the film loops that had already been made.

During the period leading up to the divorce, when Ealing were no longer commissioning new titles, OSF had strengthened their ties with the BBC and with Survival, the natural history wing of commercial Anglia Television. John takes up the story:

"Finding conditions in New York ever more irksome and unfulfiling, and increasingly at odds with the museum authorities—I had, among other irritations, become involved with the Deputy Director's mistress—I gave serious consideration to leaving. The final straw came when, fuelled by jealousy at the success that I and my assistant were enjoying through the sale of our spare-time photography, the museum suddenly announced that any and all photographs taken by employees would henceforth be deemed museum property. At this point we both resigned.

It was only a short time after I had decided to leave the museum in New York and become a freelance writer and photographer that a letter arrived from John Paling. John, who had succeeded me years before as Vertebrate Demonstrator in the Zoology Department when I became Invertebrate Demonstrator, was a director of the now independent Oxford Scientific Films.

John was writing to ask if he might come and stay with us in Old Greenwich while he was in the US on a lecture tour. I was, of course, delighted at the prospect and immediately invited him to stay as long as he could. As an afterthought, I added that his timing was fortuitous because by the following year I would probably no longer be there because I was about to take the plunge and go freelance.

When he arrived a few weeks later, John brought with him momentous news. He told me that at a board meeting a few days before my letter had arrived, there had been a discussion as to whether it might be possible to lure me back to re-join the group. Peter Parks, who had stayed with us earlier, said that he felt there was no chance—I was, he said, well settled in a good job and destined to stay there.

As a result of my letter, John brought with him a formal invitation to join the OSF board. It was an opportunity beyond my wildest dreams. It was not long before we pulled up stumps and crossed back across the Atlantic."

Arriving back in England, John quickly settled into the informal OSF way of life that so entertained visiting TV producers. Each morning Carol, the long-suffering secretary, would enter upon her first task of the day—the preparation of fresh-baked bread for lunch. As the dough for a brown loaf and a white loaf was being kneaded, Carol kept two open plastic bags beside her in case she had to answer the phone. Conscious of his 'new-boy' status within the group, John was anxious to prove himself.

"On my arrival I suggested to my co-directors that we try to interest Survival in a series of programs based on Trinidad's rich and diverse wildlife. The idea won swift approval, and once again I found myself enjoying Trinidadian hospitality while exploring the local wildlife and developing program ideas.

Recalling the help we had received in Jamaica through our cooperation with the university there, I turned instinctively to Prof Jake Kenny at the St Augustine zoology department. An experienced field biologist, Jake was among his many other talents an expert on Trinidadian amphibians and together we spent many happy hours wading through ponds and swamps at night identifying the many species by their calls. "

In the late 1930s the New York Zoological Society had established a tropical research station at Simla, high in the mountains of Trinidad's northern range. Under the directorship of William Beebe, the famous deep-sea explorer, who had reached record depths in his bathysphere off Bermuda, Simla attracted many distinguished researchers. Here Jocelyn Crane, Beebe's assistant, did her fascinating and highly detailed studies of Jumping Spider biology, and Don Griffin did his seminal work on the echo-location of bats.

"Curious to see where so much excellent research had been carried out, I expressed an interest in visiting Simla. To my dismay I learned that it had been abandoned some years earlier and was on the market. Jake told me that if I wished to visit Simla I would have to get permission from the attorney responsible for the sale—and that I might well not be successful. It took some work to discover this individual's identity and phone number, but I eventually rang him. Despite the earlier warning, I received a courteous reception, and when I explained who I was, and why I was in Trinidad, the reaction was beyond anything I had imagined.

He not only begged me to come, but better still invited OSF to use Simla as a filming base without charge, believing that our presence there would discourage pilfering and slow the encroachment of the surrounding forest.

In one short phone call, of whose outcome I had had no great expectations, I successfully resolved the two biggest uncertainties hanging over the impending expedition, namely accommodation and studio space."

An account of the Trinidad expedition has already been published in the OSF autobiographical book 'Focus on Nature', for which they were honoured by David Attenborough breaking his strict rule never to write forwards or prefaces. Having contributed many sequences to his TV natural history programs they had become good friends and David was happy to oblige on this one occasion.

"Although I contributed numerous film sequences to the Trinidad Survival programs, ranging from dark field optical bench shots of rotifers and other denizens inhabiting the water trapped in bromeliads to detailed spider material, my two principal roles were in still photography and in creating a TV program about life in Tamana, a cave in Trinidad's central range.

David Thompson and I were to spend many days underground in conditions far from congenial. The cave entrance was difficult of access, and involved a long hike up steep, muddy trails. After descending into the entrance pit there were two choices. One could either go uphill into a part of the cave inhabited by fruit-eating bats, whose droppings support one distinct food chain, or one could head down into an endless sequence of chambers and passageways inhabited by literally millions of insectivorous bats, whose noisome guano support another large and diverse food chain, of which the most conspicuous members were the giant hissing cockroaches some three inches in length, so numerous it was not possible to touch the cave wall without also touching several of them. Some dozen bat species inhabited the cave. Each evening at 6:15, just as dusk was falling, a massive vortex cloud of bats would begin to swirl out of the cave entrance, disappearing to forage through the forest. After two hours bats were still coming out, but by dawn all had returned.

Deep within the cave the bats form a solid covering of the walls, packed so tight that no trace of rock remains visible. The huge biomass of bats emits large amounts of $CO_2$ that makes breathing both rapid and unsatisfying. The deeper we penetrated into the cave, often struggling with lights, generator and cameras, the more oppressive and suffocating the $CO_2$ became as the concentration rose.

In deciding to work in Tamana, we were taking a considerable risk, for it was known to harbour the fungus *Histoplasma capsulatum*, the causative agent of Histoplasmosis or Reticuloendotheliosis, a potentially fatal lung disease of cavers. I felt that as I had never shown symptoms despite my caving experience in Mexico, I was probably immune, although I did not realize then just how serious an infection could be until a friend almost died of the disease.

David and I forced ourselves to press deeper and deeper into the cave, driven by curiosity as to what lay beyond the next bend or drop. We eventually reached a point at which our gasping breaths made it impossible to proceed further without risking unconsciousness. Gazing down into the passageway that disappeared into the darkness, all we could see were ever more bats. The journey back from this, the lowest point we were ever able to reach, was long and painful as we struggled for air.

When we returned home to Simla each night after filming we were unrecognisable, covered from head to foot with foul-smelling guano, which has a sweetish, cloying scent. We were, of course, strictly prohibited from entering the house in such a state. Instead we would be forced to hose down outside, leaving our clothes to be washed in preparation for the following day.

After my speleological experiences in the deep caves of Mexico, I was unable to resist the urge to explore further underground, my excuse being that I was seeking additional animals to film. On one such excursion I found myself peering into a crawl space about eighteen inches high and perhaps a hundred feet in length. As I started to make my way through I suddenly saw that the surface was pullulating with enormous ticks, and within a few seconds I too was covered. I waited in vain for them to bite, for ticks are renowned for their propensity to suck blood. I was puzzled by their failure to attack, for there could be few blood-filled mammals penetrating their domain, but I took it as an omen and continued my crawl.

I had gone perhaps twenty yards when the cave was suddenly rocked and shaken by a serious earthquake. I could hear boulders cascading in the distance and could not erase images of the ceiling above collapsing to crush me. That, at least, I encouraged myself, would be a swift end. More frightening was the prospect of being trapped underground, unable to find a way out should my passageway become blocked. I was already deeply committed and realized that panic would only make the situation worse. To conserve my batteries I turned off the headlamp and concentrated on the faint breeze that I now became conscious of. This, I counselled myself, might lead to an opening—although I had no idea how far away that might be. I have successfully erased (or suppressed) the memories of that journey, and recall only the intense relief at finally emerging into the now dark, mysterious but welcoming forest—through a hitherto unknown entrance.

Long afterwards, seeking information in the library, I discovered that the ticks that had crawled all over me belonged to the genus *Antricola*, the only ticks that do not suck blood directly from its mammalian host. Among the bat species inhabiting Tamana was a sizable population of *Desmodus* (Vampire Bats) whose blood-rich droppings provided the ticks with a pre-digested dinner.

An essential sequence for our program was high-speed footage of thousands of bats navigating in close formation as they streamed endlessly past the camera. We had identified a narrow constriction in the passageway along which the bats had to pass on their nightly exodus to feed in the forest. Getting the shot proved more taxing than anticipated, and required the participation of the whole team. In addition to the usual lights, cameras and tripods we needed additional special equipment—a high-speed camera, extra lights, long lengths of cable and above all, a heavy generator. Slowly, in considerable discomfort, we struggled and dragged ourselves along the steep, muddy and extremely slippery trail. Special care had to be taken not to grasp in an emergency one particular kind of tree whose trunk was covered in fearsome black spines that could cause painful injuries. With much effort the equipment was set up in place and we waited until the evening exodus of bats was well underway. Lights, action and with a fierce whine film sped through the camera gate at 500 frames per second. Within moments all went quiet again—except for the soft pulsing of a million passing bat wings.

High-speed cameras are fragile and sensitive. The smallest speck of dirt can result in film jamming into a molten ball of celluloid, so special care is needed, even in ideal conditions, to reload the camera successfully. For Sean to change film in the grime of Tamana, the air filled with a fine mist of bat guano, was no small challenge. Eventually sufficient film was in the can and we slowly descended in the darkness along a trail that is challenging even in daylight, and when one is still fresh and unencumbered with equipment.

Camera malfunction, undiscovered until the film had been flown back to England for processing, necessitated the whole, grim jungle safari being repeated, not twice but three times!"

And what of the finished program? To those not intimately connected with the filming it was hailed as successful. To those who had laboured and suffered to make it, the outcome was less satisfying. As envisioned by OSF the film would examine the two quite independent food chains based on the guano of fruit-eating and insectivorous bats respectively, and considerable effort went into keeping the two sets of raw footage clearly separate to avoid any confusion.

Survival, catering to an undemanding public, chose

to dumb the film down to satisfy a low common denominator and edited it accordingly—without reference to OSF. The two stories were mixed and blurred into an inaccurate *mélange* with little scientific merit. It was not a new phenomenon, but nevertheless those who had taken the footage felt poorly treated, their expertise discounted, their advice ignored.

"I always recall with pain and displeasure my experiences with Survival when we made an hour-long 'special' on spiders. As usual, they took our raw footage and edited it on their own, without reference to us, which was bad enough. Even more egregious was the fact that I was given almost no opportunity to check the results for factual errors. With less than twenty-four hours notice I rushed up to London and was given just one viewing, from which I had to highlight scientific and editing errors and make comment on factual mistakes in the draft commentary—due to be recorded by Peter Ustinov that very afternoon. Given the circumstances of its birth, the finished program was much better than I had dared to hope.

## Discursus Forty-Nine
## **So Excellent a Fishe**

It was news of a serious hurricane threatening to hit Bermuda that prompted John to reminisce about his time there on an OSF filming expedition.

"There had been a previous OSF expedition to Bermuda, and David Thompson and I went out to complete the programs that had been started. Our base was Nonsuch Island, a nature reserve that had once housed an isolation hospital for the Royal Navy. We went first to Tucker's Town to collect the OSF Avon inflatable and outboard motor, and by the time we had loaded the necessary supplies it was already dark. Although it was a pitch-black, moonless night, we were assured that even though we had no idea where we were going, we couldn't miss Nonsuch. The instructions did little to calm our anxiety. We would pass several islands on the starboard side. Even though we couldn't see them, we would hear the waves breaking on the rocks, so don't go too close in.

However, we were also warned not to stray too far off shore because there were rusted metal stanchions protruding above the surface that could rip the boat to pieces. Only after we had set off into the darkness did David confide that he couldn't swim.

On reaching the invisible shore of Nonsuch, we would discover, we were told, a sunken hulk that served as breakwater, behind which we could moor in safety. To our considerable relief we finally identified the hulk and edged our way to the protected inner, lee side. Clambering up, I could just make out the shape of the sunken craft in the starlight, and started to walk slowly and carefully along the deck in search of somewhere to secure the inflatable. The next thing David knew, I had vanished—while I found myself underwater inside the rusted hull, which in fact had no deck. It was a providential escape for I could easily have impaled myself as I fell on a multitude of rusted pieces of metal. Apart from some grazes, a few sea urchin spines and a dented ego I was essentially unharmed."

After this somewhat dramatic start the expedition proceeded without serious incident, although OSF learned the hard way that crates of equipment should never be too heavy to carry, especially when there were steep sand dunes to negotiate—a lesson for future expeditions.

Over the following weeks the required film sequences were steadily accumulated—principally shots of Ghost Crab and Land Crab behaviour. Part of the Ghost Crab story involved newly hatched sea turtles attempting to reach the surf before being eaten by the crabs, and this set John off on a new tack.

"When Bermuda was first discovered, it teemed with wildlife—wildlife obviously unaccustomed to human predators and all too easily caught. In 1620, after only eleven years of colonization, it was found necessary to enact legislation to preserve the turtles—"So excellent a fishe"—the first wildlife conservation legislation in the world. Even so, Sea Turtles no longer breed on Bermuda.

The life cycle of sea turtles and their extraordinary long-distance navigation has inspired a lot of research, and we were fortunate to become peripherally involved. Jane Frick, who was to die all too soon, was a dedicated and courageous biologist who was captivated by the way newly hatched turtles navigate, eventually finding their way back to their home beach many, perhaps fifty, years, later to lay their own eggs. Jane would follow hatchlings for hours, swimming alone out into the trackless ocean. She was eventually forced to follow them in a small boat, travelling ever further from shore, and we provided the radio base on shore for safety. I still have the 'Turtle Mother' T-shirt to commemorate our call sign.

Jane's turtles had arrived as eggs from Totuguero beach, Costa Rica (at enormous expense and difficulty) and been buried at various locations on Bermuda to await hatching in the hope that in the years ahead turtles would once more return to breed on Bermuda. It was a fond hope, considered by many as unlikely to succeed. However, in 2015 The Royal Gazette, a Bermuda newspaper, reported that after a number of wandering turtle hatchlings had been spotted, it was found that a nest of over 90 eggs had hatched on the beach at Buildings Bay, St. George's Island. Were these the offspring of the hatchlings we had filmed on Nonsuch, some forty years ago as they headed out to sea? DNA would be able to confirm whether the Frick family's generosity in funding the experiment had paid off. If so, it would be a triumphant, landmark conservation achievement—and a lasting memorial to Jane Frick's dedication and enthusiasm. I am saddened that she did not live long enough to share the excitement.

However, when the test results came back there

was no confirmation that Tortuguero beach in Costa Rica had ever figured in these new hatchling's ancestry, and that they probably arrived in Bermuda by chance—a navigational error on the part of a pregnant turtle seeking landfall in Mexico, or elsewhere in the Caribbean. Nevertheless, it is an important event, for it demonstrates that nature herself, unaided by human intervention, may yet be able to bring turtles back to breed on Bermuda. There seems reason to hope that the hatchlings that have just entered the surf at Buildings Bay may yet return 35-40 years hence to launch another generation of so excellent a fishe on their extraordinary oceanic voyage.

Once embarked on the subject of conservation, John could not resist moving on to yet another story. It concerned the cahow, an oceanic petrel believed to be extinct since the 1620s, and represented in museums only as semi-fossilized skeletal remains from caves. In 1951 a young Bermudan naturalist named David Wingate came across a dead sea bird he could not identify, lying at the foot of a lighthouse. Sending it to Dr Murphy, doyen of ornithology at the natural history museum in New York, he helped to confirm that the cahow still existed, and determined to discover more about it.

"It's a strange bird that spends most of its life on the wing soaring over the southern oceans. It breeds only on Bermuda, in underground burrows on inaccessible islets from which cats and rats are absent, and some of these are close to Nonsuch. The birds fly at night in bad weather and drop like a stone to enter their burrows, which may explain why they escaped notice for over 300 years. It was

David Wingate who discovered the nesting behaviour, and who has succeeded in bringing the population back from perhaps as few as twenty surviving individuals, by creating artificial burrows in which to nest. A very slow breeder, the cahow population has now risen to over 200 individuals—thus still remaining an extremely endangered species. David has won international acclaim for his conservation work.

When I was on Bermuda for my Audubon Society lecture tour years later, I made a point of renewing my friendship with David, and in the course of our conversations I told him about my interest in high-speed photography. For a brief time we entertained the possibility of recording the cahow's dramatic, high-speed entry to its underground burrow. Despite Davids excitement at the prospect, I felt obliged to kill the idea. The risk of a bird being temporarily disoriented by the bright burst of light and making a slight, but fatal, navigation error at high speed, was too great to justify the shot, considering the rarity and tenuous uncertainty of the remaining population."

## Discursus Fifty
# Stop-Motion

John has always found it painful to talk about the slow demise of OSF, for it should have had a glorious future. But the free-wheeling, unorthodox management style that won admiration from outsiders, broke all the tenets of prudent business administration. With seven strong-willed, directors and with no managing director to rein in individual aspirations and no business experience, let alone financial or managerial skills; with no focused business plan or accounting oversight, OSF was probably doomed from its inception. That it survived for almost twenty-five years despite these deficiencies is a testament to the vitality and originality that ushered in its birth.

Under the quiet but informal leadership of Gerald Thompson, the company did what it did best—innovative, technically brilliant wildlife documentation. The slow but inevitable decline began when Gerald suffered a stroke at the studio and became paralysed down one side. Gerald continued to try and film and retained his role as figurehead, but his manifest infirmity meant that the subtle restraining influence he had once exercised behind the scenes quickly evaporated as soon as he announced his retirement. Free of Gerald's common sense, wisdom and Scottish prudence, OSF soon fell prey to poor business acumen and mounting discord among the directors.

"For years I had urged the board to appoint someone with

accountancy skills and an understanding of contracts and other routine business practices. In the end the board listened and appointed Terry Downer—but it was already too late. Terry was able to exert some restraint—but only until the cancer that eventually killed him rendered him increasingly ineffective.

I was already finding OSF uncongenial and at odds with my fellow directors, when John Paling announced that he was leaving to live with his new wife in Florida. It was not long before I too sought greener fields in the United States. My legacy was the OSF picture library, the collection of still photography that supplied—and still supplies—book publishers and advertising agencies with the images they seek.

My association with the OSF library would continue indirectly for several years after I had moved on. I had created a valuable business relationship between OSF and a picture agency in New York named Animals Animals, run by the dynamic and very competent Nancy Henderson, who, when she heard I planned to return to the US, offered me space in her office. The association with Nancy, originally close—some might say too close for a healthy business relationship—soon deteriorated into one of mutual animosity, making my second New York sojourn both depressing and unfruitful."

One of the factors that fuelled John's resolve to leave was the OSF board's decision that the Picture Library did not merit the attention of a director. To John the consequences were obvious. If properly managed the library would continue to generate income from reproduction fees, regardless of what might happen to the film business. But his words fell on deaf ears, and control of the library was allowed to pass into unskilled hands. John's last act at OSF, he told me, was to prepare a report showing that the library would cease to exist as a viable business within eighteen months under its current administration without massive reorganisation. It is small comfort that the library is today the only part of the original OSF, apart from the name, that survives, albeit sold off and now under new ownership.

But I run ahead of myself. While running the library, part of John's plan to expand the business and increase its visibility to London publishers involved participating in the monthly meetings of BAPLA, the trade association for picture libraries and agencies. He was, he admits, both surprised and flattered when he eventually found himself elected Chairman of the organisation.

One of the common complaints among BAPLA members was the condition in which library material would be returned after publication. Transparencies are fragile, and very susceptible to damage from scratches if mishandled, and John felt it might be beneficial if picture researchers, publishers, printers and librarians could meet together and find out at first hand what took place between a transparency leaving the agency and its coloured image appearing in print. OSF, like all other agencies, had horror stories galore of the outrageous things that happened to their precious pictures. OSF had some quite unique and very valuable large-format transparencies returned with key parts of the image carefully cut out with a razor blade. On another occasion all the transparencies not selected for publication came back with a large hole in the middle, where a pencil had been pushed through. In such cases the client was legally liable for the damage under the agreement they had signed, but obtaining compensation could sometimes be very difficult—and the images unrepeatable.

A freelance picture researcher who had worked with OSF on a number of books for reputable publishers, set up in business on her own as a packager—essentially a small editorial team with minimal overheads who would create books inexpensively for established publishing houses, who would then oversee printing and distribution. In the 1970s this was a thriving market, and the library worked successfully with a number of packagers.

Tessa was working on a number of large projects, and had made several visits to OSF, taking with her several hundred selected images. As an old friend she was not held tightly to the six-week limit normally imposed before late fees would be demanded—at so-much-per-week-per-transparency, these fees could build up quickly. Indeed on one occasion OSF was forced to bill a major New York publisher who persistently ignored requests for the return of unused material a sum of over twenty-thousand dollars!

When Tessa did finally bring back the overdue (and very fragile) transparencies, they were all jumbled up in a big plastic garbage bag, every one separated from their cardboard mounts, and all covered in what appeared to be oily hair spray (a legacy of the scanning process, we discovered). Worse than that, it comprised material from several other libraries—with no way to tie an image to either its caption or source of origin. Tessa was duly contrite and apologetic—and did not fail to mention that her business had folded and that she possessed no assets apart from the rather snazzy sports car in which she arrived. It took days to recover OSF's material and reconnect each frame of film with its mount containing all the data as to species, location, photographer, slide ID etc. etc. Although this was a particularly egregious episode, it was not unique and John heard many similar stories of woe from BAPLA members. John takes up the story:

> "As part of my program as chairman to bring the various parties involved in the picture business together, I organised a visit to Jarrold & Son, a major printing company in Norwich. Suffice it to say that the visit was a huge success and led to greater understanding between picture suppliers and their clients. It was also an event that would lead to another important change in the course of my life. One of our contacts at Jarrolds was Denis Avon, who was also a keen nature photographer. Soon after our visit I receive a request from Denis asking if he and a friend, Tony Tilford, might come and visit OSF—such requests became quite frequent as our reputation grew. Denis and Tony had an enjoyable visit, and we remained in periodic communication afterwards.
>
> Some months later, in response to some question from Tony, I mentioned that I was soon planning to leave OSF and move back to the United States, where I

intended to work as a freelance photographer, film maker and consultant. I also mentioned that I was developing special equipment for high-speed photography.

In order to freeze rapid movement, for example the wings of birds and insects in flight, it is necessary to produce an extremely short, bright, pulse of light. It was, at that time a very specialised field in which there were extremely few practitioners. A major barrier was the lack of both electronic components and civilian engineers with experience in the field. The novice blundering into high-energy engineering ran a substantial risk of fatal accidents. I received a warning early on, and kept the blackened stump of a melted screwdriver that had vanished in a blaze of sparks after inadvertently short-circuiting a large capacitor. A timely warning, the remains hung suspended above my workbench as a constant reminder. Just as pilots are not allowed to fly for twenty-four hours after taking alcohol, likewise prudent high-energy electrical engineers.

Tony replied at once. He was, he explained, not only a prolific wildlife photographer, but also a professional electrical engineer. It soon emerged that we were both working along similar lines in the development of high-speed flash equipment, and that Tony's designs were much further advanced, much more professional and a lot safer. Recognising that collaboration is better than competition, I was relieved when Tony invited me to become a director of his company, Prestoflash, and gladly abandoned my own risky experiments to collaborate with an experienced professional partner.

As a business we were not a great success, but we

certainly enjoyed ourselves on occasion. Tony was a great believer in PR, and insisted that Prestoflash maintain a high profile at international trade fairs such as the biennial Photokina in Cologne. Hugely expensive, such involvement brought us many contacts and some business, but seldom enough to cover the costs.

For one show in San Diego we designed a machine that would periodically pour a glass of wine, allowing us to photograph the splashes in high-speed. Onlookers would then be given Polaroid prints of the captured image. The glass had been specially made with a hollow stem so that the wine re-circulated for the next shot. It proved to be a very successful gimmick and attracted a considerable crowd of onlookers. However, it did not generate the business that we had hoped for. We learned that pouring beer and other drinks for TV commercials was a very specialised art, its exponents being in continual demand. We received few orders for our flash equipment but many requests for pouring machines!"

The demand for their very specialised electronics was limited, but John and Tony did enjoy a few good contracts. In California the Naval Air Station at Alameda had just built a new multi-million dollar facility for refurbishing and testing 20mm cannons for helicopter gunships. Proud of their new toy, they wanted dramatic pictures to publicise it. Living at the time in nearby Berkeley, John was approached to see if he could photograph a projectile just as it was leaving the barrel. The answer was an enthusiastic "yes"—although secretly he had doubts as to whether his equipment was actually up to it.

"On the appointed day I arrived with all my gear, setting up the flash units behind thick protective plastic panels to safeguard them from the blast. The key information I needed to capture the image was an accurate figure for the muzzle velocity, but as this was a military secret it could not be divulged. However, on my tour of the facility I had picked up a sheet of paper from the floor of the control room—a concrete bunker isolated from the firing range—and before handing it back had noticed that it was a full report on a recent weapons test that included precise figures for muzzle velocity. These I committed to memory.

In addition to freezing the movement of the projectile, the other major problem I faced was synchronising the flash to occur at the correct moment—the precise millisecond required. Fortunately firing was electrical, rather than mechanical, so I was able to use the detonation pulse to trip an accurate timing circuit. Knowing the barrel length, and now possessing the muzzle velocity, I calculated how many milliseconds might elapse before the projectile should emerge, and set the timer accordingly. It was a tribute both to our equipment and the precision of the cannon that I froze the emerging projectile just a few inches after leaving the barrel on the second exposure.

We gathered a few more shots for good measure, but the public relations representative was on a roll. "What other shots can you take?" he asked. Showing him a selection of high-speed photographs we had previously taken, his eye lit up when he saw what happened when a bullet passed through a balloon filled with water. He promptly selected a huge meteorological balloon and ordered it filled with water. When it had swelled to over two feet in diameter, sagging dangerously, I did a quick calculation and decided that it must contain over thirty gallons—and hence weight some 300 lb or more.[10]

Because the cannon was fixed on its test mount, it was the balloon that had to be moved into position several yards in front of the barrel. Unfortunately, in the excitement of the moment insufficient care was taken to make sure the target was accurately centred. With a small balloon it would have made no difference, but in this case the consequences were catastrophic. Photographically it was a huge success—two images taken one millisecond apart showed the balloon as the projectile started to penetrate, and then the sphere of naked water hanging motionless in space just after it had exited and the rubber skin contracted.

The huge flood of water was a relatively minor inconvenience, but not well received by the facility staff. However, the trajectory of the projectile, diverted by the slightly off-centre water, had veered violently to the right and scoured the wall for over fifty yards, destroying every one of the TV cameras installed to monitor weapons tests. Anticipating trouble, I quickly packed up my gear and was just leaving when some very upset senior military personnel arrived breathing fire and slaughter in the direction of the poor PR man."

A more valuable contract came through the West German government, who were developing a system for penetrating

10    An Imperial Gallon of water weighs 10 pounds

the hulls of sunken submarines and blowing in an air supply to the trapped crew until it could be lifted. They had encountered problems in controlling their armour-piercing projectiles, which tended to veer violently off course soon after firing under water. Prestoflash were commissioned to analyse the cause.

The testing was done at the bottom of a secret mile-deep mine shaft filled with water beneath the mountains of Bavaria, not far from Hitler's Berchtesgaden retreat. Working with German engineers, who constructed a large metal framework that could be lowered to surround the launch site, Prestoflash built the necessary electronics. A nexus of sensors were designed to trigger a series of special flash units that would record the movements of the projectile during the first few moments after detonation. The flash units were required to produce pulses of only a few microseconds (millionths of a second) and operate at pressures of more than 2500 psi. The whole rig would be lowered into position by lifting gear at the head of the shaft. Massive sheets of thick armour-plating would then be positioned across the opening to prevent damage should the projectile reach the surface.

"Someone had failed to do their calculations adequately, and on the first test a projectile emerged from the water surface at high speed and pierced the armour plates destroying the lifting gear above, and leaving all our very costly equipment languishing a mile below the surface. Before the damage could be made good and our gear raised, Germany was reunified and our project was, for some reason, cancelled by the new government. Every time I read of submarines stranded on the seabed and their crews killed, I wonder whether the project that we had worked on might have saved them."

Another important commission came from the British Ministry of Defence, who were having problems with the breech of a new cannon they were developing. Each month they would order two new flash units—priced at around £8000—to monitor precisely what happened to the breech on firing. It was an excellent contract, as with each test, the flash unit would be destroyed. However, the contract came to a sudden and unexpected halt. It would only be much later that the reason emerged. It was a consequence of Prestoflash's involvement as a witness for the defense in the nuclear trigger scandal—of which more anon.

## Discursus Fifty-One
## High Nuclear Crimes[11]

I n a well-publicized press conference on the 28th of March, 1990, the United States Customs Service announced that, in partnership with Her Majesty's Customs & Excise, they had just prevented a nuclear conflagration through their brilliant interception of a consignment of 'nuclear triggers' bound for Iraq. Their revelations were calculated to attract attention, and the news media responded appropriately. Amid paroxysms of editorial delight headline writers trumpeted:

"Triggers to a Holocaust"
"Nuclear Thieves of Baghdad"
"Iraqi Nuclear Ring cracked"
"Butcher of Baghdad Threatens Britain"
"British Triumph over Plot that Menaced World"
"Madman Hoping to Blow up the World"
"Triggers of Doom"
"Nuke Bomb Gang Held"

Unable to stem the tide of hyperbole, copywriters avidly consumed, and then fancifully embroidered, the inflated and self-congratulatory press releases thoughtfully provided to them by US Customs. The fact that the resulting articles were largely speculative, absurdly confused and wholly inaccurate gave no cause for concern. This was, after all an exercise in disinformation. It had but one acknowledged purpose—to draw dramatic attention to Saddam Hussein's

11    This article has already appeared in print elsewhere.

covert program to develop a nuclear arsenal. The fact that no nuclear triggers had been intercepted was a technical detail of minor importance. Arrests had been made, and the world could once again relax.

However, the British authorities also had their own, less laudable, private agenda. In the wake of all the publicity they had found themselves uncomfortably impaled on the horns of a dilemma, victims of an embarrassing and potentially damaging political blunder. What had started creditably enough as a simple Anglo-American intelligence-gathering exercise had been allowed to degenerated into a politically motivated conspiracy of entrapment, and it had backfired. Suddenly it had become an exercise in damage control—or more bluntly, a cover-up.

. For some eighteen months past the British Government, through Her Majesty's Customs and Excise, had been collaborating with their American counterparts in what they had been led to believe was a simple operation designed to uncover links in Iraq's extensive and complex military procurement network.

'Operation Quarry', also known to British authorities by the code name 'Argus', had been established in response to a report by US Customs Senior Special Agent Daniel Supnick in San Diego, who had been persuaded that a small enquiry for electrical components received by a local company, CSI, might be linked to Iraq's covert nuclear program. It was a long shot indeed, but if correct could reap rich rewards and rapid promotion. The order had come through a small

London-based import/export company run by Ali Daghir in response to a query from the University of Baghdad.

Although it must have quickly become apparent that there was to be no pot of nuclear gold at the end of this particular rainbow, S.S.A. Supnick, intent on advancement and glory, was not about to admit to his superiors that he might have been mistaken. Instead, Operation Quarry was pursued with renewed vigour—and a determination to uncover evil-doing at any cost, even if it had to be fabricated.

The sluggish progress of Operation Quarry was suddenly galvanised and thrown into disarray by unanticipated events in Iraq. On September 18, 1989, a massive explosion occurred at a secret government laboratory in the desert thirty miles south of Baghdad. Farzad Bazoft, a young British journalist working for the Observer newspaper in London decided to go and investigate, having first obtained permission from the Iraqi authorities. As he was about to fly to London a few days later, his baggage was searched and found to contain 34 photographs of the al-Hilla laboratory, together with some soil samples from the site. Arrested on the spot, Farzad Bazoft was convicted of spying and sentenced to death.

This sentence provoked outrage in the West. Margaret Thatcher, fully briefed on the surveillance of Iraqi Businessman Ali Daghir, ordered a proposed sting operation to be brought into effect ahead of schedule so that Ali could be arrested and then offered in exchange for Bazoft. Ill-conceived and of questionable morality, this was a decision that would prove to have many unforeseen consequences.

So what was this sting? In the wake of the initial order for capacitors, Dan Suppnik had been trying, without any success, to persuade Ali to purchase krytrons. These are fast-acting electronic switches that could have nuclear applications. He even went so far as to have fake krytrons manufactured by the American EG&G company in the hope Ali would eventually agree to their purchase. Ali had no interest.

When the order came through from London to proceed without delay, two crates of capacitors—not krytrons—were swiftly packed up and flown to Heathrow. Although it was a covert operation, the TV networks were there to film the crates being loaded onto the plane in San Diego.

The day after the crates reached London, but before they could be shipped on to Baghdad, Ali and his staff were arrested, amid huge publicity. Newspapers and magazines around the world were filled with lavish accounts of how British security had intercepted a consignment of nuclear triggers destined for Saddam Hussein. With every article were published the photographs of non-existent krytrons so thoughtfully provided by Dan Suppnik and his masters.

Two objectives were achieved. The public were made forcefully aware of Iraq's nuclear ambitions, and Margaret Thatcher now had a high-profile Iraqi nuclear spy to exchange for Farzad Bazoft. However, in their enthusiasm, Margaret Thatcher and her advisors had overlooked one important fact. Ali Daghir, too, held a British passport, and as a citizen of the United Kingdom was not eligible for deportation as intended. Initially there had been no expectation of a trial, so that questions of evidence and legal niceties such as guilt or innocence had not received serious consideration. When the scheme backfired, the government was suddenly faced with the necessity of following through on their highly publicized arrest and was forced into arranging a show trial to avoid the embarrassment of exposure.

***

"I first met Ali Daghir two days after his release from prison on bail, pending an appeal against his sentence in the great nuclear triggers scandal. Little did I realize at the time how deeply I would become involved, and how much it would cost both in time, money and emotional energy?

It's a tangled tale, but important, for it vividly exposes the depths to which Margaret Thatcher and her government sank in the name of expediency."

Although the official position of the British Government was that no arms sales should be made to either side in the Iran/Iraq war then raging, in practice British and American patronage of Saddam Hussein continued unabated. The Department of Trade and Industry (DTI) were actively encouraging and granting export licenses to British arms manufacturers—a duplicitous policy dramatically brought to public attention in the famous Matrix-Churchill trial. Only in 1992 did Allan Clark, Margaret Thatcher's Minister of State for Defence (1989-92) drop his government's fig leaf of neutrality to reveal that "the interests of the West were best served by Iran and Iraq fighting each other, and the longer the better."

Ali had arrived in London as Saddam Hussein came to power in Iraq, but the two events were unconnected. A young engineer specialising in air conditioning systems, Ali had trained in the United States, but came to England nursing a deep love of Britain and British institutions. His wife, Khadija, is a Shakespeare scholar.

A natural businessman, Ali prospered. His import-export companies dealt in a wide range of non-military commodities—a £20 million contract for a factory air conditioning system in Iraq, for example. When he received a small order from the University of Baghdad for some electronic components manufactured in the United States, being worth less than $10,000, he passed it to his secretary to deal with and thought no more about it.

The American company named in the order was CSI Capacitors in San Diego, who had recently been in trouble with the US authorities for illegally importing from a Mexican subsidiary, capacitors containing PCBs (Polychlorinated Biphenyls). Once widely used in transformers and other electrical components because of their insulating properties, PCBs are highly toxic and are now completely banned. The stress of the legal proceedings against his company killed its founder, and a new CEO, Jerry Kowalski, was appointed to keep CSI alive. Operating under a cloud, Kowalski needed to find a way to redeem the company's prestige and recover its lucrative business with the US military. The enquiry from Ali's company provided just the opportunity he needed. Although he undoubtedly knew it was nothing more than a smoke screen, in order to earn Brownie points he called the CIA to say that these capacitors could be used to detonate nuclear weapons. While they might perhaps have worked for detonating the first, Hiroshima, atomic bomb, they had already become wholly unusable for the more advanced bomb dropped on Nagasaki three days later.

To the CIA, Kowalski's message presented a possible conduit through which information might be gleaned about the intelligence reports filtering in that suggested Saddam might be trying to build a nuclear arsenal—information still confidential and unsubstantiated. A joint operation was launched with US Customs, in collaboration with British Intelligence and HM Customs and Excise. Two days later US Customs Special Agent Dan Suppnik was installed at CSI under the name of Saunders to play the role of Export Manager. For more than two years the order from Baghdad went unfilled, as 'Saunders' demanded ever more technical details as to the conditions of use, ostensibly trying to clarify the technical specifications.

Meanwhile Ali was being increasingly pressured by Baghdad, and worried that the delay would jeopardise the possibility of other, far more lucrative contracts, for he felt his company was being tested by the Iraqi government. CSI, he said repeatedly, should deal directly with the Baghdad university researchers, but Suppnik ignored him.

Learning that the engineers from Baghdad would soon be visiting London, Suppnik and Kowalski flew over to meet them. At the time nobody questioned why a relatively small company in California would send two senior executives all the way to London to discuss an order worth less than $10,000.

*** 

Farzad Bazoft was hanged at Abu Graib prison on 15 March 1990 on the direct orders of Saddam Hussein, despite the fact that the military tribunal before which he was arraigned considered him innocent. This left the British government with an embarrassing problem. What to do with Ali Daghir? In the belief that he would be swiftly deported, no one had paused to consider the legality of his arrest or the validity of the spurious evidence that was used to support it.

Because of all the publicity, the government had no alternative but to proceed with a trial—but it would have to be a show trial with only one outcome. Much of the evidence revolved around technical issues related to capacitors, and in his summing up the judge effectively said to the jury "I did not understand the technical evidence, and I'm sure you, the jury, didn't either. My instructions to you are to ignore the technical evidence." He then added, "I would draw your attention to the fact that there were five expert witnesses for the prosecution, but only three for the defence."

As the basis for prosecution had been that the capacitors were designed specifically for detonating nuclear weapons, and that they could only be used for this purpose, it is obvious that the technical evidence was highly relevant. The problem for Ali was that his legal team were even more ignorant than he was on such issues and had not the slightest idea of the questions they should ask. Ali was sent to jail for five years, and his hapless secretary, Jeanine Speckman for three.

After two difficult years in prison, during which he suffered a heart attack, which was ignored by his warders, Ali was released on bail, pending an appeal. He immediately started looking for people who might act as expert witnesses on his behalf. There were remarkably few choices, and one of the first names to come up was my business partner, Tony Tilford, whose professional qualifications and experience with high-speed flash made him an ideal candidate.

Sitting in Tony's drawing room, we listened in growing disbelief to Ali's story. The capacitors that had sent him to jail were in no way unusual in design, as any first-year engineering student would know. Moreover, the crown's assertion that their only function was to detonate nuclear weapons was manifestly untrue. They were exactly the kind of capacitors that Tony and I used in our own equipment. Outraged at the way Ali had been treated, we immediately signed on to help advance his appeal.

CSI, the capacitor manufacturers in San Diego, were already well-known to me as I had purchased their products in the past. I promptly ordered a number of capacitors, giving precisely the same specifications that Ali had originally forwarded to them. Speaking to their sales manager, Tylene Williford, I casually asked whether there might be any restrictions on such a product, and she assured me there were none. Better still, she volunteered that CSI had such capacitors in stock—"left over from the nuclear trigger case". I bought the ones in stock, and ordered a few more for good measure.

Ali's appeal attracted considerable publicity, and was expected to last at least two weeks. For me there was particular pleasure seeing one of my recently-purchased capacitors prominently displayed with other evidence on the table before the Lord Chief Justice. Ali's counsel, Geoffrey Robertson QC, had prepared nine grounds upon which to base the appeal, to be presented in order of importance. Council for HM Customs, Alan Moses, QC cunningly persuaded the court to hear first the appeal based on the trial judge's misdirection of the jury.

The court had only been in session for two hours, when the proceedings were halted and The Lord Chief Justice announced that Mr Daghir might leave the court without a stain on his character. Noble sentiments indeed, which fully warranted the champagne we drank on the steps of the High Court. Two days later the Ministry of Defence telephoned us, expressing pleasure in the fact that they were once again able to purchase our flash units.

Only as the euphoria subsided was it realized what had happened. First, Ali's appeal had been upheld on a legal technicality, which meant that he would be unable to claim any compensation for the losses he had sustained—several million pounds, the estrangement of his wife, the breakdown of his son and the disgrace he had brought to his extended family. It was a heavy burden, and one from which he has never recovered. Second, by upholding the appeal on the first point at issue, the court had prevented public exposure of new evidence that would have been highly damaging to Margaret Thatcher and her government.

In 1992 Lord Justice Scott enquired into British arms sales sanctioned by the government. In the course of giving evidence, Margaret Thatcher was asked specifically about Ali's case. She assured the enquiry that she had had no knowledge of the case until she read of it in the newspapers. Even the most diplomatic of language cannot conceal the fact that this was a blatant, cynical lie. I have in my possession a photocopy of the letter Margaret Thatcher had written to the US customs investigators more than a year before Ali's arrest, offering her warmest congratulations on the progress they were making in the nuclear triggers case. Can one, therefore, be surprised to learn that in the months leading up to the appeal, the telephone lines to Ali's barrister, Sir Geoffrey Robertson, QC's chambers were being systematically monitored by government phone taps? Moreover, the laboratory in London, where the CSI capacitors were being tested on behalf of the defence, suffered a most curious break-in. Some of the capacitors were stolen and others destroyed. As this was apparently the sole outcome of the break-in, it could not have been a coincidence.

And Ali Daghir? He remains a stoical but broken man, the victim of a cynical judiciary in a country, that for all the abuses it has heaped upon him, remains wholly in love with Britain and the British way of life. He is fortunate in having friends who are able to support him, for his business empire and his family lie in irredeemable ruins.

## Discursus Fifty-Two
# The Peacock Throne

From his experiences in the Turkish highlands of Hakkiari as an undergraduate, John had long nurtured a desire to continue travelling eastwards into Iran. This dream finally came to fruition in the last years of the Shah's reign. It came about because OSF had for several years been producing wildlife documentaries for Survival Anglia, one of the British Independent television companies. The head of Survival (SAL) was Lord Buxton, who found himself attending a conservation conference at which the Shah was present. The Shah, anxious that Iran be presented to the world as a forward-looking, conservation-minded nation, had approached Lord Buxton, inviting him to send camera crews to shoot wildlife footage for a proposed series of TV documentaries. Lord Buxton immediately agreed. It was only on his return to England that he discovered that none of Survival's free-lance cameramen were prepared to work in Iran. It was at this point that, in desperation, SAL turned to OSF.

The opportunity that presented itself was too good to pass up, but would require skilful negotiations. Far from appearing enthusiastic, OSF played hard to get, and only grudgingly agreed to participate—and then only on their own terms. It was finally agreed that SAL would pay substantially more than their usual fee per program—and also, that they would cover any and all unforeseen ancillary expenses.

It was January 1977 when John flew to Teheran in the company of John Heminway, who was working for SAL, and who would later come to host his own 'Travels' series on American Public Television. An experienced traveller, John was an ideal companion, not least because he had already been to Iran, had met many of the officials with whom they would be dealing, and in addition he understood something of the complex political landscape in which they would be working—a landscape that would eventually result in the overthrow of the Shah.

"There were at that time only two good hotels in Teheran, the Hilton and the Intercontinental—and both were generally full. John demonstrated his expertise as a traveller after we arrived late in the evening at the Intercontinental, which in time became my favourite because of the cool and tranquil Japanese restaurant in the basement. Although we had reservations, the rooms had somehow been allocated to other guests. Using his urbane diplomatic skills, John entered into delicate negotiations with the manager, who had been summoned by the front desk as the temperature of the discussions rose. He was adamant. The hotel was full and there was, he regretted, nowhere that we might stay. "

Having already learned through a previous confrontation at the Hilton that Gallic wrath and outrage at such blunders gained one no ground in Iran, and that vituperation only hardened the management's determination not to yield, it was clear that a calmer, more reasoned approach was necessary.

"If the Prime Minister were to arrive at this moment and ask for a room," John began, "surely you would have one for him, would you not?" The manager was forced to agree. A room would indeed be made available. Airlines and hotels always hold back space for just such an emergency involving senior government officials.

"Well" said John, "the Prime Minister is not coming tonight and we will take his suite." And we did!

The Iran trip was clearly one of the high points of John's well-travelled and eventful life, and he frequently enjoyed reminiscing about it.

"Effectively personal guests of the Shah, we were expecting to be given red-carpet treatment. In a way we were, but the Shah's authority, we soon discovered, did not extend much beyond the suburbs of Tehran. Learning that we were to be the responsibility of Eskander Firouz, a deputy prime minister and head of the Game Department, we had felt confident that all would be well—but not for long. A wealthy businessman whose interests included cement factories and construction companies, Firouz was, like so many in the Shah's government, a rogue even by Iranian standards. Only one sixth of the annual budget allocated for running his department filtered down to its intended recipients, the rest blatantly skimmed off for personal gain along the way. On a more personal level, Firouz would take the manuscripts produced by his staff and publish them under his own name without giving any credit to the rightful authors. This we learned, along with much else, from the few remaining expatriate scientists working in the department, who had themselves suffered in this way.

It was widely believed that Firouz was under scrutiny by the authorities, who had brought in the ominous Dr Shaybani as a watchdog. A ruthless member of SAVAK, the much-feared secret police, Dr Shaybani hated foreigners and had a reputation for shooting people in cold blood. It took all our combined diplomatic skills to engineer the help we needed from him.

We soon discovered that the further from Teheran an official was posted, the less notice he paid to any orders that might originate in the capital. The seeds of revolution were already beginning to show.

Our search for suitable stories and filming locations involved extensive travelling. The possibility of a film about sturgeon and the caviar industry meant visiting the government research establishments on the shores of the Caspian Sea. Even at source, caviar was expensive—$98 a kilo. However, we were required to gain a full understanding of the industry, and the relative merits of the many different grades of caviar. In the interests of science and our television audience we nobly sacrificed ourselves by consuming substantial quantities at every opportunity, but in the end relegated the caviar program to a second filming series, should that ever come about."

The Shah took great pride in the fact that so much of Iran was designated as nature reserves and national parks. Certainly on paper it seemed impressive. There is no question that the wildlife benefited, but John was initially shocked to discover that most of these wildlife refuges were actually set aside as hunting preserves for the Shah's crazed younger brother, Crown Prince Abdurhezza. However, this apparent contradiction in function had little adverse impact in practice. The Crown Prince was only interested in shooting the largest, the most exceptional individuals with the most impressive horns. Once he had claimed his trophy, the remaining wildlife was left in peace.

The parks and reserves were patrolled by game guards employed by headquarters in Tehran, but as with everything else in Iran, the system was permeated by graft. While the filmmakers were in the department one day news came through that two guards had been shot and killed by "poachers". Upon investigation it appeared far more probable that the guards had been running an extortion racket, pressuring the locals for protection money, and that the victims had finally reacted.

From Shiraz John and John went to visit Bamoo National Park, considering a program about Ibex, but they were not suitable quarry for OSF's kind of filming. They were told by the park superintendent: "When the Prince finishes his hunting program we will open the park to the public."

By far the best thing about Bamoo was its proximity to Persepolis, the magnificent palace of Darius the Great that was destroyed by Alexander. It remains an extraordinarily powerful monument to a remarkable ruler. John was shocked to see, carved into the rock along with many other graffiti, the inscription "HMS New York Herald -1870" left by H.M Stanley of Dr Livingston fame.

"Another possible location to check out," John continued, "was Lake Pareshan, home to enormous flocks of waterfowl. We were accompanied by one of the more remarkable individuals it has been my pleasure to meet. When first introduced to Bijan Dareshuri, it was as a young graduate student studying gazelle ecology. I was immediately taken by his remarkable command of English, even though he claimed he seldom spoke it and was very rusty. It transpired that he had taught himself the language by studying the works of Shakespeare, and in consequence spoke perfect Elizabethan English. As we travelled, I learned that Bijan's father was one of the three great Khans of the Qashq'ai, the nomadic inhabitants of the Zagros Mountains, renowned for their challenging annual migration.

Along the way we stopped to look at the Sassanian relief carvings at Bishapoor, where the Roman emperor Philip is shown kneeling in obeisance before King Shapur. The massive cliff carvings, dating from about 400 AD, lie in a beautiful lush valley. Noticing a more recent monument on the valley floor that resembled a pagoda, we asked Bijan what is was. "A grave" was his short reply. It must, we observed, have been someone very important. "No" said Bijan nonchalantly, "My sister." The entire valley had, for generations belonged to the Dareshuri clan.

Some way on John H. spotted some black goat-skin tents high up on a distant hillside. Upon enquiry Bijan looked at then and said;" Oh yes. Those are my people." Pressed by John, he agreed that we might go off the track to visit them.

On reaching the tents, pandemonium broke out. It was as if the Queen had suddenly walked in unannounced on a nursery school picnic. Only then did we understand that behind Bijan's quiet modesty lay a revered traditional tribal leader. Women and children vanished in a cloud of dust as priceless carpets were spread out to welcome us. In a short time tea and refreshments were brought in, in preparation for a later feast. It was as we sat surrounded by the vibrant crowd that I suddenly realised that everyone was speaking not Farsi, but Turkish. As I was served I recalled the appropriate Turkish expression of thanks— "çoc teshekur ederim" I muttered. The impact was dramatic. No longer were John and I treated with reserved courtesy. No longer was there a suspicion that we might be Iranian. No! We spoke their language and we were at once adopted as honorary Qashq'ai. It has been one of the great disappointments of my life that I was unable to join them on their annual migration back into the mountains, for it was a rare honour to be so invited. I should have gone at once, but all too soon the Shah was overthrown in the revolution and the opportunity passed.

Indeed, in the wake of the revolution and its inescapable violence, a number of the officials with whom we had dealt were executed. Fearing that any communications from the hated West might be sufficient to indict an individual, I have reluctantly resisted the desire to write to Bijan or anyone else we knew."

At the end of our reconnaissance trip, we returned home, but before leaving Teheran, I went out to shop for some presents to bring back to the family. In a small antique shop hidden away in an alley not too far from the hotel, I found an old brass mortar & pestle that I wanted. Unfortunately other purchases had consumed most of my ready money, so I asked the owner of the shop to hold it for me. I would be back shortly, I explained, as soon as I had cashed a Traveller's Cheque at my hotel.

The shop owner absolutely insisted that I take my prize with me, and I was prompted to ask why. "Surely", I said, "is there not a strong possibility that I might go and never come back?" Looking me straight in the eye, he replied: "You are British. Of course you will return!" Glowing with pride, tinged not a little with humility, I was back, breathless, within thirty minutes."

Back in England, John advised that OSF undertake two programs, one on Hormoz Island off Iran's south coast, and one in the Great Salt Desert. Because Hormoz would present greater challenges, he recommended that two people should work there for most of the time.

"In April I returned to Iran with several crates of filming equipment, sending for John Paling and Ian Moar to join me once all the arrangements had been made and paperwork completed. This gave me two or three days in which to relax, which I devoted to learning Farsi. Just as the prospect of imminent hanging focuses the mind, similarly, nothing so prompts one to master a strange tongue when the alternative bears the prospect of starvation. I was to be on my own in the desert and my diet would depend wholly on what I could purchase in the nearest market—a five-hour drive away, as it turned out.

Farsi, written in Arabic script, appeared daunting at first sight, and I determined to master the calligraphy as a first step. This took a little concentrated effort in the hotel lobby, aided by a goodly supply of caviar and a bottle of Chateau Sardasht, a local Iranian red wine.

Once the mystique of the alphabet had been dispelled, the language seemed quite straightforward. Being Indo-European, the grammatical structure was familiar—in marked contrast to agglutinative languages such as Turkish. I practised my basic phrases on the long-suffering hotel staff, and carefully deciphered every sign and notice I saw."

As soon as John Paling and Ian Moar arrived they headed for Hormoz. It had been emphasised to them that one of the reasons for filming there was that because it was so inhospitable a spot, the survival of the wildlife there would make an interesting story. Even so, they were not fully prepared for the conditions they encountered on the island.

Situated at the mouth of the Persian Gulf, just a short dhow ride from the mainland port of Bandar Abbas, Hormoz Island was formed from a gigantic plug of salt welling up from deep within the earth's crust. Just 8 km in diameter, Hormoz has been called "The gates of Hell". When Marco Polo stopped by briefly en route to China in 1272 he thought little of it, and conditions have not improved since then. For a time the Portuguese maintained a fort there to safeguard their trade route to the Indies, and today it is home to a few fishermen and miners, most of whom are blinded by trachoma.

There is no fresh water on Hormoz—all drinking water must be shipped in—and the barren landscape bristles with massive crystalline salt outcrops coloured all shades of the rainbow by mineral deposits. In summer shade temperatures climb above 45°C and rarely drop below 38°C. Yet in spite these extreme conditions there is wildlife on Hormoz, and it was around these hardy animals that John and Ian were to weave their film.

There is little vegetation apart from scattered succulents, although Hormoz does boast a 'climax forest'— consisting of a scattering of thorn trees spaced about 400 meters apart! In the forest are found an assortment of insects and lizards, together with a herd of Gazelle, alleged to be a separate species, that go down to the shore to drink sea water—an extraordinary physiological adaptation.

As if nature and the environment did not pose enough problems, there was also an antagonistic bureaucracy to deal with. It was not so much a personalized antagonism as a desire to resist to the utmost the will of the authorities in Tehran. Thus all assurances given in the capital 1300km to the north—promises of transport, accommodation, assistance— all proved groundless. It is greatly to John and Ian's credit that in spite of all the obstacles, they successfully produced the half-hour program contracted.

## Discursus Fifty-Three
### An Iron Post

Meanwhile, in conditions not significantly better, John was happily engaged on his project in the Great Salt Desert, the Dasht-e-kavir, which occupies some ten thousand square miles of emptiness in the heart of Iran.

"When John Heminway and I had left at the end of January, we battled our way through a blizzard that dumped at least a couple of feet of snow on the desert, totally obscuring all traces of the track we were following. It was a harrowing journey.

By the time I returned the snow had gone—evaporated rather than melted into the thirsty ground—and temperatures were starting to climb. My base was a magnificent caravanserai built by Shah Abbas around 1620. A gem of Islamic architecture, its pink stones stood out against the dark, menacing peaks of Siah Kuh, the Black Mountain. Looking like a Hollywood film set, it was remote and romantic. Each stone bore the signature of the mason who had shaped it, and the whole structure was permeated by an aura of mystery and peopled by ghosts from its turbulent past.

After the nearby spring had turned undrinkably salty a few years after the building was finished, and the hapless architect executed in consequence, an aqueduct was constructed to bring water in from springs in the mountains 11 km distant. Sadly the aqueduct had been neglected over the years, and was no longer functional.

Here soldiers and merchants would pause to refresh their camels as they crossed the desert wastes, and here Shah Abbas himself stayed in regal splendour beneath the great arches and vaulted ceilings of the royal apartments. It was impossible to escape the aura of history.

Most desert creatures shun the blazing midday heat, and only emerge at night. For this reason, I too would have to become nocturnal. I would emerge onto the caravanserai roof as the sun dropped low in the sky, and making my way through the maze of domes, settling beer in hand to watch the last pink rays of the setting sun strike the cool, snow-covered peak of Damavand (18,602 ft.), jewel of the Elbruz mountains, hovering tantalisingly far off to the North.

But before I could navigate the desert successfully at night, it was necessary to familiarise myself with the broken landscape by day. Driving my Iranian-built version of the Citroen 2CV Diane, I was surprised to find that this small, light vehicle could take me to places that no Land Rover could reach. I had long ago learned to keep constant mental note of where I was, and in which direction it would be necessary to travel in the event of mechanical breakdown. While such caution obviously made sense when flying over such trackless wastes, its value closer to home was impressed on me when I came across the remains of a vehicle like my own, scattered in small pieces over a kilometre or more along a dry stream bed. The engine block was the largest recognisable component. I learned later that a young expatriate biologist had been caught by a flash flood that came raging down the narrow confines of this wadi just two months earlier. Recognising the ominous roar of crashing stones, he abandoned his car and scaled the vertical cliffs as a great wall of water raced down and carried off his transportation and supplies, leaving him alone in unfamiliar territory. Fortunately he had mentally planned ahead for such a contingency and knew that the closest help lay in a mining camp some fifty kilometres away. It was a journey that took two days and entailed some physical hardship, but it was successful. Indeed, the hardest part apparently was having to decide whether to walk during the day and risk dehydration, or walk by night and risk stepping on a poisonous horned viper. Dehydration posed the greater, more certain danger, so the journey was completed in darkness, navigating by the stars."

It had been arranged that towards the end of the expedition, Ian Moar would leave John Paling on Hormoz and join John for a few weeks in the Dasht-e-kavir. Ian enjoys gracious living and fine restaurants. He does not like to travel. Hormoz had been perdition enough for a lifetime, but the prospect of becoming lost in the Great Salt Desert filled Ian with dismay.

"Knowing his frame of mind, I made a special shopping expedition before meeting him at the airport in Tehran. Bottles of the best Iranian wines, foie gras, and caviar— everything I could find that might re-create in the wilderness something of the gastronomic delights of the Elizabeth Restaurant in Oxford, at that time the city's finest.

I jollied Ian along as best I could, and he responded

manfully, despite a deep and unrelieved anxiety. We had not been long at the Shah Abbas caravanserai when I announced that we were to head off to a new filming location—a wind pump that supplied a small oasis with water for a variety of desert animals and birds.

How far was it? Ian demanded to know. Was I sure I knew the way? I could sense a tone of desperation in his voice, and did my best to reassure him. However, his fears were well-founded. That it was several hours drive away I knew, but as to how to find it—that was quite a different matter. I did, however, possess a map. I still have it as a reminder of the trip.

From a spot not clearly marked, but situated a 45 minute drive away; we were to head off across unmarked desert in a specified direction. After two or three hours, assuming we were on course, we would come to an iron post planted in the sand—the proverbial needle in a huge, huge hostile haystack. Turn left, we were told, and follow along the base of a low mountain range and take the second canyon on the right. "You can't miss it!"

Never have those words generated such disbelief,. but we followed the instructions and just at sunset we reached the wind pump at Chaghelgerai. We had found our destination, but Ian was by now convinced that we could never navigate back the way we had come. Beyond the wind pump stretched an endless sea of mobile dunes, through which roamed feral camels. We set up camp a short distance away at the foot of a low sandstone cliff, and I produced my welcoming feast. As the champagne flowed, Ian's spirits slowly rose and we enjoyed one of the most memorable banquets I can recall. Oh yes, and the journey

home eventually proved to be largely uneventful, although
Ian's relief on reaching the caravanserai was palpable."
Leaving Iran after the expedition proved to be harder and
more taxing than envisaged. It was in late June before John
felt the filming projects had achieved their objectives. The
soaring summer temperatures made life increasingly difficult
and the thought of returning home ever more attractive
The first task before leaving was to pack up the crates of filming
gear they had brought and air-freight them back to England.
Unfortunately, on arrival in Iran all the gear for both parties
had been recorded in John's passport. Struggling to complete
the mass of paperwork required by the Iranian customs, he
was suddenly informed that because his passport contained
a record of entry, he himself would not be permitted to leave
Iran until the equipment had gone. "Oh, and how long might
that take?" he enquired casually. "Oh, probably eight to ten
weeks" was the reply.

An urgent, nay desperate, visit to the Game
Department for advice resulted in a senior government
official being dispatched to help ease the impasse. Before
returning the next morning to talk with a senior customs
official, John was advised to visit the bank and bring with
him several hundred dollars in Iranian currency to 'facilitate'
the negotiations.

"It was a revelation to see how elegantly the art of bribery was
handled by those highly skilled in this most ancient middle-
eastern craft. We sat deferentially across from the plump,
self-composed customs official at his huge, empty desk I

have no doubt that had I simply offered a straightforward bribe, I would have found myself behind bars at once. Such matters require tact, delicacy, and above all, patience. The conversation was opened in Farsi by my companion, and ranged, it seemed from my modest familiarity with the language, on all manner of subjects other than that of most immediate concern to me. Gradually, with delicate thrusts and parries, the discussion began, very gradually, to home in on how I might be permitted to leave, regardless of whether or not the equipment had preceded me.

It was, we learned, a most difficult matter. Indeed, there might not even be a solution .....unless...... At this point my companion from the ministry began sliding his hand slowly across the desk towards the customs official, both casually looking in other directions. I could just catch a momentary glimpse of a 1000 Rial note—roughly $20 worth—as it was slid by a plump hand quietly into an open drawer on the other side of the desk. As the number of notes increased, so the conversation lightened, until a broad smile spread across the hitherto unresponsive face of the official, and he announced:

"I think I have found a solution!"

$300 had changed hands over the past hour, and I was now free to leave. It had been just such contingencies of this sort that I had in mind when we negotiated the Survival Anglia contract months earlier to cover all unexpected eventualities."

John's caviar researches on the earlier reconnaissance trip were not in vain. When preparing to leave Iran after filming he managed to purchase, probably on the black market, several kilos to bring back to England. Not only had he developed an insatiable taste for it himself, he admitted, but he also knew that nothing would please his aging father more than the gift of an abundance of caviar far greater than he had hitherto consumed during a lifetime of occasional gastronomic indulgence.

It was now July, and even at 4:00 am the temperature at un-air-conditioned Merhabad airport was oppressive. Knowing what conditions would be like, and knowing how delicate caviar is, John had carefully befriended one of the British Airways flight attendants the evening before. She had undertaken to convey the valuable consignment directly from their hotel refrigerator into the galley fridge on the plane.

"As time passed, the crowd of passengers waiting to travel to London began to get restless. Something was clearly amiss, but no hint was forthcoming of what it might be. As the crowd started to become ugly, a young British Airways representative appeared, with the difficult task of soothing the mob before it resorted to violence. Apparently, just as he was about to go off duty the previous evening, there had been a hijacking. A party of disgruntled Syrians, whose flight had been cancelled, had commandeered our plane and were, even now, demanding to be flown to Damascus—taking with them all the pre-boarded caviar.

Although exhausted, having been on duty for more than twenty-four hours in very trying conditions, the BA agent was masterful. Time and time again he came forward to placate hysterical women and enraged men. He was superb. It was a pleasure to write a letter to the chairman of BA on eventual return to England, praising his even temper and conciliatory skills. It was an even greater pleasure to receive a letter of thanks, not only from the chairman himself, but also from the individual concerned.

And I should add when our plane finally returned from its unscheduled trip to Damascus, the Syrian hijackers had failed to notice my caviar, which came with me to Oxford, where as expected, it gave the greatest pleasure."

# Discursus Fifty-Four
## Historical Interlude

Wte were enjoying a leisurely lunch in a little village restaurant in France not far from Alogny when there was speculation as to the possible course of European history had Napoleon not been defeated. During a break in the conversation John commented on how rapidly events appear to pass into history.

> "Today the battle of Waterloo appears to most of us as ancient history, and yet in terms of human generations it is surprisingly recent. My father once saw a patient whose father had fought at Waterloo." She was an elderly lady, 'he explained, "begotten late in life, whose father had been a drummer boy at the battle. Viewed in this light, Waterloo seems to me as something relatively recent"

For the benefit of a visiting American, John then cited an example from across the Atlantic. He began by reminding his listeners that Arizona only achieved statehood in 1912, which being only 23 years before his own birth, to him seemed relatively recent.

> "One of the first white settlers in south-eastern Arizona was a man named Herbert Read. He had passed through the Chiricahua Mountains on his way to the California gold rush in about 1850. He later returned to settle there, building a log cabin in what is now Cave Creek Canyon. This was at a time when Geronimo and his Chiricahua-Apache tribesmen were actively resisting white incursions into their territory, and seeking revenge for an earlier attack

by the Mexicans. Somehow Herbert Reed established a close relationship with Geronimo, who would visit his homestead in friendship, even though subsequent settlers in the area were attacked and killed.

I have not only stayed myself in the Read cabin, but was fortunate enough to know Herbert Read's son, who was born there. When I met him he was in his eighties, and had only recently retired as postmaster in nearby San Simon. Is it surprising, therefore, that I am totally captivated by the romance of the American southwest?"

With a typical non-sequiter, the conversation suddenly turned to the unrelated subject of practical jokes. It was agreed that the best examples combined both elegance and simplicity. To illustrate this, John told of a classic Oxford joke (although I have also heard the story attributed to Cambridge). A group of labourers were busy doing road works in the High Street, when a couple of undergraduates approached them with a warning that students dressed as policemen were soon to appear and order them to stop digging. Shortly afterwards the same undergraduates confided to the police that students dressed as workmen were busy digging up the High Street—before retiring to observe the confrontation between, as it were, an immovable object and an irresistible force. Not all practical jokes are so innocent.

"We were in Costa Rica on a filming expedition, and were staying at the La Selva Research Station, where we joined the resident staff and visiting research workers. Conditions were a bit basic, and everyone slept on bunk beds in a huge dormitory housing perhaps fifty people or more. From time to time the peaceful routine would be interrupted by visiting groups of blue-haired seniors from New England, busily adding to their 'life list' of bird species. One such group became victims of a particularly cruel, but vastly entertaining, practical joke.

Many of the party, upon retiring, placed their dentures overnight in a mug beside the bed. During the night, somebody wickedly moved the mugs around, creating confusion and anguish next morning when the breakfast bell sounded, and nobody's false teeth would fit."

Most practical jokes go unpunished, the perpetrators remaining anonymous, but occasionally there comes wonderful retribution.

"In my third year at Oxford I shared digs with an American Egyptologist from Brown University. By strange coincidence it was the same digs my father had had in 1920—but a different landlady. It was reported that at Brown, someone had been away for the weekend, and returned to find his room packed tight from floor to ceiling with innumerable balls of waste paper. Discovering the instigator, the victim plotted an appropriate response.

It was sometime later, perhaps at graduation time, when the victim-to-be let slip that his girl friend would be coming to visit. On the appointed day he came with her, opened the door to his room and ushered her in. In his absence the room had been stripped bare and contained only a bed—with retaining straps at each corner and a large whip!'

## Discursus Fifty-Five
# Reflections on Mortality

As the years have passed, John and I have had cause to reflect on the ever increasing number of our mutual acquaintances whose names have appeared in obituary notices. In childhood, death was something dark and malignant, a mysterious force that carried off favourite aunts and uncles; something that brought tears, even to the eyes of grown ups.

> "I shall always remember with pain the death of my grandfather. He was, admittedly, ninety-three. Even so, he seemed hail and hearty until one day, while polishing his dining room table, he dropped down dead. While my parents rushed down to Canford Cliffs, near Bournemouth, to handle funeral arrangements, I was sent to school, and I do not think that I have ever again experienced such grief as consumed me then, but I look back with gratitude for the outpouring of sympathy from the master who found me sobbing uncontrollably in a remote corner of the school changing rooms. Since then I have found death much easier to handle."

For some people, death maintains the horror that it engendered in childhood, tightening rather easing its grip as the years pass. For John the opposite is true. One of his favourite quotations is Woody Allan's observation: "I'm not afraid of death—I just don't want to be there when it happens."

In the course of his life, John has come close to death on several occasions—in motor accidents, climbing accidents and during serious illness. Drifting in and out of consciousness, with death hovering nearby, there was only peace and no fear. It is John's firm conviction that most blame for a fear of death may be firmly laid on church teachings. In bygone centuries, when life for all classes of society was short and brutal, the prospect of a benign afterlife in paradise held strong attraction. As a political tool, it became a powerful incentive for extracting the last ounce of labour from the oppressed peasantry.

How much simpler is the life of a Balinese, to whom the body is but a temporary home for the *atman* or spirit. Discarded like a worn out suit of clothes, the physical remains are cremated, while the spirit is recycled, appearing again within forty days in a new-born infant within the extended family.

For John, so he is happy to assert to those who ask, death as such holds no fear—provided that the end is swift, painless and unexpected.

"The hardest aspect of death is anticipation of the sorrow to be felt by those left behind. It can be imagined, but never experienced. It is hard to accept that one will have no knowledge of what happens when one is gone, and yet this of itself is some comfort. I have no doubt that once dead, I will exist briefly only as a memory in the mind of friends, before fading into oblivion when they too die."

John rarely looks forward to death (and then only briefly in passing bouts of depression). For the most part he is simply saddened by the realisation that he will never know the answers to all those mysteries that make life so fascinating and scientific research so rewarding.

Why, he wonders, is suicide considered to be so wrong? While it is always shocking to those left behind, for the deceased death comes as a blessed release, an irreversible end to a growing litany of mental and physical agonies.

"I have known," John observed, "very few friends who have killed themselves, and have very little insight into the inner torment that drove them to kill themselves. Indeed, from the outside it appears a rather extreme solution to a relatively straightforward problem, but onlookers generally remain in ignorance of other people's demons.

It's true I've known several elderly men, sound in mind, who have chosen the exact hour they wished to check out, and I admire, almost envy, their determination to flaunt custom and recognise when their time had come. However, my father, bedridden some whie before reaching his century, asked his physician for help in leaving, his vision and hearing severely impaired. He was told 'boredom is no excuse for euthanasia", and was forced to live unhappily for a further year or two.

Very different was the case of Ramon, whom I had known when he worked as a film editor at OSF, but years had passed before I re-connected. I learned that he and David Thompson had purchased an estate in France, and as it was only about three hours drive from us, I went to see them. It was anold mill near Saint-Yrieix-la-Perches south of Limoges, with several large lakes well-stocked with fish, and we received a warm welcome. Ramon, I learned, had negotiated a very substantial loan from a French bank to make the purchase, apparently intending to run the place as a vacation spot for keen anglers and their families. David had been brought in manage the grounds and the angling, and was rewarded with a minuscule percentage shareholding.

When we returned the following year, Ramon was dead. He had driven to a remote spot on the property and run a garden hose from the exhaust pipe into the car, leaving his unwitting business partner, David Thompson, to resolve the resulting cauldron of problems. David told us a story that was almost beyond belief. Ramon's wife, who had worked with me at OSF, had left him, and he had become obsessed with revenge. The property (and its 1 million euro bank loan) were part of a complex plot to ruin her financially, in the belief that with his death, she would inherit the debt. It was a bizarre plan that ultimately destroyed only David, whose tiny shareholding made him responsible for clearing up the mess. Ramon had overlooked one key point, namely that under French law, his estranged wife need not accept the property he maliciously bequeathed to her. Throughout the months, nay years, that Ramon was developing his planned revenge, he never gave the slightest hint of his twisted mental state."

It was in the wake of these discussions about death and what might follow, that John felt obliged to mention some of the questions that have sprung to mind when meditating on an afterlife.

"There are many theological questions to which I long to hear authoritative and convincing answers. Thus those of us raised in the Christian tradition are taught from infancy that when life ends, if we have been 'good', we shall go to Heaven, there to dwell eternally with angels amidst abundant milk and honey (a questionable diet for calorie counters). In this context, heaven is portrayed as a paradise possessed of everything one has ever longed for in our earthly existence. Is Heave thus filled with Ferraris and Lamborghinis, and the best champagne? This picture of a blissful eternity, while perhaps comforting to the poor and oppressed, nevertheless raises some difficult questions. In reality the thought of an eternal, unending life is actually far more frightening and depressing than the prospect of death, eternal peace and oblivion. What pleasures can there possibly be that would forever continue to provide delight without the spice of novelty? Even if one were to find the answers for which one thirsts in life, observing the world forever without being able to influence or participate in terrestrial activities would soon induce a depression from which even suicide could not provide relief.

If I die in great pain, crippled by disease or physical trauma, perhaps with extremities detached, am I destined to bear such burdens for eternity? As this would surely negate many of the pleasures I have been assured are in store for me in paradise, one must assume my deficiencies will have been made good. Thus I am, in effect, taken back to the days when I was still whole. Likewise, are infants never to progress beyond utter helplessness? What heavenly rules govern such advancement or retardation of aging?

For those to whom the pleasure of good food and fine wine is a major element in the enjoyment of earthly life, there must be concerns about eternity. Is heaven well-stocked with good wines, and how well do fine vintages age in eternity? Is heaven well-supplied with skilled and creative chefs? If not, are gourmets and gourmands alike destined to be denied for eternity that which has given them the greatest joy? Surely this would seem more like Hell than Heaven.

There are many other human activities that appear to raise questions when translated to the heavenly sphere. Are antagonistic couples doomed to quarrel for ever, and will mistresses remain permanently unrequited in love? Does sexual intercourse lead to pregnancy, and if so, is heaven populated with baby angels that have never had an earthly existence? At this point one might justifiably enquire about the career prospects for angels, namely by what qualities and through what intermediate steps may an angel expect advancement up the career ladder to the rank of archangel—and can they progress any further?
It is not the physical you, it may be claimed, that ascends to Heaven, but some mysterious 'spirit', a phantasmagorical distillate of the mind, a disembodied intellect. Is this 'spirit' a phenomenon inherent in all living things? If so, can we recognize it in an Amoeba, a Cane Toad or Bristlecone Pine? Is Heaven likewise populated with the spirits of extinct flatworms, trilobites and pterosaurs? If it is indeed a uniquely human characteristic, then at what stage in human evolution did it first appear? Do Neanderthals and Denisovans share Heaven with Ützi and the Tollund man—and if not, why not?

## Discursus Fifty-Six
# Once Upon a Time

Those of us close to John know the true story of the acquisition of his château in France, but for the benefit of his more gullible American guests he would sometimes embroider a more romantic, albeit utterly fanciful, explanation of how he and Joyce came to occupy so imposing an historic pile. While there can be no question that his ancestors successfully survived the Hundred Years War, there is also no firm historical evidence that they ever actually participated in it. Applying a statistical line of reasoning, seasoned with no little fantasy, he would argue that the small population of England following the Black Death, combined with the evident quality of his known ancestors, made it highly probable that members of his family would have joined the Black Prince in his victory at the battle of Poitiers in 1356

'You will recall," he said, adopting his best professorial manner, "that in the Hundred Years War England's Plantagenet kings, successors to the throne of William the Conqueror, were fighting to reclaim what they considered to be their ancestral lands—lands to which the kings of France also laid claim. At the heart of the conflict lay the question of whether royal inheritance in France could, or could not, pass through the female line. Edward II of England laid claim to French lands through his marriage to the daughter of Phillip IV of France after her brother died without an heir in 1328. French nobles, quoting the harsh Salic law of Clovis I (481-511) disputed Edward's claim—the theme, you will recall, of the opening scene in Shakespeare's King Henry V$^{th}$. The result was war. When the Black Prince, the son of Edward III defeated John II of France at Poitiers the great Duchy of Aquitaine passed once more into English hands."

So it was, he embroidered, that in the rape and pillage that followed the battle his ancestors had (albeit briefly) acquired (or more properly seized) the lands of the noble d'Alogny family. That being so, he maintained, he had merely reclaimed the ancestral family home, and was even now busily engaged in making good some nine-hundred years of neglect to the fabric.

The actual circumstances of the château's acquisition were somewhat more prosaic. "You aren't going to buy a château are you?" John and Joyce asked in evident disbelief. They had just arrived in France and were breakfasting with the Poiriers, old California friends. "Oh no!" they replied, "We heard it was on the market and simply thought we'd go to have a look. Do you want to come along?" It was this disarmingly simple invitation that was to initiate a new phase in John's life.

Alogny had been on the market for some time. Situated on a hilltop, it had spectacular views in every direction, but was run down and very overgrown. Until the Revolution, it had been reached by a drawbridge over the moat, but today, a mere shadow of its former glory, it retained but a single tower, and was of habitable size and irresistible charm.

Anyone possessed of common sense and a grain of fiscal prudence would have hesitated, but for John, reality and fantasy are often indistinguishable. In that moment of sublime lunacy, he and Joyce made a life-changing decision. It would, they convinced themselves, if rented out provide much-needed financial support to the educational charity they had founded in Bali. Their confidence would quite soon prove to be misplaced.

Sitting in the realtor's office, the purchase documents had just been signed when an Englishman popped his head around the door, demanding whether they had any châteaux for sale. Mme Destouches, the realtor, looked up, smiled sweetly, and replied "Oh dear! So Sorry, but we've just sold the last one!"

John would soon discover more than he wished to know about the French tax system, labour laws, mediæval construction methods, and the intricacies of plumbing, electrical wiring and sewer design. He also had to learn the French word for blackmail.

It was not long before the castle's solitary toilet ceased to flush, bringing with it an urgent need to learn about French sewage disposal. After several days of uncomfortable digging in search of a *fosse septique*, the garden had taken on the appearance of a major archaeological site, with pits and ditches spread out across the landscape. In time it was discovered that the very first hole had been barely twelve inches off target.

The problem was found to result from the inadequate

do-it-yourself skills of the previous owners, who had misaligned the main sewer pipe and compensated with a *coudée* or double elbow bend in the last couple of feet that became all too easily blocked. "All it took," reported John afterwards, "were a few hours of pick-and-shovel work to realign the pipe." He was filled with admiration for the *vidangeur*, who unhesitatingly leaped into the freshly drained cesspit and began probing up the inflow, seemingly untroubled by the strong possibility that in disturbing the blockage, he might well be engulfed by the substantial volume of backed-up sewage.

Ignorant of French labour laws, when work first began, John employed a number of young people. The first was Jerome, who had been recommended as a gardener, and he was soon followed by a host of unemployed friends. Jerome's gardening skills, it was eventually discovered, were confined to the many flourishing marijuana plants growing in the more remote corners of the property.

One day Yan, self-appointed leader of Jerome's band of helpers, appears and asks—nay insists—that John buy him a car. He has, he says, been grossly underpaid and heartlessly exploited—but a car would make things right! A few quick enquiries revealed that Yan was actually being rather well paid for his work.

When Yan returned a few days later he brought with him a letter—a threatening letter setting out the possible consequences should John fail to give him a car. Quoting the maximum penalties that might be exacted under the French legal code, he explained the massive fines that could be levied for employing 'black' (=untaxed) labour, additionally mentioning that one might also find oneself forever banned from entering France again. Playing for time, John told him to return the following evening, seemingly needing some time while sufficient money was rounded up.

Calling Jerome, John explained that if Yan were to blow the whistle, Jerome himself, and the other members of the team, would all be at risk for working *en noire* and themselves face significant penalties—and be out of a job.

Yan returned next evening, and while John sat talking with him out in the garden, a friend slipped out of the bottom of the tower and noted down the license number of the car by which he had arrived. The gendarmerie, on being consulted, volunteered the potentially valuable information that owner of the car had only just been released from prison.

John takes up the tale:

> "I asked Yan whether his friend knew the nature of his visit? Was he aware, I wondered, that Yan's activity made him a *complice par instigation*—an accessory before the fact—in a blatant case of *chantage*—blackmail—thereby making him (and Yan) liable for a protracted return to prison? Perhaps, I suggested to Yan, he might like to reconsider. He slunk off muttering threats into the darkness.

Fortunately, as it so turned out, the gendarmes were called to an emergency elsewhere and never made it to Alogny. Later the same evening, Yan was summoned to a meeting—essentially a tribunal of his peers—who impressed upon him the unwisdom of his actions, and the probable consequences for all present. Under duress, Yan agreed to drop his claim, and further agreed never to visit Alogny again nor have any further communication with John or his friends. "It was an interesting experience," John observed later, "and added at least one new word to my French vocabulary, although" he observed somewhat wistfully, " I have never yet needed to use *chantage* again in conversation."

The tower, sole reminder of Alogny's tumultuous past and its crowning glory, was in terrible condition when John arrived. Uncertain foundations had, in centuries past, yielded to the weight of massive masonry above, creating a marked scoliosis in the central column of the spiral stairs and giant cracks in almost every step. Massive baulks of timber, emergency first-aid, placed at intervals stand testimony to the ingenuity and skill of mediaeval artisans.

Soon after moving in John was visited by an elderly lady who had spent her childhood at Alogny, and wished to see it again for her eightieth birthday. Clearly the castle had already fallen on hard times when she lived there, for three different families occupied three separate floors—none with running water or indoor sanitation.

When she was young, she said, no one was allowed in the tower for fear it might collapse; she refused to set foot in it. John too had originally had reservations about its safety and consulted with several experts. The structural engineers grimly assured him that the tower was in imminent danger of collapse—that no remedy existed. The only solution, they said, would be to pull it down and build a new tower from scratch. On the other hand, local stone masons whose lives were spent working on such structures were more sanguine, and were in no doubt that even if nothing at all were done, the tower would be in exactly the same condition fifty years hence.

Ultimately it would be a solitary English mason, chronically depressed and uncommunicative, who laboured alone through the winter to stabilise and strengthen the tower with steel reinforcement and much concrete. In the years since Keith worked on it, not one single crack has appeared in the stonework and it is widely believed that long after the rest of the castle has fallen down, the staircase will remain standing in solitary glory, a testament to his masonry skills.

## Discursus Fifty-Seven
# The Eastern Front

For years John's only association with the Orient was the knowledge that his grandfather had captained one of the closest ships to survive the cataclysmic destruction of Krakatoa on August 27th, 1883, but in time the Far East would come to figure prominently in John's life. He has always regretted the fact that his grandfather died before he was old enough to ask intelligent questions about his long life.

John reminded me, not for the first time, that the Crimean War end on March 30th 1856, with the signing of a peace treaty at the Congress of Paris. When news of this auspicious event reached London there was universal rejoicing. So that John's grandfather, then barely four year old, should not forget the occasion, his father, John's great-grandfather, took him from his bed and beat him soundly.

"The family was staying with grandfather when the Second World War ended following the atomic bomb attacks on Japan—an event sufficiently significant that it merited a small announcement on the front page of the London Times, which at that time still kept news confined to the inner pages. I recall being very impressed by how much my father knew about atomic bombs, bearing in mind that the whole subject had been top secret. Only with the publication of his autobiography, 'My First Seventy-Five years in Medicine,' did I discover the source of his information. He had been asked to monitor the health of scientists working on some secret wartime project, who might have been exposed to radiation—although this fact was never revealed. By asking a few pertinent questions of each patient he was gradually able to build up a comprehensive picture of the project they were engaged on, and gained a general understanding of the broad principles upon which the proposed nuclear weapon was to be constructed. To him it underlined the futility of trying to maintain secrecy.

Remembering how grandfather was to be permanently reminded of the end of the Crimean War, my sister Jean prevailed upon him to exercise a similar *aide-memoire* on me. She was quite upset next morning when I had absolutely no recollection of having been beaten the previous night. Either I was a very heavy sleeper, or grandfather showed more compassion than his own father."

\*\*\*

Returning to England after a filming trip in Australia with OSF, John took the opportunity to break his journey in Singapore. This gave him the chance to renew his friendship with Ivan Polunin.

"A student of my father's in 1942, Ivan's interests extend far beyond his medical work as an epidemiologist. An avid collector of eastern ceramics, he is also a leading authority on fireflies with an insatiable curiosity about all natural history.

While in Singapore I was anxious to find *Misumenops nepenthicolis* a curious crab spider that lives inside the bowls of certain Pitcher Plants, poaching their insect victims before the plant can digest them. Ivan knew exactly where to find them."

Malaysia is also home to another spider John particularly wanted to find. *Liphistius* belongs to a small, aberrant group of spiders that in several features resembles fossil species from the Devonian, some 400 million years ago. Like the coelacanth, it is a true living fossil. Again, Ivan Polunin knew exactly where to look. He described the location of a colony on the island of Penang, and another deep within the Batu caves near Kuala Lumpur. John still nurtures the hope of one day finding *Liphistius* on Bali.

> "Although none have ever been found on the island, I remain convinced that they must be there—unless they were wiped out on April 10th, 1815 when Mount Tambora erupted. The largest volcanic eruption in recorded history—its dust cloud was responsible for Europe's 'year without a summer' and Turner's dramatic sunsets—it covered Bali with ash to a depth of three feet, destroying agriculture and initiating plagues and widespread famine."

It was whilst exploring the Batu Caves that John witnessed the famous Thaipusam festival, in which devotees of Subramaniam, the son of Shiva, perform extraordinary acts of penance. Cheeks and tongues are pierced with metal blades, and huge burdens, attached by innumerable fishhooks, are carried in procession. There is seemingly no limit, he commented, to the excesses of religious fanaticism.

> "In Penang I made the acquaintance of an elderly amateur hymenopterist, whose interests included spider-hunting wasps. It was through him that I first met Sjovald Cunyngham-Brown, a man as unusual as his name suggests. I was invited to join him for breakfast at the swimming club,

but not forewarned that I would be required to swim for a mile in conversation before eating. A man already in his mid-eighties, he was unusually fit. After a necessarily large breakfast, I was invited to join him for a walk in the hills. We set off at a fine pace, climbing ever higher into the forest. From time to time we would come upon peasant farmers tilling their patch in a clearing. Cunyngham-Brown would engage each in long and animated conversation in fluent Chinese. He was, I learned, godfather to many children up here, for he had at one time been mayor of Georgetown, the capital.

Despite his advanced age, his mind was undimmed. He had recently acquired a new Chinese dictionary and spent two hours every morning learning new words to add to his already impressive vocabulary. We would have long conversations ranging over topics without number. It was in the course of one of these that he paid me a compliment that I have cherished ever since."

Cunyngham-Brown had been in Singapore at the time of the Japanese invasion in February, 1942, and gave a moving first-hand description of the event. Knowing that all was lost, and that the next day they would be rounded up and imprisoned, the British community held a magnificent farewell ball at the Raffles Hotel, everyone in full evening dress. The following morning he described how he came downstairs, gazing wistfully at the debris from the previous night before going to spend the rest of the war in a Japanese prison camp.

"Conditions in Japanese prison camps were notoriously harsh and as he described his experiences, I commented that I did not think I could have endured such hardship. I was flattered beyond measure when he replied that, on the contrary, he was convinced that I possessed the necessary characteristics that would have enabled me to survive the hardships successfully—I doubt he was correct, but I was flattered."

## Discursus Fifty-Eight
# Island of the Gods

When John is not in France or California, he can often be found in Bali, and one evening the dinner guests were curious to learn more about what drew him there. Many people travel to Bali for the vacation of a lifetime, but far fewer have reason (or excuse) to return again and again.

> "The first visit was an accident. A friend, in anticipation of a substantial legacy from a very elderly grandmother, had asked for suggestions as to where she might travel. Giving voice to a long-cherished private dream, with one voice we exclaimed "Bali".
>
> "Oh", came the reply. "Very well then, if you will come with me to Bali within the week, I'll pay your fare."
>
> "How very inconvenient. Yes!" was the response, and so began a whole new chapter in my life."

Bali exerted its magic immediately, with the result that instead of staying two weeks, as planned, John and his wife Joyce stayed for two months, leaving then only because their visas expired. By good fortune and good friends they had by-passed the usual tourist experience of Bali—isolated in luxurious resort hotels—and in time established close friendships with several Balinese families, and undertaken exploratory journeys into remote valleys in search of new and little-known archaeological sites. Anxious to find excuses for returning, they decided to form a tour company that would introduce very small groups of visitors to those aspects of Bali that truly set it apart as a rich, vibrant and wholly unique culture. So it was that 'Hidden World Tours' launched *Bali Beyond the Guidebooks*.

Munduk, high on Bali's volcanic spine, was a summer station in the days of Dutch colonial rule. Here officials would bring their families to escape the coastal heat—particularly oppressive in the heavy, high-collared formal attire that custom of the times demanded. Far from the tourist routes, Munduk slumbered. A short time before John and Joyce first came to Bali, a local businessman, anxious to attract some of the tourist dollars, and even more anxious to see them benefiting his community, started a small hotel. Here visitors could watch a dance teacher instruct local children in the intricacies of this quintessential Balinese art form. Those with culinary curiosity could attend a Balinese cooking class given by a local teacher in her own kitchen in the village. Musicians were encouraged to visit Made Tripp, a leading musician on the island, to take lessons and watch how instruments, notably bamboo flutes, were made. Those with a spiritual bent were encouraged to discuss Balinese religion with the local priest. For those anxious to immerse themselves in the more arcane aspects of the island's culture, arrangements could be made to see how the abilities of fighting cocks might be improved by cross-breeding with wild jungle fowl.
Warming to his subject, John continued:

"Like many cultures in the East, the Balinese have a passion for cock fighting. Although nominally outlawed, cockfights are permitted in the context of certain temple ceremonies, when blood must be spilt to appease the spirits of the earth. In practice cockfights are widespread and often managed by a local mafia. For a peasant population with little income, the bets are substantial— and sometimes huge. Royal families have been ruined through an addiction to cockfighting, and whole villages bankrupted.

There can be few men in Bali who do not own one or more fighting cocks. Although their lives may be brief, the cocks are like sumo wrestlers in Japan, and have every luxury provided—special food and a rigorous training regime. During the day, particularly in the mountain villages, prize birds are raised high above the tree tops on long bamboo poles. As 'top bird' it will enter the arena with a pronounced psychological advantage.

The sight of many parked bicycles, some with the characteristic cages and baskets used to transport birds, is a hint that there is a cockfight not far away. Pausing to listen, one is soon directed to the cockpit by a characteristic sequence of sounds. It may be in a local temple, but more likely in a private compound. The rare appearance of a police uniform will bring proceedings to an immediate conclusion, but most often the proceedings follow an age-old routine.

Arriving between bouts,one finds a dense crowd packed around the arena in lively conversation. Owners will be crouched ringside, massaging and encouraging their prize fighters by blowing into their nostrils. From time to time they will be goaded to lunge at nearby birds in a display of ferocity. Rival owners will be harangued, the merits of their birds disparaged.

Two birds will be being prepared for the next bout. Long, curved, razor-sharp blades, called *taji* are attached to one leg by a specialist versed in the ancient method of tying. As the time draws near for the next round, the volume of sound rises to fever pitch as bets are laid verbally across the ring. Everyone is shouting and waving money——it is form of betting that few anthropologists have tried to understand. No written papers change hands, for all bets are verbal——and upheld by a traditional honour system.

Suddenly, at some invisible signal, the ring goes silent. The two combatants enter the ring——or more usually find one another face to face as their wickerwork cages are lifted. Usually the birds fly at one another with terrible ferocity, their wicked *tajis* glistening. Within seconds it's all over and one bird lies dead——the winner perhaps bleeding. Occasionally, like Ferdinand the bull, one, or sometimes both, birds prove reluctant and must be caged together to produce the needed animosity. If both birds are evenly matched, the contest may continue for some time, but the rounds are timed. Not by a wristwatch, but by a coconut shell with a hole in it that measures time by how long it takes to fill and sink.

The match settled, the winner is praised and fêted for he has brought his owner substantial winnings. The loser, having lost, is no longer accorded celebrity status. His corpse, dangling from his owner's handlebars, is taken home for dinner."

From the *bale* or elevated platform where one sits to consume glasses of deliciously cold Bintang beer——a welcome legacy of

Dutch colonial rule—at the Puri Lumbung Hotel in Munduk, one looks out across a sublime landscape. Rising to the left are a series of densely forested volcanic peaks, the tallest being Batu Karu, which houses near its summit a particularly sacred temple. Falling away steeply below is a wide expanse than contains countless terraced rice fields, that cascade in profusion down the valley, vanishing into the distance, where the sun glints off the Java Sea. Floating like clouds in the far far distance are the great volcanic peaks of East Java. On a still evening the sounds of a distant gamelan orchestra drift across the valley from the village of Gesing, nestled among the trees on the far ridge. John cautioned me against making frivolous wishes, warning that things passionately envisioned have a habit of coming to pass. He then continued:

> "Many times I have sat looking out across this blissful vision of paradise, and said to myself (and anyone else nearby) if I were ever to own a house in Bali, there is where I would want it to be." He then continued, "We had gone to visit our friend Nyoman Witama in his village one morning. In the course of conversation he mentioned a family whose home was about to be seized by the bank. Innocently enquiring further we learned that the equivalent of $500 would save them, but that it was needed that very afternoon. Their financial problems were vastly greater and more pressing than our own, and we immediately volunteered to help.
>
> Later in the day we accompanied Nyoman on foot down a narrow muddy trail that ran alongside a rushing stream. The house was a simple structure with tiled roof and four rooms, positioned amidst the rice terraces, with

sweeping views down the valley. All we could hear was the sound of running water.

Completing our mission, we were preparing to leave when the conversation took a new turn. Like most farming families, their language was Balinese, with some limited understanding of Bahasa Indonesia, the national lingua franca, so we were dependent on Nyoman for a translation. Slowly we gathered that the family actually owned another house, located in a nearby village, but in very poor repair. Their dream was to sell the present house in order to have sufficient money to make the village house habitable."

"How much?" we enquired.

It should be explained at this point that there are roughly 10,000 rupiah to the dollar, making exchange calculations somewhat confusing. We thought that at $30,000 the property, despite its attractions, was rather overpriced. It took several minutes before Nyoman pointed out that we had our sums wrong. The price was $3,000!

Blinded by this revelation, we forgot at least temporarily our own precarious financial situation and agreed to buy. It was at this point that the old, very old wizened grandmother came and hugged Joyce with tears streaming down her face. Kissing that weathered, mud-spattered face with its salt tears was like embracing mother earth herself, she told me afterwards."

"Now technically it is not possible for foreigners to own property in Indonesia, so the agreement was drawn up in Nyoman's name, but we kept possession of the documents. It has proved a most serendipitous purchase.

Nyoman undertook the improvements to the house that we had only dreamed of, demolishing walls, installing electricity, well water and sanitation. His brother, Made, who lives nearby, took charge of the garden, making forays into the high forest to bring back orchids and other decorative plants. In a moment of daydreaming about the future, we rashly mentioned that a small pond might be an enhancement at some distant date. It was some three weeks later that we arrived to find not just a pond, but sizable lake, complete with island on which flourished a Norfolk Island Pine tree.

But that was not all. In our absence Nyoman had started to worry that, as we grew older we might find the narrow, muddy path a problem. The solution? A complete flagstone and cement path some seventy-five yards in length running to the property, that now boasted a fine gate—and a *padmasana;* a stone altar on which offerings could be made daily to prevent our being troubled by evil spirits. Even though the offerings are not made on a strictly daily basis, there have been no assaults by denizens of the nether world—although we did discover that in our absence, the house was being used for illicit liaisons periodically."

SUBLIME LUNACY

## Discursus Fifty-Nine
# Birth of a Dream

Here is John's description of the origins of 'The Bali Children's Project', the educational non-profit he and Joyce started. Although this has appeared elsewhere, John feels that it merits repetition here.

"In an oft-repeated ritual, the last thing recalled before being swallowed by the all-enveloping tropical night is the incessant drumming of heavy rain. It cannons off the tiles and gurgles along the bamboo gutters, where its soothing music merges imperceptibly with the more distant voice of the stream that tumbles down the gully beside the house to the accompaniment of a multitude of amorous frogs—or could they be toads perhaps? Before a decision can be reached on this important matter, sleep will supervene, carrying me off once more to a blessed Nirvana of rich Balinese dreams.

A distant insomniac rooster, unduly anxious to welcome in a new day, intrudes briefly on my slumbers; just long enough to let me share the enchanted vision of sinuous rice terraces cascading in profusion down to the distant Java Sea by the light of the full moon. The mysterious bulk of the mountains hang as a dark backdrop to the scene, the fine detail of their forested flanks lost in shadow. An occasional firefly still flashes hopefully above the *sawa* in search of a mate. The insect voices that clamoured so loudly for attention at nightfall are now muted, only the echoes of their urgent song remaining, as if tangled among the myriad silhouetted palm fronds hanging limp in the still night air. The nocturnal transition from torrential rain to brilliant moonlight occurs with the same imperceptible rapidity with which the white-bellied swiftlets soaring in profusion at dusk are seemingly transmuted into bats, even as one watches.

This is Sanda, our sanctuary high in Bali's untouristed mountains, lying within the ancient kingdom of Gobleg—surely a name that would have delighted Tolkien. We settled here, by happy accident rather than by design, after a passion for natural history and archaeology had led us along many winding forest trails to remote backwaters, to communities in which many farmers were still unable to speak Bahasa Indonesia, the national lingua franca, but only the difficult local Balinese language.

The disparity between the Bali portrayed in lavish hotel brochures and the realities of life for most of the rural population is palpable. Here there are no pristine white coral beaches, only hour upon hour of backbreaking toil in the oozing mud of the rice terraces, interspersed from time to time with colourful, complex rituals to ensure the gods look favourably on the endless cycle of labour.

It was up here in the mountains, nurtured by dramatic scenery and the irrepressible smiles of our neighbours, rice farming families for whom the tourist boom has brought little material benefit, that the seeds of the Bali Children's Project were first sown. We knew from experience that in times of economic hardship, it would invariably be the girls who would be withdrawn from school first to labour in the fields. Yet we felt sure that the key to breaking this cycle of agricultural poverty

lay in education, for without education the future held
no vision beyond motherhood and farming; no dreams of
college, university and a possible profession. It would take
a sudden epiphany to make us try and do something about
it.

We were sitting with our old friend Nyoman
on a narrow wooden bench in front of the warung
run by his wife, Ketut, in the village of Tamblingan. It
stands close beside the road, stocked with all manner of
simple merchandise the neighbourhood might call for.
It also provides a meeting place where the affairs of the
world might be discussed at length and placed in proper
perspective. Here on the very crest of Bali's volcanic
mountain spine, swirling mists keep the temperature in
check and frequently conceal the adjacent fields of rich
blue Hydrangeas that form a major contribution to the
local economy, being in high demand at lower elevations
for temple offerings.

Today, however, the sun is shining and our
conversation is correspondingly bright, covering many
topics, including education. Commenting on the insatiable
thirst for learning among poor families in his community,
Nyoman illustrates his point by telling us of two little girls
he knows.

"Each day," he says, "they must walk for well over
an hour to get to school," adding simply "They go without
breakfast and without shoes." Clearly there was more to
the story than he first told us. Our curiosity aroused, we
asked for more information, and whether it might be
possible to visit them.

"It's quite a long hike to get to where they live, and the path is very muddy—but if you really want to go I could take you there tomorrow."

"Why not now?" we demanded impatiently, and with only token resistance Nyoman agreed.

It was, as predicted, a challenge to negotiate the steep and muddy winding forest trails. From time to time we passed by rudimentary thatched sheds hidden in the undergrowth, some housing cows, others improbably housing families. At last Nyoman turned off the trail and followed a narrow path towards what appeared to be yet another dilapidated cowshed. A pathetic row of washing, the merest rags, hinted that the occupants might not only be cows.

The world we entered at that moment was worse and more disturbing than anything we had previously seen in Bali—or could possibly have imagined. Peering inside we were just able to make out two small figures, two little sisters, huddled together in the darkness. Softly, Nyoman spoke to them in Balinese, seeking to reassure them. Their fear was palpable.

As we waited quietly outside Nyoman explained that we were the first westerners they had encountered, and that with our bleached faces, to them we were indistinguishable from certain demons known locally to inhabit the forest. Between Nyoman's quiet, repeated reassurances, their story began to emerge.

Their mother had died some years earlier, and they lived alone with their father. A simple labourer earning perhaps $25 a year, he owned no land of his own and hence was obliged to work in other people's fields. He often had to travel far to find work, and was sometimes forced to leave his children alone for days on end.

"They must leave to walk to school before daybreak," Nyoman explained, "and generally there is nothing to eat."

"Don't they get anything to eat at school?" we immediately asked.

"They have no money to buy food." Nyoman explained. "If they are lucky, they will get a bowl of rice when they get home at night." We were speechless.

After a long interval, two little faces appeared in the doorway, studying us intently. Very slowly, very cautiously, with patient encouragement from Nyoman, the two small sisters emerged into the light. They were both tiny and manifestly undernourished. It was hard to imagine from her size that the older sister, Iluh, might be eight years old. We sat motionless as the drama unfolded. It was only with difficulty that they were persuaded to approach us—and still further encouragement was needed before they would sit near us.

As the slow minutes passed and their confidence grew, they gradually edged closer—then closer still. Suddenly we each found ourselves with little arms reaching around us. It was an embrace like no other, and we found ourselves instantly in love as our eyes filled with tears.

For quite some time we had nursed a growing desire to give back to the people of Bali some tangible mark of recognition for the pleasure and delight with which we had been blessed through their friendship. In this moment of sheer joy in a forest clearing everything fell into place for us. Our immediate impulse was to adopt Iluh and Kadek and for a brief, ill-considered moment we even considered bringing them to live with us in California. But then wiser council prevailed. It would not be simply wrong, we realized, but almost criminally irresponsible to remove a child from a culture as rich and all pervasive as their Balinese society. Far better to improve their lot within the world they knew.

Within days arrangements had been completed for them to become, with some support from us, a part of Nyoman's family—a solution to which their father gave his blessing. Two days later, after buying them new sarongs, the sisters had their first lesson in traditional Balinese dance, a fitting introduction to their new life.

Over the years that followed we watched with pride the growth and development of our two new daughters, Kadek the more artistic and Iluh clearly academic—it was not long before she had taken over management of Nyoman's warung.

It would be many years before we learned that the girls had promised their mother on her deathbed that whatever the sacrifice, they would continue to go to school and pursue an education. The wisdom underlying this promise would be manifested when Iluh graduated top of her private high school class, fluent in several languages.

Spurred by our first meeting with Iluh and Kadek, it took little imagination to realize that we had glimpsed only the tip of what must be a widespread iceberg in rural Bali, and we soon found ourselves starting to support other children in need of help to stay in school. Our own severely limited resources were not sufficient to go far, for money has never been a priority in our otherwise rich lives, and soon our friends found themselves being importuned to help. We quickly learned that by becoming a registered non-profit, friends and acquaintances were more readily parted from their disposable income. However, being formally registered with the US Internal Revenue Service as a '501 (c) (3)' non-profit in California may lend a necessary air of respectability to the enterprise, but is of limited consequence when it comes to practical issues deep in the Balinese countryside.

The Children's Project had not been in existence long before we began to meet other people with similar good intentions. From them we heard a growing litany of horror stories, of funds donated for education being diverted to provide motorcycles and televisions for a growing circle of extended family members. Indeed, several informants, even those married to Balinese partners, assured us that the task was hopeless, and that they had reluctantly been forced to abandon their own plans.

By good fortune rather than good management, the Children's Project had hit upon a protocol that worked. Unquestionably this was due to the exceptional qualities of our first Balinese assistants, whose dedication and enthusiasm laid the foundation for future success. Foremost was Ketut Resni, the first girl in her village to go to high school, who worked with Yudi. Yudi, who was functionally blind throughout childhood) taught himself English and computers. Together they provided ideal role models for the children we supported, visiting each child monthly to distribute the funds needed for continuing education. By monitoring closely the needs of each child, and making necessary payments either to the child or directly to the school, donations were applied where needed.

Even so, vigilance is always needed. We chanced to meet the headmaster of a rural school some years ago, and made enquiries about the needs of his pupils. He was most anxious to solicit our help. Upon closer enquiry, it transpired that what he was really seeking was not help for the school. "I need a new roof for my house" he admitted under further questioning. It should be added that despite this lapse, we subsequently became close friends, filled with admiration for the sacrifices he and his wife made to ensure their three daughters obtained a university education, despite their humble upbringing in a remote mountain village.

We have come a long way since that time. We still sponsor individual children, and with the help of partners, are currently supporting over two hundred, some going on to high school and even university. However, our programs now extend far beyond individual sponsorship. We soon discovered that if girls in particular were ever to have a vision of the future that went beyond rice farming and motherhood, the seeds had to be sown long before the age at which our sponsorship for school was required. It was in recognition of this need that the Children's Project began creating village kindergartens and pre-schools. To date we have over a dozen of them, with more on the horizon, each serving some 30 to 40 children—and sometimes significantly more—each day.

Concerned at the erosion of traditional Balinese music and dance through the impact of television, BCP has created two children's gamelan orchestras, and provided help to music teachers.

Responding to urgent contemporary needs, BCP has initiated an HIV/AIDS awareness and sex education project that has been invited to schools in all eight Balinese regencies.

Like many non-profits, The Bali Children's Project runs a volunteer program, and this too has evolved over the years. We have been fortunate in having the benefit of some remarkable, dedicated individuals, but we have also learned that some applicants come with their own private agendas that do not fully accord with BCP interests. Today we are more discriminating in whom we accept, placing well-qualified individuals, who are willing to commit to at least two months, in village schools, where they teach English and exercise any other special skills, particularly computers and teacher training. Future plans not only include the creation of village learning centres, equipped with libraries and computers, but a wholly new program catering to artists with disabilities. Dedicated to the memory of Judith Scott, the world famous artist, and twin sister of BCP founder Joyce Scott, it is hoped this will eventually help change attitudes towards disability in Balinese society, while fostering self-esteem among the disabled by acknowledging their innate creativity.

And what of Iluh and Kadek, who were catalysts in the creation of BCP? Following enrolment in a high end spa training school, Kadek now dreams of opening her own establishment. Iluh, happily married, attended university to learn how best to teach teachers. In a fitting closure to the story, Iluh is now the BCP Regional Manager serving the scattered mountain communities among which she grew up, and her father has come to live out his years beside her in the compound she shares with her husband's family. Truly, nothing good happens without first dreaming!"

## Discursus Sixty
# In Good Company

Just the other evening the conversation at dinner turned to the unusual and the distinguished people that one had met. John was uncharacteristically quiet as others recounted their experiences, and feeling that perhaps he was waiting for a cue, I suggested that he might have something to add to the conversation.

It turned out that his reticence was genuine. In a quiet aside he explained that he had met so many such individuals—"Nobel laureates abound at Oxford", as he put it—that he felt it might sound pretentious to talk about it. Not to be silenced, during a lull in the conversation I demanded that John make a contribution.

"One of the best features of the old Zoology Department at Oxford was the tradition of a wholly democratic coffee break each morning, at which the merest freshman could initiate a conversation with a Nobel Laureate or overhear a contentious discussion between leading academics. There was one such occasion, I recall, when Sir Julian Huxley was in earnest discussion with Prof E.B. Ford, doyen of Ecological Genetics, and Arthur Cain, a leading researcher into snail population genetics. Ford, I should explain, was eccentric, even by Oxford standards and spoke in a high-pitched and extremely precise and idiosyncratic manner.

Huxley was pontificating about a new, very long paper on snail polymorphism and wound up the conversation by saying "Well, I think it is a very weighty paper." To which Ford very quietly responded with "There is a certain class of mind [pause] to which the mere avoirdupois of a paper implies [sniff] weight!"

Another encounter he enjoyed recalling was his first meeting with Dennis Leston. Denis was a self-taught, very self-opinionated and contentious entomologist from London's East End, with a big chip on his shoulder who appeared one day in the departmental library.

"Hello, I'm Denis Leston. I'm the world's authority on Hemiptera. I've been invited here by John [Prof Pringle]—I suppose it's on account of my international reputation"
Shocked by such a blatant display of self-aggrandisement, John felt there was only one possible form of reply:
"Oh, I'm John Cooke. I'm the world's authority on spiders. How nice to meet you."

This exchange laid the foundation for a friendship that would last several years until they went their separate ways. John also recounted another, later encounter with Dennis.

"Dennis Leston appeared one morning looking very much the worse for wear after a night of partying. I greeted him with the words "My God, Dennis, you don't look a day over sixty seven!" believing him to be some twenty years younger than this. The jest fell flat when it transpired that it actually was his sixty-seventh birthday that he had been celebrating!"

Convinced that there must be more anecdotes about interesting people he had met, I pressed John again. After a brief pause to collect his thoughts, he began:

"As a teenager I chanced to read 'The Story of San Michele" by Axel Munthe." He paused, looking around the assembled company for an indication that anyone at the table might be familiar with the work. "When it was published in 1929," he resumed, "it became an instant best seller and the name of Dr Munthe widely known. Today both Munthe and his book have largely sunk into undeserved oblivion."

It seemed highly improbable that John had ever met him, but not wishing to spoil his story, I held my peace. It was well that I did. Painting a backdrop to the story he was about to tell, he explained that Axel Munthe qualified as a physician in his native Sweden, but set up practice in Paris. Here he soon built a flourishing practice in Parisienne high society, using the income that this provided to work without charge among the destitute. In 1882 he went to Naples to treat the poor during the great cholera epidemic.

Following a spiritual awakening during a visit to the island of Capri as a young man, he eventually bought the hilltop site of a palace constructed by the Roman emperor Tiberius and built himself a sanctuary there that he called San Michele. Here he would entertain the cream of European artistic and literary society. Among his guests was the self-invited Marchesa Louisa Casati, who arrived one day without warning and refused to leave.

The Marchesa was perhaps the most notorious woman in Europe. Fabulously wealthy, highly eccentric and wholly devoted to self-advertisement, she threw extravagant parties and behaved outrageously, including wandering around

Venice clad only in a fur coat, while leading her pet cheetah with its jewelled collar. Not surprisingly she became a legend in her own time. Despite Munthe's attempts to dissuade her, she became a regular visitor to San Michele, and on one occasion brought him a highly unusual and somewhat bizarre gift.

It seemed an uncharacteristically anticlimactic ending when John suddenly abandoned Capri, and switched attention to New Zealand, but as we would discover, the story had not ended. A friend had invited John and Joyce to join her on board a 145 ft. Brigantine, the Soren Larsen, that she had chartered out of Auckland to welcome in the new millennium.

"I had always," said John, "wanted to sail in a square-rigged ship, if only to experience something of my grandfather's life. Although guests on board, we were invited to join the regular crew in standing watch and participating fully in the ship's management. Joyce and I always seemed to get the midnight-to-four am watch, sometimes taking the wheel, but more often finding ourselves lashed to the cabin top as forward lookouts. Heavy seas meant we were often soaked in spray, but we had an unrivalled view of the southern hemisphere's night sky and its unfamiliar constellations. By day we joined the crew in furling sails high up the mast and out along the yardarms. On the last night of the old millennium we were riding at anchor off the town of Gisborne and came ashore for midnight festivities in the central square. We then moved down to the shore, taking up position to catch the first rays of sunlight of the new dawn. As we waited, Kiri Te Kanawa sang to the accompaniment of the New Zealand Symphony Orchestra. When the sky began to lighten, a fleet of thirty or more Maori war canoes swept ashore, with the Soren Larsen as backdrop. There followed dramatic Maori welcoming dances and ceremonies.

We were quick to report back to friends and family around the globe, anxious to describe all that we had seen at the first town of any significance to welcome in the new Millennium "Oh yes" came the response several times over, "we know all about that—we watched it happening on television."

After laying this suitably distracting verbal smoke screen, John then revealed that on the voyage he had chanced to meet Axel Munthe's grand-daughter, Katriona. Some years later, when they went to stay with her at her old mill house in Tuscany, they were offered chocolate biscuits from a battered old 'Cadbury's' tin. Unsuspecting, like so many before, their hands alighted on soft bundles of tissue paper, within which reclined the Marchesa's gift—two shrunken heads from Amazonia, their power to shock undiminished by the passage of years.

Axel Munthe was a great story-teller, and a particularly favourite is the tale of the Leichenbegeiter or Corpse Conductor. As a doctor, he had been asked to accompany a boy with advanced consumption from San Remo back to his home in Sweden. His patient died in Heidleberg on the way, and after performing his first embalming, sent the body back to Sweden for burial, coincidentally travelling on the same train himself to visit his brother. It transpires that no corpse can be allowed to travel on the Germany Railways without its leichenbegleiter. (It remains unclear whether one leichenbegleiter can travel with two corpses). After a series of mishaps, Munthe accidentally finds himself in a locked car with a professional corpse conductor accompanying the body of a distinguished soldier back to Russia for burial. It is a long, hot journey to Lübeck, where the bodies will take ferries to their respective destinations, and Munthe and his companion drink more than is prudent. Following some confusion, the packing cases containing the two bodies become switched, with the result that the poor Swedish boy receives a full-blown military funeral in Russia, while the distinguished General is buried in Sweden with a simple rustic ceremony. The vicissitudes of Munthe's journey are wonderfully recounted.

## Discursus Sixty-One
# Parental Tales

John's father had been educated at Merchant Tailors' School in London, which was founded in 1561 by members of the Merchant Tailors' Company. The Worshipful Company of Merchant Tailors, which had its origins as a guild in the Fourteenth Century, is one of the twelve great livery companies that originally regulated trade in the city of London. Through being a member of the school, John's father automatically became a member of the Merchants Tailors' Company, which conferred on him the freedom of the city of London. Whatever other benefits may accrue from being a Freeman of the city, perhaps the most significant is that it allows you to be drunk in the streets without fear of official retribution.

Today the Merchant Tailors' have become largely a philanthropic and social organisation, but still retain much of the pomp and splendour it enjoyed in mediaeval times. Nowhere is this more manifest than in the banquets given in the Merchant Tailors' Hall.

> "My father had invited his older brother Alfred to a Merchant Tailors' dinner, which was naturally a full evening dress affair. Alfred had run away to sea at the age of sixteen and had the misfortune to fall into some machinery. After hanging by his hands for many minutes he was finally rescued—but only after his right leg had been mangled and eventually torn off. His return home

with a wooden leg caused his mother great distress.

Merchant Tailors' dinners were, before the war, very grand affairs with many courses. Part way through the evening a liveried waiter would murmur into a diner's ear "would you care for a cool seat, sir?" and replace his massive leather chair.

It was in this rather splendid setting that Alfred raised his hand to summon a waiter, and quietly asked him to bring something. Properly trained, the waiter didn't bat an eyelid and disappeared, returning a short time later with a silver salver on which rested the requested hammer and tacks.

Alfred bent down, pulled up his sagging sock, secured it to his wooden leg with the tack provided, and carried on dining as if nothing unusual had happened."

Mention of the Merchant Taylors School prompted John to return to his favourite topic of spiders. Among its distinguished old boys, he told us, was the Elizabethan physician, Dr Thomas Muffet (b.1553), who wrote the earliest book on British spiders. He held that a spider "gently bruised and spread on bread" or hung in a walnut shell around the neck, was efficacious in curing the ague. It is believed that Little Miss Muffet of nursery rhyme fame was his step-daughter, who has a memorial in Westminster Abbey reading simply "Dear Child".

Of his father, John told many stories, including an explanation as to why he himself never gambled.

"As children my father would sometimes take us with him when he went to visit patients in the country. He was a very busy man, and this would provide an opportunity to spend time together with his children. One of his patients lived in a very fine Georgian mansion near Henley, with swan-covered lawns sweeping down to the river, and where champagne was served promptly at ten o'clock each morning.

My father had only to mention that his patient was a bookmaker for me to draw the obvious conclusion—namely that a large number of punters had lost a great deal of money in order to keep him in this style. Consequently I have always considered gambling to be a fool's pastime."

Only in late middle age was this rule of life briefly abandoned. John was on a filming assignment in Nevada one summer. The only public pay phone in the little town of Yerrington stood in open sunshine, and was unbearably hot. However, someone suggested visiting the local casino, where sure enough, there were pay phones in air-conditioned luxury.

"I had just finished speaking to Joyce, my wife-to-be, and was in high spirits as I headed out through the casino towards the parking lot. As I passed the rows of brightly coloured slot machines, with their flashing lights beckoning to me, I pondered on what the attraction might be. At the same moment I happened to feel a 25-cent piece in my pocket and out of curiosity pushed it into the waiting slot of the nearest machine. The sudden appearance of a huge pile of money flowing from the machine made it all too clear the reason why people gambled. Anxious to repeat the pleasant experience, I fed my hoard piece by piece back into the waiting machines—but of course they gave nothing further back. I estimate my gambling debt to stand at about three dollars.

> Some years later we would occasionally use Reno as a base for skiing, the casino hotels offering inexpensive food and accommodation in the expectation that their guests would then gamble heavily. My belief in the unwisdom of gambling would be strongly reinforced on such occasions. We would observe zombies working several slot machines simultaneously for hours at a time— we would see them at bed time, and they would still be there at breakfast next morning, still feeding in money in a catatonic daze. From time to time they might hit the jackpot, and the machine would ring as coins tumbled out. Now any normal person might be expected to demonstrate some sign of jubilation at such bounty—but no. We would watch in disbelief as money continued to be fed back into the machines without the slightest flicker of emotion passing across anyone's face."

This talk of sudden wealth prompted another memory. John began by explaining that in the old days, before the National Health Service in Britain, doctors in the country would often treat poor patients without charge. From time to time grateful patients might later leave, as a token of appreciation, a brace of pheasant, or wild duck, a hare or a box of fresh fruit and vegetables on the front steps.

> "One morning during the war my father came down to find a fat envelope in the letter box. Inside were two thousand pounds in cash (an immense sum in those days) together with an anonymous, illiterate note saying: 'This 'ere is for wot you done for our Mum while she was alive". My father, unable to identify the patient, immediately

handed the money in to the police as lost property, but was obliged to receive it back six months later when, not surprisingly, it remained unclaimed. He said that as a result of this experience he felt morally undermined, for each morning thereafter he would open the letterbox with the expectation that he might find there another gift from a secret admirer.

It was one of father's colleagues who, on entering the ward in a mental hospital, was asked by a patient "Were you at the battle of Waterloo, doctor?" Before an answer could be given, the patient said "Well, it was like this!" and promptly began to throw a fusillade of hard, heavy ivory billiard balls at the poor man in simulated cannon fire.

Father himself told of one of his own ward rounds, which in those days was a very formal occasion, in which the presiding physician was treated as a revered and exalted personage. After the patients had been tidied up and their bedclothes smoothed, father entered the ward. To Matron's horror, the silence was broken by a voice from the far end calling out "Dr Cooke, you're old, you're bald and you're ugly, and I hate you, I hate you, I hate you!" He took it in his stride, but later said what irked him most was the reference to old age.

*** 

Talking one day about his son Richard, John recalled his first day at school in England after returning from Connecticut.

"Remembering my own return, we were concerned to make the transition as painless as possible. After making enquiries, my mother found a convenient school for Richard and the girls, apparently well-regarded, although unaware that it was Roman Catholic and taught by nuns. For better or worse she enrolled them.

Richard had just mastered the first half of the alphabet shortly before his first day, and on being quizzed on his reaction to the school responded "God. God. God— and a lot of letters you've never even heard of!"

Joyce, during a discussion about children, told a tale that reinforces how hyper-vigilant parents must always be. While she was resting briefly, Lilia had discovered a way to climb up to the bathroom cupboard. There at the back of the top shelf she found a bottle of 'Baby Aspirin'. Noticing how dangerously quiet the house had become, she went and caught Lilia red-handed, bottle still in hand. "How many did you eat?" she demanded.

"Two"

"Are you sure?"

"Two", was the emphatic reply, several times.

As a good mother, she remained unconvinced and went immediately to the doctor, who confirmed that on such occasions one should never trust the word of a three-year-old.

It was just as well. On having Lilia's stomach pumped it was clear that she had consumed an entire bottle-full.

For John this story reinforced his oft-repeated injunction "Find out what the children are doing, and stop them!"

## Discursus Sixty-Two
## **La Grange aux Dîmes**

John's excursion into French real estate began when the Poiriers, long-time mutual friends in California decided to buy an old farmhouse in central France. On impulse several of us, including John and his wife, offered to come and help in its renovation. We were not alone, and for several summer weeks the house party swelled to seventeen souls, who more than occupied the available space. The teenage members of the party camped unwillingly with numerous bat families in the attic space, while one elderly soul sought uncomfortable sanctuary beneath the kitchen table. 'Tammy Faye', so named for her uncanny resemblance to the wife of disgraced tele-evangelist Jim Bakker, came unenthusiastically with her new (and soon-to-be-temporary) partner and was forced to camp in a field across the road. Each morning in tight hot pants, her Buffon-style hair in disarray and false eyelashes dangling, she would come teetering across the dewy grass on high heels for a late breakfast.

Anxious for peace and privacy, John and Joyce carved out their domain in the pigsties. Straw bedding from the last porcine occupants still lay thick and mouldering on the cobblestone floor, and spider webs hung thickly everywhere, but the whitewashed walls, he consoled himself, were not too badly stained.

"A small niche in which a candle might be decoratively placed for nocturnal illumination contributed the sole Homes & Garden touch. Once swept and tidied, the sty became the envy of the entire household, a tranquil oasis in a sea of chaos. It was even possible, with care, to position the bedding to avoid the raindrops that fell through gaps in the tiles. It was a situation that brought to mind that obscure Scottish legal term 'stillicide', meaning "to be dripped on from one's neighbours' roof.

That first year we cleared the undergrowth together to discover the property boundaries, and between long, leisurely meals beneath the giant Chestnut tree, improving our masonry, carpentry, plumbing and other craft skills through a combination of necessity and practice. The following year, in self-defence, high priority was given to putting a new roof on the *porcherie.*"

John's first real estate purchase was to follow a few years later, memorable for being perhaps the only property ever purchased with a credit card. It was a small house attached to a sizable barn in the hamlet of Les Poulets—aptly named as the sole street, which runs down to the river Anglin, was thronged with chickens. It took Joyce only a few trips to the ATM to withdraw the necessary cash for its purchase. To this day it remains without sanitation—but has recently attracted attention from conservationists because of its original and unmodified mediaeval features.

Not long after this, John's attention was drawn by our mutual friend David Martin to another, closer and more remarkable property in the village of St. Pierre-de-Maillé.

Even among our circle of unusual friends, David stands out. By profession a mason, by avocation artist, musician, and above all, a born teacher. It must be more than thirty years ago that David was driving with friends through nearby Angles-sur-l'Anglin, hailed with good reason as one of the ten most beautiful villages in France. "Stop!" said David. "I'm getting out. This is where I will spend the rest of my life!"

David's enthusiasm is irresistible, although John successfully stood out against his insistence that he buy a derelict alcohol factory—last used by the Germans during the war to provide fuel from sugar beets to power the Paris trams—it had lain deserted for many years. "It has," enthused David, "a steam engine that alone is worth more than the property." It was only with great difficulty that David was persuaded that steam engines didn't figure prominently in John's plans for the future. However, with his next suggested purchase David hit the jackpot—even though the French taught long ago in school did not include the neologism beloved of the casino in nearby La Roche Posay: "Jackpotez-vous!" cry their posters.

"In 1415, or thereabouts, the Bishop of Poitiers had ordered built an enormous tithe barn in which to store his share of the ten percent of everybody's produce demanded by the church. At first sight it might seem strange to construct such a building beside a river renowned through the ages for its periodic catastrophic flooding. However, it proved a sound investment. To enhance his investment, the Bishop also had built a bridge across the river, levying a toll on all traffic that crossed it—doubtless including those delivering their tithes. Built on massive foundations resembling a bridge abutment, and including accommodation for clerks and toll collectors, the Bishop's barn has withstood the floods that swept away lesser structures—including his bridge. However, his barn could not withstand the wrath of the oppressed populace, who in the French Revolution rose up and commandeered it, defacing the bishop's *blazon* or coat-of-arms, whose remains are still visible."

For more than ninety years Mme Gervaise had lived in the toll collectors rooms overlooking the river and its mill. A cesspit in the adjacent barn provided all necessary sanitation, and at some distant date a pipe had been installed to bring town water to the house. When she finally moved into the village *Maison de Retraite* (old folks home), Mme Gervaise placed her house on the market—at a price that would undoubtedly have seemed substantial when she was young. It was this property to which David drew attention, emphasising its unsurpassed location, historic significance and exceptional price.

Twenty-eight-thousand dollars sealed the purchase. Considerable work would be needed to restore it to its full mediæval glory, at the same time upgrading the services to acceptable modern standards. John and his friends had just removed some unnecessary modern internal walls, stripped off the false ceilings to reveal the massive oak beams, and opened the wall behind the single cold-water sink to expose an original fireplace. It was in the midst of this work that Mme Gervaise came to call. Standing tall despite her years, she was a veritable *grande dame*. Holding her long walking *baton* she gazed thoughtfully at the chaos and remarked "Oh, now it looks as it did before we improved it."

"Regretfully, she did not live to see the work completed—
the great oak beams exposed and cleaned, the native
flagstone floor that overlaid her bilious green ceramic
tiles, the curved cherrywood staircase released from its
closet-like enclosure and stripped of its hideous dirty-
cream paint—and above all the magnificent fireplace and
chimney-piece that David designed and built to replace
the original that had been long removed.

It was not long after Madame Gervaise's visit that
we unexpectedly learned about *les jours de patrimoines*. This
proved to be a day when the historic buildings of a village
are thrown open to the public. No one had thought to
warn us that St. Pierre was to have such a celebration. The
first intimation was the appearance of a large sign in the
road outside giving the history of the house, to be quickly
followed by most, if not all, the inhabitants of the village
and its surroundings, who thronged through, anxious to
see what we were doing."

The house, like that of several neighbours, had a garden
running down to the riverbank. A pair of pigsties that came
with the property introduced John and Joyce to one of many
curiosities of French property ownership.

"The two pigsties had a small walled yard in front, as
one might expect. However, it turned out that the yard
belonged to our neighbour, M. David, across whose
property our access lay. M. David, a wizened old man
with a captivating smile acquired a Norfolk Terrier, which
he kept in a cement doghouse in the yard. Terriers are
sociable dogs, and 'Minou' was desperately unhappy
at being left alone for days on end. For hour after hour

she would howl in misery, and being within easy earshot, we were constantly reminded of her situation. It was not that M. David was cruel, but as a retired farmer, he had a somewhat cavalier attitude towards animal welfare.

In time we could stand the howling no longer, and issued an ultimatum. "When she howls in the night, we will come and tell you so you can take care of her—or if you prefer, we will take care of her. So it came about that we acquired a delightful canine companion, on whom we doted. However, she came with strings attached. Early every Sunday morning, M. David would come to collected her to go hunting, and late in the afternoon, he would return her again. Invariably I would enquire about the success of *la chasse,* and each time M. David would reply with a wonderfully mournful, expressive Gallic shrug of the shoulders. The hunting, we discovered, was a social event, participation in which required the possession of a dog for form's sake, and in which little, if any wildlife was harmed.

In time we acquired by default, sole ownership of 'Minou'—also known as 'Little Dog' to distinguish her from 'Bella', a large Golden Labrador with a touch of Rottweiler. There was no question that despite her size, 'Little Dog' was the dominant presence. When 'Bella' flew from California she had to travel in a large cage, and before departure she was given a sedative to ease her anxiety. The check-in line was long, and before Joyce reached the counter, Bella had subsided unconscious onto the floor, and required several airline staff to lift her into her cage.

M. David was a man of habit. Every morning around 6:00 am he would walk the fifty meters to his garage, almost adjacent to our house, and take out his car. At midday he would drive 300 meters across the bridge to eat lunch in a small café, before returning the car to the garage. In time, he became so old and bent that he had to go into a retirement home. When he finally went to meet his maker, we bought his small house, thereby acquiring, after a delay of some fifteen years, ownership of the pigsty yard. Even more important, we acquired his garage, which we had for many years looked at as king Ahab had lusted after Naboth's vinyard. For all its usefullness, it was not waterproof. On the first of June, 2016 the river gods lost control of the Gartempe, which overnight rose some eight feet and flooded the courtyard to within an inch of entering the house. The van parked nearby was filled to the top of the windshield, while within the flooded garage we lost all our garden machinery, and much else besides. We filed an insurance claim that went for many months unanswered because the mayor had failed to declare a natural disaster on the grounds that too few people in the village had been affected. A year and a half later we received some (inadequate) compensation.

## Sixty-Three
# A Taste of India

Not infrequently dinner conversations would drift to India. John, biding his time, would wait until a convenient pause in the flow allowed him to interject a few anecdotes of his own. It transpired that in the sediments of memory, India lay as a thick geological horizon that would periodically reach the surface, to prompt a series of discontinuous recollections. As usual, his approach to the subject was oblique rather than logically direct.

"The dons at many Oxford colleges," John observed one evening, "maintain an exalted standard of living that was the norm for persons of quality during the reign of Queen Victoria, but which has long since vanished elsewhere.

Merton was no exception, and employed a chef of outstanding abilities, amply supported by a magnificent wine cellar. I have no moral grounds for questioning this status quo, for I was for much of my life a beneficiary. My father, who became a Fellow of Merton in 1942, for many years sat on the college wine committee, selflessly tasting the finest vintages as he help lay down bottles for posterity. Maintaining his close association with Merton for the best part of fifty years, he himself eventually became posterity—enjoying with his family the fruits of his earlier labours.

The only voice I ever heard raised against the gastronomic indulgence of senior common rooms was that of Nikko Tinbergen, who had received a Nobel prize with Konrad Lorentz for his pioneering work in Animal

Behaviour. Although a Fellow of Merton, he refused to dine in college on principle, feeling the college resources would be better employed in education."

The Indian sub-continent first came to John's notice because his Aunt Grace, one of his mother's sisters, had lived in what was then Ceylon for many years. Inextricably interwoven with visions created by Kipling's Jungle Book, her life appeared wonderfully exotic.

"I've always harboured a healthy respect for monkeys, regarding their endearingly human appearance as subterfuge to conceal a malevolent and vindictive personality. They positively delight in biting an incautious finger proffering nuts, fruit or other monkey delicacy. The seeds of this opinion sprang from a story of Aunt Grace's experience with a monkey that had allowed her to befriend it. Each day it would come to accept the nutritious gifts that she would carry, the bonds of apparent friendship bringing the two of them into ever-closer proximity. Thus lured into a false sense of security, Aunt Grace allowed her guard to drop, until one day the monkey chose to strike. Without warning it lunged at her and buried its teeth into her cheek. The wounds were deep and extensive. Moreover, they became infected, leaving horrible scars.

As a budding scientist, I was fascinated to learn that Aunt Grace had been subjected to the unusual treatment of radioactive irradiation with radium, in the belief that it might alleviate scarring. To my critical childlike gaze it did not appear that radium had provided much benefit.

Aunt Grace and her husband had returned to England at the outbreak of the second world war and

retired to a small cottage on Dartmoor. Later, they ran a
Dr Barnardo's Home for orphans in the middle of Windsor
Great Park, and it was here that I came to know them at
war's end. Staying with Aunt Grace and Uncle Tom was
a special treat, not least because their only transportation
was a pony and trap, in which we would set out to do
the shopping. Tom had been a Judge in Colombo, and
always seemed a bit distant. However, he won my heart
with cherished gift—a beautiful native dagger—the prize
evidence in a murder trial that had come before him. It
had a strange, romantic aura, a palpable, evocative link
that bound me to the mysterious land of Serendip."

John's association with India was strengthened during his
undergraduate years at Oxford through his passion for Indian
cuisine, and he would often reminisce nostalgically about the
Cobra restaurant.

> "Although the dons may have dined well, undergraduate fare
> offered little incentive to eat in Hall. Besides, my frequently
> crepuscular existence demanded feeding at unorthodox
> times. There were in Oxford in the mid-50s several Indian
> and Chinese restaurants owned by an entrepreneurial free
> spirit named George Halcrow. Married to the daughter
> of best-selling mystery writer Edgar Wallace, George's
> numerous business enterprises were more of a hobby than
> necessary sources of income. His "Cobra" restaurant, deep
> in Oxford's old, as yet unrestored slum district of St. Ebbes,
> became almost a second home, where I would eat virtually
> every day—and sometimes even twice a day."

George Halcrow delighted in the company of a large circle of
undergraduate and post-graduate friends, who would gather

nightly in the back room at the Cobra, which became, in effect, a private club. The restaurant closed officially at 12:30 am, but this had no impact on the denizens of the back room, who would continue talking or playing chess until the small hours. From time to time, George would disappear into the kitchens to create some dish of Indian snacks for his guests.

"The back room attracted a diverse crowd, which often included individuals destined in time to play a role on the world stage; for instance Sadik el-Mahdi, who subsequently became prime Minister of the Sudan. Whenever there was a slight lag in the conversation—which was not often—it took only the most oblique reference to the Black Hole of Calcutta to enliven the evening. Sunil Bahttacharya was convinced that this noteworthy event during the Indian Mutiny had been an atrocity committed by the British on innocent Indians. He could be relied on to maintain this fiction with increasing animation for at least half an hour —and often much longer.

When Ali, the head waiter, presented the bill it was customary to simply sign it. Periodically, generally at intervals of two or three months, one's conscience would begin to prick, until one felt obliged to settle up. George would disappear into the kitchen and reappear with a menacing fistful of signed bills, often splattered with curry stains. Flipping through them, George would say, "That looks like about ten pounds", when in all truth the real total was probably many time this.

One evening the conversation had turned to banking, and I maintained that printed cheques were an unnecessary luxury, and that the banks were bound to honour a properly worded manuscript cheque. To prove my point, I took a partly-used curry-stained paper napkin and wrote George a cheque to cover my (alleged) total. As I had predicted, the bank honoured it."

As the conversation gradually died down and the evening came to a close (often around 4:00 am) George would pile the last of his guests into his Land Rover and drive them back to their 'digs' scattered across the city.

John often voiced his opinion that everybody should drink to excess at least once in his or her life, for nothing is more effective in instilling a desire for moderation. However, he also conceded that for some people once was not sufficient. In his own case, it had taken perhaps three occasions when the room refused to stop rotating before the lesson was fully learned. But there was, he said, one notable occasion when the room should have revolved uncontrollably for hours, but for some reason didn't—at least he had no memory of it doing so!

> "I had volunteered my services to some experimental psychologists who were interested in playing different sound tracks into each ear while the subject was asleep, and recording the resultant brain activity on an electroencephalograph. Following instructions, I did not go to bed the night before and presented myself in a suitably sleep-deprived state the following evening. To induce sleep still further I was given some fast-acting barbiturates and settled down comfortably while the electrodes were attached. When I showed absolutely no signs of sleeping, the dose was repeated—and eventually

a third time. At that point, the investigator's' patience exhausted, I was dismissed and sent home.

"At the time I was living at home. When I returned, my parents were busy clearing up after a small dinner party, and my father enquired whether I might like a small glass of Vintage Port to empty the decanter so he could wash it up. In my semi-drugged state I failed to remember that barbiturates and alcohol don't mix well. In a very short period of time I began to feel the effects, and anxious not to disgrace myself, slipped out of the house to get some coffee at the Cobra. I strode purposefully down the Woodstock Road, but by the time I reached St Giles, I was hopelessly drunk. I have only the faintest recollection of feeling my way along the massive stone abutments of the Ashmolean Museum, and wondering how on earth they had managed to move it so that it completely blocked the open space of St. Giles – and why?

My subsequent route through the city remains shrouded in mystery, but sometime after midnight I appeared at the Cobra. The back room was reached down a short flight of steps, and as I appeared in the open doorway about to descend, I raised my arms to announce my arrival. At that very moment, the chandelier in the centre of the ceiling emitted a brilliant flash and fell to the floor. Ever afterwards I was treated with special respect by Ali, who remained convinced that I possessed supernatural powers. I've often wondered whether he might not be right."

On another occasion, when the subject of alcoholic excess came up in conversation, John repeated the story of Kenny— one that I have heard on several occasions. John and some friends were dining in New York one evening. It was quite a good restaurant, and one of the house traditions was to have a bottle of liqueur on each table, to which diners were invited to help themselves at meals' end.

"One member of the party was an outgoing Korean. Like many people of eastern descent, Kenny had inherited a pronounced sensitivity to alcohol. Before long, he was the life and soul of the party. Having finished the bottle of liqueur on his own table, Kenny began to wander around the restaurant entertaining other diners and consuming whatever liqueurs remained on their tables. At the end of the evening, as we were preparing to head for our respective homes, Kenny confided to me that he couldn't remember where he had parked his car. This I took to be a somewhat ominous sign. Encountering a member of the party the next day I enquired solicitously about Kenny, wondering whether he had made it home all right. Eve looked a little puzzled and questioned why I should be so concerned. As I explained his anxiety about being unable to remember where he had parked, she hesitated a moment before announcing in disbelief: "But Kenny doesn't have a car!"

SUBLIME LUNACY

## Discursus Sixty-Four
# Go East Young Man

John was not a little surprised when Prof. Pringle, head of the Zoology Department at Oxford, announced that he had submitted his name for a scholarship to India, not least because there had been no prior discussion. ,

"It was, he explained, a 'Junior Scientist Exchange program' run by the British Council, and he was anxious that I visit the zoology department at Sri Venkateswara University in Tirupati. The head of the department was an Indian friend of his from Cambridge, an electro-physiologist, and he needed supporting. In addition, I was to keep an eye out for young researchers worthy of a scholarship to work in Britain. In short, I was being recruited for academic espionage!

When asked by the British Council whether I had any other particular institutions I wanted to visit, I replied that I corresponded with scientists in several parts of India, and would welcome the opportunity of visiting any of them. To my delight—and considerable surprise—I was given the opportunity to travel widely in both North and South India. Even better, my request to travel by train rather than plane, was agreed to."

In Chandigarh, the Punjabi city designed by Le Corbusier, the zoology department was focused on microscopy, and was well-equipped to section and stain specimens. Somehow, the department had managed to acquire an electron microscope. Sadly, though, it contributed nothing but prestige. The electricity supply proved far too erratic and uncertain for its operation. Likewise, an expensive Zeiss photomicroscope, its objective lenses sticking out like the arms of a Hindu deity, remained locked away unused. In this case, the department did not have sufficient funds to cover the cost of film, paper and processing materials.

"My principal destination was, of course, Tirupati. Here too, there was a very fine photomicroscope—a Leitz, as I recall. It too was on prominent view, greeted frequently with "*namaste*"by those who passed by. Like its counterpart in Chandigarh, this instrument also remained unused—albeit for different reasons. In Tirupati it was feared that if it were to be used, it might get broken, and hence be unusable. For this reason it was not used.

Sri Venkateshwara University is located in Tirupati, a bit north of Madras (Chenai). The site of a particularly holy temple, it is automatically assumed that everyone arriving in town must be a pilgrim, and hence liable for a pilgrim tax. If it were possible to buy stock in the temple business, this is where I would invest.

The temple is located high in the hills, and could originally be reached only by a particularly arduous seven-mile hike. Each of the thousands of granite steps are covered in carved inscriptions. Recognising that many pilgrims, and particularly those old enough to have accumulated some wealth, were also infirm, the temple authorities called in a Swedish civil engineering company, who constructed what must be the finest road in India, an impressive series of switchbacks, which serves a fleet of buses that carry thousands of pilgrims daily. For the wealthy there are cool, comfortable bungalows close to the temple, for the longer one can stay, the more ceremonies one can arrange and pay for. At the entrance to the temple, guarded by fierce men with swords and spears, hangs a huge *hundi,* a container into which the faithful fling money. How much money? Well the temple not only funds the university, but a host of hospitals, schools and other institutions around India. It is said that there are never less than fifty-thousand pilgrims on any day of the year, and often many times this.

Two episodes in the Tirupati experience remain particularly vivid. I had been out doing fieldwork in the hot sun for several hours, and returned to my bungalow exhausted and caked in grime—a combination of sweat and dust. I was surprised to find an agitated graduate student waiting for me. Nobody had thought to tell me that the university had arranged a formal reception for me, and that even now the vice-chancellor and assembled faculty heads were anxiously awaiting my arrival. With no time to wash or change, I was rushed to greet the assembled dignitaries, all clad in their academic finery. As if that were not bad enough, I was then told that I was expected to deliver an address—and for Indians, to whom speaking comes easily, it should not be brief. Seldom have I wanted more earnestly, for the ground to open up and swallow me.

After leaving Tirupati, I took the train to Bombay, a journey of some 48 hours. I was not feeling well when I left, and as the journey progressed it became clear that I was going down with Dengue or Breakbone Fever. In Bombay I was almost unable to walk, but by a happy stroke of luck had on this occasion acceded to the British Council's

wish to put me up in a good hotel. Lying helpless in bed
awaiting the arrival of a doctor, my room suddenly filled
with steam. The hot water geyser had gone berserk and
created an overheated sauna. I was, with great difficulty,
just able to reach the bedside phone and call the front desk
for immediate help before passing out.

It turned out, once back in England, where I
was rushed to hospital, that in addition to Dengue, I also
had Chikungunya Fever and Hepatitis. The source of the
latter I had no doubts about. Returning unexpectedly early
to my bungalow in Tirupati one day, I found the cook's
young assistant chopping vegetables for my salad on the
concrete floor of the toilet – a simple hole in the floor."

John's Indian sojourn provided him with many stories. He
was, for example, highly taken by the Indian railway service,
which allowed for five different classes of travel, of which
'Air Conditioned' was the top. The individual compartments,
unconnected by any corridor, would become one's universe for
the journey—and no train journey in India lasts less than 24
hours, regardless of distance. Thanks to the British Raj, India
is united by widespread use of English (often spoken with far
greater skill and artistry than one finds in England) and so
one is able to enjoy long, often fascinating, conversations with
one's fellow travellers. However, each compartment carries a
prominent sign warning against accepting any refreshments
from strangers in case they might be drugged. John's greatest
enthusiasm, however, was reserved for the catering service.

"At the appropriate moment the train stops at a station and
waiters come on board, visiting each compartment in turn

to take orders. Experience has shown that the vegetarian meals served in South India are much superior to the non-vegetarian ones. Once the orders have been taken, the train continues on its way. Meanwhile the orders are being telegraphed ahead to the next stop. On arrival, the train is overrun by swarms of small boys delivering everybody's meals. Under way once more, the meal is consumed at leisure as the endlessly fascinating countryside drifts by. Later, at another stop, an army of small boys again swarms through the train to gather up the dirty dishes. It is a masterly demonstration of organisation, all the more striking amid the chaos and confusion that is India."

## Discursus Sixty-Five
# Famous and Not-so-Famous

I n the course of his life, John has crossed paths with many
kinds and conditions of men. Graced thus with a goodly
cross-section of society, he has no hesitation in voicing
sweeping, outlandish opinions. 'I can't help it," he says, "if
people live up to their racial stereotypes. Don't overlook
the fact that the best Jewish jokes are always told by Jews."
Adding as a provocative afterthought: "But of course there are
no Polish or Irish jokes—they're all true!"

'The current preoccupation with political correctness I
cannot but view with mild amusement and a touch of
disdain. I have no objection to being the butt of jokes—
particularly if they are good jokes, or they effectively
penetrate my armour of conceit. I have little patience with
the thin-skinned whose inability to laugh at themselves
reflects not only no sense of humour, but also a chronic
lack of self-esteem.

The pendulum of political correctness, regardless
of its merits, has a tendency to swing too far. Thus
praiseworthy intentions often overstep the bounds of
reason and expose themselves to ridicule."

"Gender equality," John has observed, "is both
admirable and desirable. However, I am in no doubt
that the feminist movement did itself a disfavour when
it started to fiddle with the English language. Words
that had graced our common vocabulary for centuries
without trace of gender bias suddenly became targets for

graceless reform, replaced by jarring neologisms. To insist that mankind, for centuries a word quietly connoting the whole human family without hint of race or gender, be replaced by personkind is no less absurd than insisting on personhole covers or the island of Personhatten, which are personifestly ridiculous. In the rare situations where gender assumes a significant role in the meaning of a sentence one can always fall back on such cumbersome forms as Lady doctor, or Male nurse. The English language is so rich and convoluted that devices of this kind are usually unnecessary."

Although John has rubbed shoulders with the rich and famous from time to time, he does not seek out their company. There are, of course, notable exceptions, but he is quick to proclaim his admiration for the under-privileged.

"It is amongst those who have the least in terms of material possessions, that one encounters the greatest generosity. It is embarrassing to be the recipient of gifts from those one knows cannot afford to give without significant sacrifice, yet to refuse would be far more wounding. I have witnessed such selflessness in many communities—among peasants in Mexico, nomadic tribesmen in the Sudan and North Africa, in the slums of Calcutta, in the mountains of Bali, and in the now-vanished slums of Oxford.

In my student days, many of the best rock climbers came from working-class families in the British Midlands, and it was a tribute to my parents that they would welcome such friends when I invited them to stay. When you put your life in the hands of a climbing partner, you want someone solidly reliable. The superficial façade of respectability counts for nothing when your very survival is at stake. It is confirmation of the views voiced by Vladimir Peniakoff in 'Popski's Private Army'. A classic account of daring missions behind the German lines in the North African deserts, Col. Peniakoff had no hesitation in choosing working class companions, on whom he could rely in a crisis, over the more effete upper-class officers seeking to join his units."

John's upbringing and travels have made him equally at home in the company of peasants and patricians. In both, he admits, one has to be selective—but it is easier among the former. He makes a distinction between the Idle Rich and the Incidentally Rich, who work for pleasure without the need for profit. It is amongst the latter that John has formed several lasting friendships.

"Adrian and I first met at Merton, where we were both members of the Myrmidons, the college dining club. Our friendship grew after I was invited to dinner with the family—just an informal event one Sunday evening, " but by the way, Black Tie."

Dinner was seven for seven-thirty, which I discovered meant arriving at the lodge gates soon after 7:00. It would be close to 7:30 by the time one had driven through the park and reached the house. A beautifully proportioned Georgian pile, built onto the remains of an old Cistercian Abbey, Thame Park had a magnificent double staircase extending up to a formal entrance on the upper level. Just as we were wondering whether to mount the stairs, a less pretentious doorway at ground level was opened by a footman in livery. Invited inside, we were relieved not to have made the wrong decision. Mounting past suits of armour, we were eventually shown into a big room lined entirely with large views of Venice by Canaletto. Here we were to await the family—an opportunity to examine and enjoy the pictures that was to be repeated on many subsequent occasions.

Being an informal supper with the family, we were served by only three servants (in livery)—and on the second-best silver dinner service. We could not have been more welcome or placed more at ease. The only embarrassment came when her ladyship spoke with obvious pride and delight of her collection of amber. We were invited to admire several pieces, noteworthy for their inclusions. The study of insects and spiders trapped some 40,000 years ago, when the amber was still liquid pine sap, is a legitimate area of scientific study, and I was happy to examine such an admirable collection. Then came the *pieces de resistances* in her collection. A number of enormous lumps of some clear plastic material in which were embedded frogs and snakes, so manifestly pickled and set out as rather poor museum specimens, as to be embarrassing. These creatures had not struggled to escape some Oligocene entrapment, but had obligingly extended their limbs, and neatly coiled their bodies while being preserved in formalin.

It called for every ounce of diplomatic *sang froid* to avoid bursting her ladyship's bubble, and find words expressing pleasure at having been vouchsafed the honour of seeing them, but without in any way hinting that she had been the victim of an obvious fraud—and doubtless at considerable expense."

At a time when Shell Petroleum was promoting their product with the slogan "Put a tiger in your tank" there was a craze for having large tiger dolls lying across the rear windowsill of cars. Adrian and his family went one better. They used to drive around with a live Cheetah. John had many stories to tell of them—for instance the construction of a private racecourse around the park in which Adrian's custom Ferrari could speed unimpeded. Adrian's younger brother inherited his father's interest in militaria. In some manner never explained he acquired a pair of enormous cannons from a defunct battleship—perhaps 16 inch or even greater calibre. During the troubled years of Labour government the entire mounting sat in the park, aimed directly at Downing Street. Today, they grace the entrance to the Imperial War Museum in London. However, there was one family occasion at Thame Park that eclipsed all others.

"Sir Frank was a renowned collector and authority on Japanese arms and armour, and had Japanese connections at the highest level. One day his dinner guests included junior members of the Japanese royal family—in all probability the late emperor—and we were invited along to help balance out the "younger set". This was a dinner worthy of royalty. We ate off the gold dinner service, drank the finest wines that money could buy, and were waited on by seven liveried servants. It was a memorable evening! But it subsequently became an evening of acute embarrassment. After dinner, Sir Frank issued his usual invitation for the assembled company to visit the armoury.

Sir Frank's superb collection of Japanese swords and other militaria occupied the chapel of the old monastery, and was always a delight to see. On this occasion, however, delight turned to dismay. As each outstanding blade or display of sword furniture was viewed by the royal party, his Royal Highness would comment: " Oh yes, that came from our collection", or "that belonged to our family." We were looking at the cream of the Imperial armoury, a major display of sacred historic heirlooms, abducted, stolen or looted after the war, an unparalleled assemblage of national treasures. It was embarrassing beyond description.

I am happy to say, however, that in due course the cream of Sir Frank's collection was eventually gifted back to Japan—some slight compensation for that painful evening."

During the war, Thame Park, like so many other great houses, was taken over by the military. At war's end when the family returned to take up residence, they found the house had suffered considerable damage through theft and neglect. John tells of meeting the attorney responsible for negotiating with the government for reparations.

"He told of the protracted discussions needed to convince the authorities that the taps and other bathroom fittings that had disappeared during the war were indeed of solid gold—and not merely gold plated."

# Discursus Sixty-Six
## Peak Pictures

I once asked John, which of his photographic images bore the greatest significance for him. It was, he replied, a difficult question to answer because it all depended upon which criteria were to be used to make such a determination. Some images bore deep personal significance because of the place, person or event with which he associated it. Others, because of the technical difficulties involved in capturing it. In this regard, he observed:

> "If your intention is to produce a marketable image, the problems associated with getting it are an irrelevance. If it is not well-framed, well focused and well-exposed, it is worthless. The fact that the photographer sat for thirty-six disagreeable hours in a wet ditch threatened by all manner of noxious insects and venomous reptiles carries no weight in determining if it will sell."

Likewise, an image that is damaged has little chance of being sold. John lamented the loss of one irreplaceable subject that still continues to grieve him after many years.

> "I was down in Big Bend National Park in Texas shooting a program on roadrunners. It was after nightfall, when any self-respecting roadrunner should have returned to its nocturnal resting place—perhaps a protected hollow in the middle of a spiny Lechuguilla plant. There was a brilliant full moon just starting to appear over a low cliff some short distance away. To my surprise a roadrunner appeared on the skyline and stood still. I positioned myself so the

roadrunner was silhouetted against the full moon, set my 35mm camera on the tripod and in greatest excitement put on a 500mm lens. The moon and roadrunner filled the screen and I managed to get off half a dozen frames before the bird moved off. When the film came back from the processing labs every frame had been ruined, with deep scratches that suggested the film had been allowed to fall on the floor and been walked over. Today, I would summon the magic of PhotoShop, and pixel by pixel remove the blemishes, but in those days there was no alternative to committing the whole roll of film to the bin. Invariably, such accidents always seem to happen to one's most valuable pictures.

An image that retains special significance is one of a shield bug warming up its wings before taking flight—a shot that was reproduced in the Time-Life Photography series Nature volume. I had been invited to help teach a photography field course in the Everglades with a distinguished wildlife photographer who shall remain nameless. One evening, over a post-prandial glass of wine she confided to me that I had saved her life—something I was totally unaware of. She went on to explain that before becoming a photographer, she had been overcome by a deep depression and was on the verge of committing suicide, when she chanced to come across this image. It was, she said, such a revelation to realize just how wonderful the natural world can be that she changed her mind and determined to learn more about it. I cannot but wonder how many other photographic images have contributed to saving a life so directly"

Once the seed of Big Bend had been planted in his mind, it began to grow, and soon started to unleash further reminiscences. Named for the great loop of the Rio Grande in Texas as it marks the border between Mexico and the United States, it is the largest, most remote (and least visited) of all the American National Parks. The whole of the rugged Chisos range of mountains lies within the park boundaries.

"Big Bend I had first visited with the family when driving to Arizona from New York, en route to the Natural History Museum's Southwestern Research Station in the Chiricahua Mountains. The memory remains deeply embedded because of a cactus spine that had penetrated my calf during a moment of carelessness while taking a picture. Over the next couple of years it would move slowly around my leg before finally disappearing.

Many years later, while filming tarantula behaviour at the Southwestern Research Station in Arizona, I chanced to meet Martha Whitson, who was studying roadrunner biology. Inspired by what she told me, I suggested roadrunners as a possible film subject for television, and was delighted when Survival Anglia, the British TV company, took to the idea. On Martha's advice, Big Bend appeared the most suitable filming location. Two or three events stand out in my memory.

Roadrunners are not easy to approach, but if one can find where they spend the night and are in position when they start to warm up in the first rays of the sun, exposing their in-built solar panel—a patch of dark skin on the back—one can follow them as they forage for insects. This was made much easier by playing recordings of their calls, kindly provided by Martha. It was possible to walk only a few feet away from the bird, and if one lost it in a dense patch of vegetation, playing the right call would quickly re-establish contact. One day as we were tracking together, we came over the crest of a low ridge, the roadrunner leading. On the far side was a Bobcat, who took off in surprise, while the roadrunner launched into a 100-yard level flight —the only time I've ever seen the species in powered flight."

It was around the public campgrounds that Roadrunners were most abundant, and it was here that John hoped to film the courtship behaviour, in which the male entices the female with the gift of a snake or lizard. It took a lot of patient observation to locate a filmable nest with a potentially receptive female on it. Eventually, a suitable site was found.

"After hours of patient waiting, a male roadrunner came into view bearing a gift. Just as the female was preparing to leave the nest to greet him, my camera viewfinder went dark. Lifting my head, I found an elderly couple had stepped in between me and my subject, and were trying to engage me in conversation about hummingbirds. They seemed deaf to my entreaties to move away, and I missed the climax of the sequence. Seldom have I been so tempted to commit geriatricide. At the time I felt it nigh impossible to witness another courtship, but being better prepared in knowing what to look for, I actually observed it several times subsequently and got what I needed on film.

One of the sequences required for the program was a parent bird feeding the young—bringing in snakes for them to eat. The most accessible nests were in one of

the public campgrounds, and I had set up the camera on
an ideally situated nest. Through the camera I could see a
parent bird coming in with several small snakes, which the
young consumed voraciously. Something about the scene
did not seem right, and so I looked again more closely.
They were not small snakes that were being brought to the
young, but a tangle of discarded spaghetti, collected from
the adjacent campsite."

In those distant, happy days there was far less concern about
illegal border crossings. John would often go down to the hot
springs, and not infrequently wade across the Rio Grande for
an evening in the Mexican village of Boquillas. More often
the journey would end at the hot springs.

"Often I would be there alone, having braved a path that
was alive with rattlesnakes, invisible in the darkness, but
making their presence known by their disquieting rattle.
The hot springs had been developed in the early 1900s as
a health resort, but the river eventually swept away the
buildings, leaving only the bathhouse foundations, which
created a pool some three feet deep. In theory one should
not have been there, but the not infrequent presence of
off-duty park rangers showed that the prohibition was
largely theoretical. On some evenings small groups would
come down with beer and, wrapped in a pleasant haze of
marijuana smoke, enjoy a relaxing evening naked under
the stars. From time to time, when the heat of the water
became too intense, all that was needed was a quick jump
over the low wall and into the river to cool off—followed
by a return to the inviting ambience of the spring."

During John's Roadrunner stay in Big Bend, he had had the good fortune to meet some Parks Service personnel from headquarters in Harper's Ferry, Virginia, who were anxious to produce a film about the park for the visitor's centre. It was not long before they approached John to enquire whether he could return the following year to make the film. A contract was arranged with OSF, and the next spring John moved into an empty cabin—an old ranch house from pre-park days—with total freedom to roam the park in search of suitable subjects—a wonderful opportunity to explore a region of boundless interest.

"There were many high points, ranging from the sublime to the ridiculous. A keen historian, I was delighted to discover the first vehicle inspection pit in America. This was built by the military during their campaign against Pancho Villa in the second decade of the last century—the only time the US mainland has been invaded. More rewarding was a rafting trip through the Santa Elena Canyon, where the US and Mexico are barely twenty feet apart in places. We explored a chamber formed from a fallen slab of rock, that had served as someone's home for several years—until the discovery of a floating human body had scared him into leaving, never to return.

Sequences of spadefoot toads burying themselves until roused to surface again in response to rain, tarantula courtship, spider-hunting wasps—the filming opportunities were legion and the scenery magnificent. The only blot on the expedition was a failure by the US Park Service to honour their commitment to report back on the

---

rushes. Once the film had been dispatched for processing, nothing was heard regarding its content and condition— no possible advance warning of equipment malfunction or other defects. Indeed, I never even had an opportunity to view the final, edited film, although I am sure I would have heard had outcome not been satisfactory."

## Discursus Sixty-Seven
# Low life in High Places

John asked his guests one evening "what do you know about Grylloblatids," I watched with some amusement, the blank expressions on everyone's face as they confessed their total ignorance. It was a question that only a trained entomologist might have been expected to answer with confidence. I recognised immediately where the conversation was headed. John went on to explain that the insects are divided into thirty-two major groups or Orders—such familiar ones as beetle, flies, butterflies & moths and bees, ants & wasps, together with some less familiar ones such as silverfish and booklice. The Grylloblatids are quite the rarest and least seldom encountered of all the orders.

"Few people have ever seen Grylloblatids in the wild (or even in museum collections). This is because they are only active at night on snowfields above 10,000 feet in a few mountain ranges in Russia, Japan, Korea and the United States—a habitat that receives few observant visitors. Not only are they the rarest group of insects, but despite living in such inhospitable, challenging surroundings, they also have the lowest range of temperature tolerance—surviving only in an environment just a few degrees above and below freezing.

I had happened to meet John Edwards, a biologist in Seattle, while on assignments filming spiders—whereby hangs another tale. He was doing research on Grylloblatids, and persuaded me to propose an article on them for

National Geographic Magazine. My proposed title proved irresistible—Low life in High Places—and so the following summer I found myself on assignment on Mount Rainier."
For John, wandering about on giant snowfields alone in the moonlight proved to be a blissful enterprise, and one that he ranks highly among his top experiences, and one that he delights in sharing with anyone who will listen.

"An immediate question that springs to people's minds is "How do animals survive in such bleak and seemingly inhospitable environments?" The short answer is 'aerial plankton'—a term unfamiliar to most listeners. Large numbers of small insects and spiders get carried upwards on rising air currents, often travelling considerable distances by this means. Those unfortunate enough to be wafted over mountain ranges may find themselves deposited on rocks and snow as the air cools at dusk, and few will survive long once landed. Thus there accumulates on the snow a substantial deposit of deep-frozen insect protein.

Now nature abhors waste, so it is not surprising to learn that such an abundance of nourishment does not go unused. During daylight hours several bird species forage for appetising morsels, selecting the larger, more conspicuous corpses. After night falls, a whole new community of foragers takes over, including specialized beetles and harvestmen. However, the dominant members of this nocturnal guild are Grylloblatids, which prove to be quite abundant. During the day they remain hidden in the narrow gap that exists between rock and snow. Here they must move constantly to keep within the extremely narrow range of temperatures that they can tolerate."

Grylloblatids are not the only surprises awaiting the enterprising biologist who ventures onto Mount Rainier's snows. From time to time mountaineers in Alaska and the Cascades have reported in amazement that occasionally they encounter areas where the snow takes on a pinkish hue. If one pauses to examine the phenomenon closely it turns out the colour is caused by the presence of huge numbers of tiny transparent annelid worms belonging to the genus *Mesenchytraeus*. Found only in western North America, Ice Worms feed on wind-blown pollen grains and red algae, which gives them colour when concentrated in the gut.

When asked about publication, John shakes his head sadly and says that the article never appeared. The official reason given by the editors was that National Geographic had commissioned too many natural history articles and was abandoning those that could not be published within the time constraints set by their contracts. Privately, John reluctantly concedes that neither Ice Worms nor Grylloblatids have the visual appeal needed to hold a mass audience. Nevertheless, on a personal level he is grateful for the opportunity they provided to experience Rainier's mountain environment for a couple of months.

John's base for his nocturnal explorations of Mount Rainier's snowfields was a hut at about 10,000 feet, frequented by the many climbers bound for the summit—a further 4500 feet higher up. It was inevitable that he would eventually be unable to resist the lure of the mountain. It is not a very challenging climb if one is fit, the main danger being ice falls as the temperature rises during the day. This means making an early, very early, start in order to descend before the risk increases too much. "As dawn broke we found ourselves on a steep, narrow ridge, which gave an exhilarating sense of exposure. A woman in the party, seeing the world spread out beneath her between her legs, had a sudden panic attack and was unable to continue. John, knowing that he would be able to make the climb another day, volunteered to remain with her and help an off-duty Park Ranger in the group lower her to safety while the others went on. Gripped by paralysing fear, it became a difficult task to persuade her to make any movement, so it was a slow, painful descent. Once off the ridge it became easier and they were able to collect another, earlier casualty, who had been overcome by exhaustion brought on by altitude sickness and who had decided to bivouac by the trailside.

"To my great regret, I never did find time to make another summit trip. I had particularly wanted to see the ice caves created by volcanic fumaroles. My interest had been aroused by reading about them when they provided shelter to two men who had inadvertently crashed a light aircraft on the summit. Clad in ordinary street clothing, they could not have survived long without such shelter. Not surprisingly, they paid a heavy price for their folly. Not only did they suffer both steam burns and frostbite, but they also incurred the substantial cost of removing the remains of their plane—it being forbidden to leave litter in a National Park."

This was not the last of John's adventures in the Cascades Range. It had been some years since Mount Saint Helens had erupted in May 1980, and John was invited to join a research team studying the return of wildlife to the mountain. This was at a time when it was still closed to visitors, and would be a unique opportunity to see at first hand just how extensive the damage had been.

"There were many points of interest. Trees, both fallen and standing, had been sand-blasted by the force of the eruption, leaving bark only on the downhill side, the other smooth and often lightly burnt. Flattened trees, all lying parallel to one another, and Spirit Lake, such as remained, clogged with fallen timber. However, one of my strongest memories of this memorable occasion had nothing to do with the eruption. Those accustomed to living and working in the mountains generally carry the minimum weight possible, sometimes going to extremes to economise—I've even met people who as a matter of course, cut off the margins of their maps to save weight. One of the graduate students in our party, who spent much of his time in the mountains amazed me when he produced a heavy, old-fashioned cast-iron coffee grinder from his pack. A coffee addict, he allowed nothing to compromise his morning brew. I was thankful I hadn't mocked him earlier when he shared one of the tastiest pots of coffee at first light high on the flanks of Mount Saint Helens. He clearly knew where his priorities lay".

After a few days on Mount Saint Helens, John returned to his assignment on Mount Rainier, where he became involved photographing a conservation project the Parks Service had initiated. With some ten thousand people each summer seeking to make a summit attempt, almost all of whom needed to spend a night at the Camp Muir hut, human waste disposal becomes a major concern. Few people realize how persistent are the organisms that inhabit the human gut, when deposited in snow. They can persist for years, gradually infecting the melt-water with *Giardia* and other noxious parasites so sanitation at the hut was of great importance. The toilets were designed so that the contents could be carried down by helicopter, but this was far from ideal. Not only did helicopters destroy the tranquillity of the mountain, they were not a reliable disposal method, as became apparent when a load of waste was accidentally dropped, polluting a huge tract of snow. The solution, it was decided, should be a new solar-powered toilet, that would reduce the waste to a dry, easily transported powder.

"I was invited to record the installation of this new facility, from its pre-construction at lower altitude, to its completion at Camp Muir. A vital step in this Eco-friendly project was removal of the dry residue, and rather than helicopters, it was decided to use llamas. Alexander and Einstein were government employees, who could each carry 50 lb. loads. Strong-willed, they would only work at their chosen pace, best described as a slow walk.

The prefabricated solar toilets were carried up to Camp Muir by helicopter in a series of flights. The work crew to assemble and install them were obliged to hike up to the job site, but I was given the privilege of traveling by helicopter. The pilot was a very experienced Vietnam veteran, with whom I had flown on several previous occasions, and in whom I had great faith. He found routine chauffeuring very dull after the excitements of war, and at days end would sometimes try to recapture the thrill of earlier years. On several occasions I was permitted to travel outside the plane, riding on the skids for a better view while photographing, as the pilot would break free and fly at low altitude while weaving along canyons and gullies at high speed, providing a welcome adrenaline rush.

I had just been deposited at Camp Muir, along with some toilet parts, and the helicopter took off to pick up another load. I watched it but before it had risen a hundred feet off the ground, there was a terrible bang as the tail rotor shattered and the aircraft started to spin and fall. With my finger on the camera motor drive, I recorded the whole descent, which ended in a terrible crash before my eyes just a few feet away. The pilot and co-pilot survived, with a broken back and other injuries, and had needed first-aid until a large military helicopter capable of operating at altitude, could be alerted to fly up and take them to hospital. I did not remain on Mt. Rainier long enough to christen the solar toilet installation, but have no doubt that it has since given great satisfaction to many mountaineers—and continuing employment to Alexander and Einstein."

## Discursus Sixty-Eight
# Natural and Supernatural

J ohn has always observed a healthy scepticism about the supernatural, preferring instead what he calls "the infinite delights of the natural world." Such scepticism is hardly surprising in view of his impatience with what he regards as the manifest absurdity of most theological discourse—even when expressed in the beautiful language of the King James Bible. Wishing not to appear discourteous in company, he is reluctant to participate actively in discussions where people recount their own out-of-body experiences, encounters with ghosts and other supernatural phenomena. However, when challenged specifically, he will sometimes submit and recount his own story.

"I have often mentioned my close friend George Lampel. We had become firm companions at school, sharing a common interest in natural history; and much else beside. Following a two-year interlude for National Service, in which George served in the RAF and I in the Royal Navy, we renewed our companionship at Oxford, George reading physics and I zoology. Having successfully foiled the examiners in our respective disciplines, we both embarked on post-graduate work for the degree of D.Phil. While my choice was simple, George's diverse interests posed a dilemma—biology or physics? The question was resolved by examining the options through a single, simple financial lens. Natural History involves little capital outlay, whereas low-temperature physics research necessitates a lot of expensive laboratory facilities. Better, therefore, to be a professional physicist, with Natural History as a hobby rather than be a professional biologist and dabble in low-temperature physics as a hobby."

George's chosen area of research was the arcane subject of "Flow and turbulence in liquid Helium-3", but in the summer of 1961 the university's Helium liquefiers, on which his research depended, were shut down for servicing, and so during the Long Vacation George decided to head off on a Natural History excursion, as he not infrequently did. On this occasion his chosen venue was Iran.

"It was the end of the long vacation, and Oxford was stirring in preparation for the new academic year. I had dreamed a particularly vivid and disturbing dream about George, in which he had been killed, and in my dream I was obliged to go through his belongings to eliminate items that might have proved distressing to his mother. These included several handguns and a substantial pornographic library. It was a complex dream and unusual in that it remained to haunt me long after I had awakened. Knowing that George was due back in Oxford about that time, a couple of days after my dream I wandered over to his lab to get a report on his travels. I was met by doleful expressions, and someone said, "Hadn't you heard? George was killed in a car crash in Iran a couple of days ago."

Almost at once my dream returned—but this time it was for real. I received a call from George's mother, announcing her imminent arrival in Oxford and I found myself re-living in the most minute detail each scene that had figured in my dream."

John dismisses any supernatural agency underlying this event, preferring a more mundane explanation, triggered by a vivid imagination and subconscious concern that George was late in returning. Once the seed of disaster had been sown, the dream followed a completely logical path—as subsequent events demonstrated when repeated in real life. John never ceases to marvel at the readiness with which listeners to the tale prefer to favour a supernatural explanation involving messages from beyond the grave.

As a postscript, John reports that years later, while filming in Iran, he set out to find George's grave so that he could take back photographs for his mother and sister. After making himself a nuisance at the British embassy, convinced that they alone would know its whereabouts, he finally discovered that the graveyard no longer existed, having been taken over for development some years before.

On another occasion when talk of the supernatural surfaced in a social gathering, John was pressured into telling of an event in which the religiously superstitious were all too ready to see the Almighty's hand.

"We were attending the Christening of the new-born son of an old Oxford friend in the parish church at Wytham. It was a big family event, with some imposing elderly aristocratic relatives in attendance, and it was hardly a stress-free afternoon.

By an unhappy coincidence, as the officiating cleric reached the point in the service when the godparents are called upon to renounce the devil and all his works, poor Oliver experienced some sort of seizure, emitting a penetrating scream before falling back unconscious onto the pew, his eyes rolled back out of sight. Sitting in the pew behind, I had an uncomfortably clear view of events. To me it was clear that Oliver, who was recovering from a nasty attack of testicular cancer, and was still very frail, had simply been overcome by the strain of the festivities—but nevertheless, it was an unnerving experience."

Reference to Oliver Impey triggered several reminiscences, for he was a contemporary of John's at Merton, where he had also read zoology. A man of diverse interests and well-developed aesthetic tastes, towards the end of his graduate work at Oxford, he got employment in the furniture department at Sotheby's. He would travel by train to London each day, and apparently drove his fellow first-class passengers to the brink of apoplexy by dictating his thesis on "The form and function of the jaw-suspension of Varanid lizards".

Oliver was apparently sanguine about the ire he generated, happily pointing out that there was no restriction on conversation in first class carriages, and that it was neither here nor there that his conversation just happened to be wholly one-sided.

"In time Oliver became Keeper of Oriental Art at the Ashmolean Museum. He was delighted when I loaned the museum a samurai sword attributed to the 13th Century master swordsmith Masamune, and gave it pride of place in his new exhibition. His special field of expertise was early Japanese porcelain, and he was able to identify the works of master potters by the faint fingerprints, barely visible, left on their work—a truly esoteric speciality."

It was one evening when the conversation had once again turned to the supernatural that somebody asked John about his encounter with Big Foot, an event that he was unusually reluctant to describe until pressured.

"We were spending the summer *en famille* at the Southwest Research Station in Portal, and had gone out one evening 'roadruning'. This was a regular event, cruising the roads after dark in search of spiders, snakes and other wildlife. Driving slowly up Cave Creek Canyon, we rounded a corner to find ourselves facing a large bipedal creature that fitted the popular image of 'Bigfoot'. Witnessed by two adults and three children, there was unanimous consensus on what had been seen so clearly visible in the headlights— approximately eight feet tall, dark and covered in fur, with a slight greenish tinge. It immediately lumbered off into the shadowy undergrowth, dropping down into a dry stream bed. I at once leaped from the car to follow, but was unable to see where it had gone.

Once back at the station it was agreed that we would not mention what we had seen, for reporting a mythical creature in such scientific company would have invited ridicule and reflected badly on my professional reputation. However, over the next two weeks rumours began to circulate, and it became apparent that our experience was not unique. Campers on a nearby side canyon had reported about the same time a similar sighting to the local Ranger Station, and slowly it emerged that several scientist at the Station had also seen something—but like ourselves, were reluctant to jeopardise their reputations by talking about it."

As the hesitant witnesses gathered to discuss what they had seen, several possible explanations were put forward. Although there was a suppressed wish that it truly was a 'Bigfoot', the notion received little public support. Someone suggested that it might have been a practical joker among their colleagues, who had ventured out dressed in an animal costume. The idea was soon dismissed on the grounds that it would have been the height of lunacy to do such a foolish thing in an area where so many people carried firearms. It was finally agreed that most probably what we had all seen was a very large bear that had briefly wandered down from the mountains. It is well known that bear fur sometimes carries a coating of lichen that can impart a greenish tinge. Suffice it to say that no further sightings have been reported to the rangers in the years since. Nevertheless, John in private still wonders whether there might have been more to the story than just a large, bipedal bear. He secretly wishes there was.

Many years later, when John and Joyce were living at their Sierra sanctuary in Dutch Flat, they had several encounters with bears. On one occasion Joyce opened the front door and inadvertently touched the big bear on the other side, who was feeding on food left out for the cat. It is not known who moved fastest, Joyce or the bear?

On another occasion, a bear became trapped in the laundry room one night, causing bedlam. Opening the door a crack, it appeared that it was huge. Eventually it turned out, it was only a baby bear—standing tall on the washing machine.

# Discursus Sixty-Nine
## Webs of Intrigue

As a recognised authority on spiders, John would from time to time, be called upon for professional advice. Most often there would be questions about spiders and venom, concerning which the general public harbours many false convictions, both in Britain and in the United States. Given that some spiders do indeed possess a poisonous bite, curiosity and concern are not unreasonable, but John has little patience with people who declare with absolute certainty that they (or their aunt, friend or close acquaintance) has been bitten by a spider, the alleged culprit frequently being identified as a 'Brown Recluse' across the Atlantic, or a 'False Black Widow' in Britain.

"Did you witness the spider biting, and if so, who identified culprit?" John always asks.
"Well, I didn't actually see it bite—but the doctor assured me it was a poisonous spider." To which the proper response is "Rubbish!" John challenges any physician to correctly distinguish a spider bite from that of a host of possible biting insects, let alone correctly identify which species might be responsible.

Doctors all too frequently revel in being thought to be the guardians of profound ancient wisdom, and are very reluctant ever to admit ignorance, even though identifying any one of the more than 600 spider species inhabiting the United Kingdom is an arcane skill that few possess. No, the determination that a spider was responsible is a convenient way to silence an insistent patient and maintain the monopoly on wisdom.

> "With a few notable exceptions, such *Hyptiotes*, all spiders possess "poison glands". Their secretions may help quell a victim's struggles, but their principle role is to reduce the victim's tissues to a liquefied soup-like consistency. Spiders digest their prey externally and only imbibe the resultant fluid. I have been bitten by many spiders, including *Phoneutria fera*, a Brazilian species renowned for its aggression and toxicity. Although several species of British spider can deliver a painful bite when antagonised, the pain is very largely due to physical trauma rather than any chemical substance injected. Few things so infuriate me as the wildly exaggerated, unsubstantiated reports in the news media of hysterical attention-seekers claiming to be victims of horrendous spider bites. From time to time people collect spiders that are supposed to substantiate their claims—not the actual biting spider, but other ones found around the house or garden. In every case that I have seen, they prove to be widespread, common, utterly harmless species. The news media thrive on exaggeration."

Spider stories always catch public attention and make a regular appearance when local news is in short supply. It is also a seasonal phenomenon, peaking in the autumn, for this is the time of year when many species reach maturity and are at their maximum size. Who has not seen a large *Tegenaria* unfortunately trapped in the bathtub? These are spiders that usually live on a sheet-like web, but leave it to search for mates when they mature. It may also be that as the weather becomes cooler, spiders seek protection from the elements and come indoors. As web-dwellers, some species lack the adhesive pads that allow more peripatetic spiders to climb smooth surfaces. Attracted by the presence of moisture, they descend into the bathtub to drink but are unable to scale the smooth enamel surface when time comes to leave. A common response is to try and flush the offender down the drain, but frequently the spider is able to escape the flood and enter the overflow system, from whence it might spy on bathers unnoticed (were its eyesight good enough). It is all too easy for the spider to emerge during the night from its hiding place and resume its futile efforts to scale the vertical walls of the tub. As one spider looks much like another of the same species, it is widely believed that an endless convoy of spiders is crawling up the drain each night to invade the tub. For the tender-hearted, it is now possible to buy special little ladders, designed to help spider escape from the tub. A more economical solution is to drape a towel over the edge.

"While at Oxford Scientific Films, my colleague John Paling decided to make a small film about spiders in the bathtub. John is a born communicator, with fine sense of humour, and needless to say his film told the story well. Sadly, the film never got the circulation it deserved. Indeed, the only public showing I know of was in a Christmas lecture I gave at the Royal College of Physicians in London. The occasion was deemed a great success, but came close to being a disaster. Misjudging the London traffic. I arrived with the family barely minutes before the lecture was due to start. My father, having initiated the idea, was undergoing paroxysms of anxiety, and contingency plans were already being drawn up in case I failed to appear.

It was a light-hearted lecture aimed more at the physicians' families than the physicians themselves, and the film made a fitting climax. The scene opens with a young lady, a hired model, entering her bathroom in anticipation of taking a leisurely soak in the tub. Horror of horrors! There is a big *Tegenaria* house spider in the tub. Quickly she turns on the water and flushes the spider down the drain. With the spider gone, she fills the bath and disrobes (most decorously). All the while, the spider is climbing up the overflow pipe until it is positioned behind the perforated cover, from whence it can watch the bather unbeknownst. The shot is skilfully taken over the spider's shoulder, as if were, with the bather visible in the background through the overflow.

To make the film, John had acquired an old bathtub and laboriously had it sawn in half longitudinally, so exposing the plug hole and overflow to view, enabling the spider's movements to be followed. The script called for underwater shots of the bather's feet, and rather than incur the expense of a professional model again, it was our long-suffering secretary, Carol, who was asked to dabble her feet in soapy water while perched uncomfortably on the rim of the sectioned tub."

I once heard somebody ask John about his most memorable experiences filming spiders. It was not an easy question for him to answer because there have been so many. He was then pressed to give some examples.

"In some ways the most memorable event was only peripheral to filming. We had been on an expedition to Costa Rica, and were preparing to leave the following day. Very early in the morning, a couple of hours or more before dawn, I set off alone through the forest, conscious of every rustle and animal call in the undergrowth. My destination was an emergent giant tree that had had a platform built in the upper branches. On arrival, moonlight barely penetrated to the forest floor, but I was able to locate the nylon climbing ropes, which stretched invisible some two hundred feet up into the darkness. Attaching myself, I slowly climbed, using two ratchet-like jumars to grip the rope. The higher I climbed, the lighter the star-filled sky became, until I reached the 8-foot by 8-foot platform. Here I sat, watched and listened, every sensation magnified beyond reality. I experienced, once again, the same bliss and awareness that made nightclimbing on Oxford buildings as an undergraduate so addictive. Very gradually, almost imperceptibly, the first light of dawn filtered through the branches, awakening the life of the forest. Orb-weaving spiders were putting the finishing touches to the night's construction. The distant voice of a Howler Monkey triggered replies, which came nearer and nearer, until the troop passed by, scarcely noticing the unaccustomed observant stranger in their midst of their domain. I lingered, spellbound, for as long as possible before abseiling down to begin the homeward journey, the experience forever etched in my memory.

Another memorable experience was filming time-lapse sequences of spiders spinning their orb-webs.

Araneid orb-weavers generally spin during the night, a behaviour seemingly triggered by temperature change. I had introduced spiders to frames some three feet in diameter, made from thin, supple branches. The spiders were encouraged to lay down a basic framework of silk, in the hope this would encourage them to stay and spin. The frames were set in a small draught-proof room, with filming lights positioned to illuminate the web from behind, making it stand out against a black background. The lights were controlled through a variac, allowing them to brighten very slowly so as not to alarm the spider. The camera was operated by an intervalometer, set to fire at a predetermined frame-rate so that in the finished film, the action would appear speeded up.

Night after night I would sit in near darkness, beginning around midnight, with just sufficient illumination to see when the spider started to move. This was more demanding than one might imagine, for staring at a small spot in the blackness, I found myself regularly starting to hallucinate, imagining the spider to be moving when in fact it was stock still. At the first sign of movement, I would turn the variacs up very slowly, for at this stage the spider could be easily alarmed, loosing the urge to spin. Once web construction began in earnest, however, the spider would continue regardless of the bright lights, the whole task taking about twenty minutes. The spider's first task was to lay down a series of threads radiating from the centre, followed by a loose temporary outward spiral. Then the spider would start from the periphery and lay down the finely spaced sticky spiral. As each inter-radial section was attached, the spider would pluck it, the vibrations causing the outer adhesive film to break up into discrete droplets. The spider would end its nocturnal labours at the centre of its web, where it might sit waiting for breakfast to arrive, before spinning a signal thread up to a retreat beneath a convenient concealing leaf."

Perhaps the most challenging filming project was for the 1992 World's Fair in Seville. It was a short segment in a visually stunning film without commentary that carried a conservation message. A rowdy carload of people, an allegory for humanity, drive unheedingly past a sign warning of dangerous cliffs ahead. As they go rushing by, they toss out cans and bottles.

"I was contracted to direct the filming of a sequence in which a coke bottle passes in slow motion through an orb web, then hits a bird's nest, scattering the eggs, before landing in a pond next to a frog, that had to jump out of frame in surprise.

It was late summer, and *Araneus diadematus* was common in Berkeley, California, and a fair number were captured and taken down to Santa Cruz, where the filming was to be done. All went well, but later it was found that the special synchronised lights used for the slow-motion filming had developed a fault and the resultant footage was unusable. By the time this was discovered, and plans made to re-shoot, it was late autumn—and the production had moved north to Vancouver, where adult spiders could no longer be found. It was also the end of the season for *A. diadematus* in Berkeley, but diligent searching produced a few hangers-on. These were then smuggled across the border into Canada, where they refused to spin in our over-heated hotel room. Joyce, self-appointed wrangler, overcame her natural hesitancy about spiders and spent each night riding herd to keep them on their frames. Time was running out and production was due to end in a couple of days. Things looked desperate. We then found somebody with a garage we could use. Although not heated, it was connected to the house, and by leaving the door open, the spiders were spared frostbite but still subjected to the usual daily temperature cycle. The next day we were rewarded with a single perfect web.

Filming was scheduled for a local park, and with infinite care the frame with its web was transported and placed in position, carefully protected by a large golfing umbrella, from the giant Maple leaves that were falling in profusion. There would be just once chance to get the shot of the coke bottle, its label visible, flying in slow motion through the centre of the web—and nobody would take responsibility for throwing it! In the end Baily Silleck, the producer, had to undertake the task himself. For half an hour he practised lobbing coke bottles, looking ever more anxious. Finally it was time to try for the shot, and the tension was intense. Taking careful aim, after deep breathing, the bottle was thrown, and to everybody's relief, it passed through the web as planned. After the spider shot, bird's nests and frogs were almost an anti-climax."

## Discursus Seventy
# The Criminal Classes

John immediately caught everyone's attention at dinner one evening when he announced "I will never forget the first time I had to appear in court."
"My parents were long-time friends and admirers of Bernard Gotch, the Oxford artist well known for his beautiful watercolours of Oxford buildings. A meticulous craftsman, he would sometimes delay the completion of a painting for a year or two if bad weather interrupted the work, returning again on the same date to ensure that the shadows and lighting would be exactly the same when work resumed.

When it was decided that a family portrait—a conversation piece—might be a desirable addition to the family collection, my parents instinctively turned to Bernard Gotch. When he came to discuss the project, we all gathered in the drawing room, each without thinking, assuming a characteristic position. I was sitting behind my mother on the back of the sofa; my sister Jean sat at the piano, against which my father leaned in a typical, thoughtful pose. These, it turned out, would be the way in which the artist wished the family to be immortalised.

Being used to painting immobile buildings, Bernard Gotch worked slowly, which probably accounts for the rather bored, distant gaze of some of his sitters. My sister Judy was caught in riding habit as she entered the room—and could never shake off the caption of: "Oh God, the horse has died". I myself was reduced to keeping mental count of the number of cars, buses and pedestrians, visible through the front gate, passing in each direction— and my boredom is obvious. The best likeness, it was universally agreed, was the portrait of my grandfather hanging in the hall, just visible through the open doorway .The first requirement, before painting began, was to turn the carpet over as the artist was offended by its colour.

Work was progressing slowly but steadily, as each family member was required to adopt their original pose and hold it for several hours. As I was so sitting, I was somewhat startled to see a rather disreputable figure enter the driveway and approach the house. I was even more startled when he ostentatiously threw a brick through the drawing room window, missing Bernard Gotch by a hairsbreadth. I immediately leaped up and rushed out to confront him, only to find him in an aggressive posture and muttering in some unrecognisable Slavonic language. As he walked casually out of the gate and up the road, I followed a short distance behind. Meanwhile the police had been summoned and in due course arrived to make an arrest, telling me that ours was but the last of several houses whose windows he had broken—along with the windscreens of a couple of parked cars.

As a teenager, it was an interesting experience to be summoned to court as a witness—my only vision of the proceedings being coloured by Hollywood movies, it being before the days of universal television. The prisoner was Polish, and had approached the police some time earlier demanding that they give him a ticket to return home. When they, not unnaturally, refused, he set out on his destructive walk up the Woodstock Road.

His stratagem worked! He spent the winter well-fed in a warm prison and in the spring, six months later, he was deported back to his homeland."

Because we move in relatively law-abiding circles, we tend to be taken by surprise when we fall victim to criminal activity. I don't mean violent street crime, like the time John's girls were robbed at gun point in Berkeley, just a block from home. Such an event is inevitably traumatic, particularly as two students were killed by the same robbers at the same spot the following week. No, I am talking about identity theft and confidence tricksters. When the outcome is good, it is possible to look back in amazement that one was so gullible—or that the tricksters were so skilled in their craft. There are also occasions when the malefactors are so stupid that one has to laugh at their naiveté. The episode that springs to mind took place in France.

"Many years ago we joined with a group of friends to purchase *Les Tardes,* an old farmhouse—or more accurately a hamlet that comprised three conjoined houses. Positioned on a low hilltop, it enjoyed panoramic views and stood in splendid isolation. Unoccupied for nigh on sixty years, it was in the words of one of our partners, "not so much a renovation, as an archaeological dig".

The original concept was simple. The six partner couples would have a place in which to vacation, and when not so used, the houses could be rented out at a healthy profit. Blinded by the promise of substantial returns, we set to work, investing incalculable sums in 'sweat equity', oblivious to the pitfalls that lay ahead.

We soon discovered that we had joined a growing community of foreign investors in French rural real estate who were doomed to disappointment. Although continental holidays had become *de rigeur* for many, with over half a million British families now owning second homes in France, each justified by the fantasy of rental income, there now appeared to be more *gîtes* available than holidaymakers in search of accommodation.

From time to time we welcomed guests at *Les Tardes,* and periodically partners would come to claim their rightful vacation. However, there was one eventuality that had received inadequate attention. Old buildings, particularly those renovated by inexperienced amateurs, require constant upkeep, and even when working properly, are forever in need of cleaning, housekeeping and welcome services. For those partners unfortunate enough to have homes of their own within a thirty-mile radius, there proved to be countless calls on our services and goodwill, a continuous need to perform those tasks that already occupied too much time at our own properties. Gutters and downspouts would become solidly blocked for no obvious reason, tiles would fall and circuit breakers trip. Lawns needed frequent mowing and weeds thrived on the gravel driveway. For some guests, unaccustomed to country living, the presence of bats, flies and spiders were a source of disproportionate concern and anxiety.

Reluctantly it was decided, despite the expense, that a resident couple might simplify our lives, she for the housekeeping and he for maintenance and gardening. The first couple proved skilful at cultivating marijuana, and introduced us to a widespread, but generally inconspicuous, sub-culture of French society—an itinerant band of self-proclaimed artisans whose chief abilities lay in partying and minor criminal mischief.

In time the young folk moved on to more profitable pastures, and were replaced by an older, but no less criminal, couple. They had first come to us as potential investors, who would not only join the partnership, but become resident caretakers. We were to provide the care, we eventually discovered, while they did the taking. The promised investment proved to be a figment of their imagination, maintained by endless excuses. Such accomplished liars, they were allowed to move in, despite an agreement that their investment must be banked first.

How, one might ask did two such obese and inactive individuals acquire their criminal skills? She, it transpired, had been a bank vice-president, which some would say was a self-evident explanation. He, as a parole officer, was in daily contact with the criminal classes, and had clearly assimilated his clients *mores*. Their days were spent weighting down the livingroom sofa to ensure a sudden typhoon didn't blow it away.

When the decision was eventually made to place the property back on the market, it was clearly necessary for them to move out, which they resisted to the last. The eviction notice was served by the local *huisier* (bailiff). We accompanied her when, having served the notice, she went to check that they had left, and that the property was in good order. Imagine our surprise (a word totally inadequate on this occasion) when we discovered that our caretakers had totally stripped the property of everything moveable, including every stick of furniture!

A quick mental inventory of mutual acquaintances with empty barns, coupled with a few tactful enquiries, soon suggested where the missing items might be found— at the home of a friend's daughter living some distance away and who was not party to the earlier saga. In a carefully-worded message, not mentioning any names, I let it be known that an insurance claim would soon be submitted for the absent furnishings, and that this would, of necessity, require a police report—adding that whoever was accommodating the missing items would risk being charged as a *complice après le coup* if not the more serious *complice avant le fait*. My arrow found its mark. The next day, fearing that the property might be torched out of spite, we arrived early. During our absence a miracle had occurred. The missing furniture had all reappeared, in its appointed place during the night.

There was some satisfaction in realising that our resident criminals must have incurred not inconsiderable expense in hiring a large truck—and a team of workers, for they could not have moved so much themselves, even if they had been fit."

The outcome of this particular encounter with the criminal underworld had no painful consequences, and was, in retrospect, mildly humorous. Whereas in France, John and his partners were dealing with amateur do-it-yourself rogues, the consequences were rather more painful when crossing paths with professional criminals. It all began innocently enough when John and Joyce were going with old Berkeley friends to visit family in Latvia, and decided to rent their house to cover the expense. Wrong!

"We had put up a small notice in the village store a few weeks before leaving, and to our delight it attracted a potential renter. Charlene came with two young children to look at the house. Her husband was unable to come because as vice-president of a nation-wide plumbing company he was away on business. She explained that they lived a few miles down the mountain and were building a house near Dutch Flat. Their property had sold unexpectedly quickly and they needed somewhere to live for 3-4 months while the new house was being finished.

It sounded very convincing, but in reality nothing that she said was true. The house had not been sold, but had been foreclosed, and Jim's plumbing company was his father's small, local enterprise that had actually folded.

Accepting their cheques for first and last months rent, plus a healthy security deposit, we set off to stay with my niece & family in Riga.

We had not been there long when problems surfaced. Not only were Jim & Charlene's cheques not honoured, but worse, our bank accounts suddenly held no money. Checking on-line, we found that not only had our savings been stolen, but substantial sums had obviously been paid to on-line sites that were clearly pornographic— which for a time led to some potentially acrimonious discussions!

It quickly became clear that our tenants, far from being the sweet young couple they appeared, were in reality hardened professional criminals. I will not attempt to catalogues their misdeeds, for a few choice examples will suffice to illustrate the point.

As tenants, under California law they had rights that were heavily weighted in their favour. They could not, for example, be evicted, and any retaliatory action we might take could be construed as 'harassment'. Thus we could not cut off the phone. All we could do was block long-distance calling. They bypassed this by simply calling Directory Enquiries, who would then offer to put the call through—for an additional charge. Happily the phone company finally dropped their demand for several hundred dollars after somewhat tense discussions.

Amongst our tenants' more outrageous affronts was the writing of large cheques to me on a non-existent account, and then after presentation, pretend to be me and withdraw equally large amounts in cash before the cheque had cleared, repeating the ruse several times. Ultimately the bank were forced to admit their error and make restitution.

Breaking into a locked storeroom, they had discovered an old chequebook of mine in a file cabinet and used it to purchase a Range Rover costing over $40,000. As the account has been closed for ten years or more, the cheque was not honoured, but when the vendors came to reclaim their vehicle, it had already been sold on for cash.

When Pacific Gas & Electric company discovered that the electric meter had been bypassed, shortly after we had regained possession, I was given about 30 seconds to pay $600 to prevent power to the property being discontinued—in mid-winter.

It turned out that they already had a criminal history, for which Jim had received a custodial sentence. However, he talked the judge into allowing him to spend only weekends in jail so he could "provide" for his family. While serving time, he would call Charlene by reversing the charges—on our phone. When winter came, he would call in sick and spend the weekends skiing. We found receipts showing that they spent over $2000 for a weekend at Squaw Valley—money, of course, that was not theirs.

Needless to say, we had long discussions with the county Sheriff, who finally decided he had sufficient grounds to make an arrest. The first time he had them come to his office, they talked themselves out of it—winning the officer's grudging praise that they were the slickest con artists his department ever encountered.

Not believing that the Sheriff might actually come to evict them from our property, they made little preparation to leave, renting a U-Haul truck only one day before the given deadline. As they paid for it with a dud cheque, U-Haul came and reclaimed it, complete with contents, before it had been unloaded.

In their haste they left a lot behind after they were forced to depart. Included in the haul were boxes of papers, which provided, albeit late in the day, a detailed picture of their criminal activities. We discovered that the house they had previously lived in, which had been foreclosed, belonged to her grandfather, who had been forced to live in the garage—before he died unexpectedly from a blow to the head, followed by immediate cremation. His will was unbelievable. Charlene, as executrix, had altered it to make herself the sole beneficiary, which amazingly had been accepted. The day after the grandfather's death, credit card applications were made to some thirty companies in his name, all to be run up immediately over the maximum credit limit. The catalogue of Jim and Charlene's misdeeds could be continued for many pages. They had joined the local Baptist church, which was duped into helping them financially. At the same time they befriended individual church members and 'borrowed' substantial sums from each.

Jim confided to me later, after his (temporary) release from prison for other frauds, that while volunteering at a church-sponsored camp, he was using 'crank' and 'crystal meth' behind the woodpile. Their cell phone records, running to thousands of dollars each month, showed clearly that they were not only using drugs, but were also dealing—information the police were happy to make use of. After Jim returned to prison and Charlene left for a new partner and probably further criminal enterprises, we lost touch. In time we received a letter from the court to say that Jim was now legally responsible for a debt of some $36,000—and that it would be repaid from his minimal prison wages. Sure enough, two or three checks arrived before all went quiet. I have recently—after an interval of more than ten years—received two checks for $28 each! From this it was clear that Jim had recently returned to prison and thereby to gainful employment. The wheels of justice turn slowly."

## Discursus Seventy-One
# Of Babes & Sucklings

There can be few families indeed that have not gathered into their collective archival memories accounts of the improbable and entertaining things that children have said. I refer not to the transitory pronouncements widely reported of new, mispronounced words that fond parents circulate among relatives, or of grammatical novelties perpetrated by their growing offspring. No. I refer to those rare, wonderful remarks that have stood the test of time and passed into family history through repeated telling.

"My sister Jean" John reported, "had gone to stay with an old school friend, who had married a clergyman and lived in a small, remote parish in rural Shropshire. It was somewhere in the hinterland near Cleobury Mortimer; the sort of village that A.E.Houseman had in mind when he wrote "Clunton Clunbury Clungunford and Clun are the quietest places under the sun." In so secluded a community, the children had few companions, and were largely left to find their own amusements. Not unnaturally, they were influenced in their play by what they had observed their father doing. So it was that Jean, walking unnoticed down through the orchard one day, came upon the children at play. They were conducting a funeral service for the doll in their little perambulator. At the appropriate point in the service, tipping up the perambulator, they were overheard to say: "In the name of the Father, and of the son—and into the hole he goes!"

A mutual friend told of the time she took her young son to the eye doctor. As they sat in the waiting area, the little boy was restless and fretful. Pointing to the adjoining play area, she urged him to make use of it. Above the door hung a sign that read 'No Children Without Supervision'. The suggestion to play only provoked further anguish, and repeated urging only made the situation worse. Finally, in desperation, the mother demanded to know why her son refused to go and play. The explanation, broken by heavy sobbing emerged. "But I don't have super vision!"

Not long after John and Joyce had met on the long steps to the Elephanta Caves on an island near Bombay, they were reunited when he came to visit in Berkeley, California. Joyce's daughter Ilana was ten years old, and had hitherto always slept with her mother. The new sleeping arrangements now relegated her to a bunk bed off the kitchen, which did not meet with her approval.

> "Each night we would hear the doleful mantra: "I hate you.... I've always hated you.... I'll hate you for the rest of my life." Shortly thereafter Ilana would lapse into a deep sleep. The next morning she would become once more her usual loving self."

Ilana was about nine. She and Joyce were in the car with the dog, Dustin, when they decided to go to the movies. Turning to Dustin, Joyce said reassuringly "We'll be right back." Outraged, Illana responded "My God! Don't lie to her!"

It was while speaking of Ilana that John reported on the splendid scene at Stanford University as Ilana went to receive her doctorate. Soon after completing her thesis, she had been offered a tenure-track position at the University of Oregon and moved to Eugene. When she returned to Stanford for the graduation ceremony, she was accompanied by Kodi, aged three and Juniper eighteen months. As they were all preparing to mount the dais, Ilana was explaining that she was about to become a doctor—to which Kodi announced firmly "Then I'll be the dentist!"

Kodi continued to surprise the family with her sayings, but perhaps never more so than when she announced to her grandmother when about five years old "I'll bet you don't know, but I've got a vagina!"

While reminiscing about humorous highlights, John recalled a time when he and Joyce had kept chickens at their mountain home in Dutch Flat. Unable to leave the chickens alone when both she and John were in Berkeley, she would bring them down with her in a large box and allow them to roam the apartment. At that time they still had the large house on Benvenue and rented out rooms to students, with whom they would share meals when in residence. One day, Flavio from Brazil, always anxious to improve his command of the language, asked "What is it in English for 'house chicken'? It was in telling this anecdote that John was reminded of another memorable occasion.

"Among our many Balinese friends, 'Wayan of the wall eye' was exceptional. He came from the isolated Bali Aga village of Bangle, up in the mountains of East Bali. When we first met him there was no road to the village, only a rough track up which we would hike for a couple of hours to visit him. He and his brother were master performers on the Genggong or Balinese 'Jews Harp', a curiously versatile instrument whose single note is modified by harmonics produced by altering the shape of the mouth. Perhaps the most remarkable thing about Wayan was his command of English, which despite his isolation, he had mastered on his own at a time when foreign visitors to that part of the island were a rarity, and few outsiders ever visited his village. My regard for Wayan, already considerable, was enormously enhanced when, unable to recall the English word 'calf', he created the marvellous neologism *Kitten cow*."

When John was four years old the family spent their summer holiday at the seaside at Canford Cliffs near Bournemouth on the South coast. After John had been allowed to visit the 'Gents' on the front unaccompanied for the first time, he was overheard telling his little sister: "When you're a big girl, Judy, you'll be allowed to go to the gentleman's lavatory too." In late middle age, she would sometimes ask when she might be permitted to enjoy this promised privilege.

On another occasion, reminiscing about life in the post-war austerity, John recalled one of the passing legion of his mothers cleaning ladies.

"Mrs Smith was a curious woman, who always wore a knitted pixie hat. I recall little else about her, except that she used to take a bath ( I assume with my mother's connivance) in my bathroom. I did not object to the bathing, which was often clearly needed, but what I did

take exception to that she would cut her toenails in the tub
and then fail to remove the clippings before I next bathed.

When enquiry was made one day about her life,
she replied with the classic aphorism:

"Appy? Who wants to be 'appy? Comfortable's all I ask."

It was a natural progression to continue talking about other
family retainers. John recalled Hill, the gardener, who came
and sat with him when convalescing after an appendectomy,
and helped plot the progress of war in the Pacific with little
home-made American and Japanese flags, which were stuck
into a National Geographic Society map of the region.
However, foremost among the staff recalled was old Annie
Edney, who had come during the war, when help in the
house was impossible to find because all suitable women had
been co-opted for war work. Annie had recently received
shock treatment for some mental condition, and her doctor
felt it would be good if she could work for a while in a
medical household, where her condition could be constantly
monitored. It was never envisaged that she would continue
working in the Cooke household to the end of her days.

"Annie lived with her older sister, Mrs. Beezley, who as
a dressmaker was still agile into her nineties, vigorously
kneeling to measure hemlines like someone half her age.
They lived in a small row house in Plantation Road that
lacked all modern amenities (but which in the years
following their deaths would become highly desirable
up-market yuppie accommodation). Every Thursday
evening they would heat water for a hip bath set in front
of the fireplace in the sitting room, in preparation for their

weekly visit to the theatre, where they had season tickets in the front row of the Balcony, regardless of the play. Thus they would see the Christmas Pantomime repeatedly throughout its two-month season.

Annie lived in a universe of her own, and in consequence was prone to producing startling *non sequiters* when suddenly pulled back into the real world. There was a memorable occasion when my mother, intent on making conversation, mentioned that it was Prince Charles' second birthday, and that the band of the Grenadier Guards had played 'Happy Birthday' outside his window at Buckingham Palace. The unexpected reply was: "And the man says the rat will be dead in the morning." Clearly a domestic rodent problem in Plantation Road was dominating Annie's mind. This delightful *non-sequiter* has long been adopted by the family as a phrase to highlight apparent lapses in logic.

As the years went by, Annie became ever more of a responsibility. If any of her dusters were moved, she thought that her work must be unacceptable and that someone else had been brought in to replace her, necessitating careful soothing of her ruffled feathers. The half-eaten apple cores she left on the staircase were a minor inconvenience, but as she became increasingly frail, my mother would have to go and transport her to and from the house, carefully taking her arm to lead her in as she could barely see where to go.

To the end of her days she could list her before-breakfast duties as a housemaid at the age of sixteen in lady so-and-so's country house, yet had no recollection of events occurring only five minutes previously. She might well have been a beloved character from such TV series as Upstairs, Downstairs or Downton Abbey."

John's father was renowned as a raconteur, and I cannot resist the temptation to perpetuate a few of his anecdotes here. There was the occasion, as a very young physician, he was asked to serve as locum for a rather up-market country doctor. He was told that if her ladyship at the manor house called, he was to take the Rolls-Royce. Sure enough, her ladyship did call, and my father set off feeling rather grand in the big, old stately car. On arrival at the manor—calamity of calamities— the driver's door would not open, trapping father inside in his tail coat and striped trousers.

In desperation, as the butler appeared at the front door, there appeared only one option. In Rolls-Royces of that ancient vintage, the windscreen hinged at the top and could be opened forward, leaving a narrow gap above the dashboard. With great aplomb, father slowly slithered out across the gleaming bonnet of the car, dusted himself off and set off to visit his patient, the butler remaining solemnly deferential and seemingly unmoved. Some time later, when it came time to leave, father slid himself as elegantly as possible over the bonnet and re-entered the car through the windshield before driving off down the great house's winding driveway.

There was an occasion when his father was examining a rustic farm-worker patient and noticed an old surgical scar. Enquiring about it he received the memorable response: "Once them surgeons gits inside, they just 'elps themselves."

"When I was young" John recalled one day, "it was a long-standing Christmas tradition that the whole family would head down to the hospital, the Radcliffe Infirmary, where father would carve the turkey on his ward. It was valuable training as children to learn to have conversations with strangers—often semi-comatose patients with little interest in the life of the ward. I have always thought that this was similar to the possibly apocryphal tale that the Royal Family practised the same skills on trees in Windsor Great Park.

We children would range from ward to ward, collecting offerings of turkey, gravy and stuffing at each in turn, but always making sure we spent as much time as possible in the children's ward, which despite its bright colours and airy atmosphere, was nevertheless burdened by a heavy feeling of gloom as one knew that many of the little patients forced to remain in hospital at the festive season were sufficiently ill that they might never survive to the following Christmas This was an early lesson in how to handle the prospect of death.

On father's ward—Cronshaw—not only did he carve the turkey, but was obliged by tradition to hand out presents to Matron and the nurses. Tradition also dictated that he should submit to being dressed up in some ridiculous costume. For my mother it was a custom that provoked great anxiety lest the holes in his elderly underwear be revealed for all to see.

When distributing Christmas presents to all the nurses he would give each a kiss. It was from observing this ceremony that my younger sister, Jane, developed the conviction that father's job in the hospital was to kiss the patients better; as he did to her in times of pain.

# Discursus Seventy-Two
## Art and Miracles[12]

No account of John's life would be complete without mention of his sister-in-law, the famous artist Judith Scott, for she has played a major role in the convoluted course of his life. Through her, he has become increasingly immersed in the study of art and disability. Judith's remarkable story has been told in the book her twin sister, Joyce, has written[13], and it seems particularly appropriate to reprint here the review that John had written under the title: 'Judith Scott - A Modern Fairy Tale of Art and Miracles.'

"Long ago and far away, so legend tells us, giants walked on Earth—heroes who had arisen from anonymous poverty to undertake epic journeys beset by overwhelming challenges and hardship before conquering the forces of darkness to emerge triumphant onto the world stage.

These are mankind's classic stories, told and retold in the darkness, around the dying embers of countless campfires, passed down from generation to generation, forming the universal mythology of human history. It is no exaggeration to say that Judith Scott's life story is cast in same mold as these mythic tales.

Who could ever have imagined that the deaf little girl with Down Syndrome, cruelly labelled in the heartless language of the time "a Mongoloid Idiot", might one day become famous; hailed around the world as an artist of

---

12    Retains its original American spellings

13    Entwined—Sisters and Secrets in the Silent World of... Artist Judith Scott. 2016. Beacon Press

extraordinary vision and originality? And yet this is the remarkable arc of Judith Scott's life story—a story of which her twin has written:

> *"When I think back to the dreamtime of our distant childhood and reflect on the twin journeys along which the fates have brought us—the tangled, lonely paths we've traveled before finding each other again. I begin to realize that my childhood prayers, so earnestly besought, have indeed been answered. Judy and I are living in a nebulous galaxy of miracles extending far beyond anything I had ever dreamed, or could possibly have imagined.*

It seems appropriate to begin Judith's story in the traditional manner thus: "Once upon a time, in a distant land long ago"—Cincinnati, Ohio in 1943 to be precise—twin girls, Judith and Joyce Scott, were born. They lived with their mother and father and three older brothers in a semi-rural community on what was then the outer edge of the city. When Judith was sent home from the hospital, the wise and caring family doctor advised her parents that she would be 'a little slow, and to give her lots of love'. It would be years before Judith's slowness could be ascribed to her possession of the extra twenty-first chromosome that characterises what would come to be called Down syndrome. Her emerging difficulties were heightened by an attack of scarlet fever in infancy which unknowingly deprived Judith of her hearing. It was a loss that would remain unrecognised for many years.

The advice given to her parents by the family doctor would be only the first of the many miracles that have followed Judith's star. Conventional wisdom at the time of her birth dictated that such children be taken away and placed in state care—or more accurately, to be warehoused by the state. Fortunately for her, and the world, Judith was allowed to stay with her twin sister Joyce, and be raised in her family. For seven-and-a-half years the twins inhabited a blissful world, a primeval garden of Eden in which every stone, leaf and blade of grass was alive with meaning; a paradise awaiting exploration and discovery. With her twin sister as guardian and interpreter, Judith felt and tasted her way through her new world. Together the twins poured water into holes, painted box turtles with the juice of crushed mulberries, discovered the joys of exploring and sharing. It was an enchanted childhood.

Then struck tragedy. Under cover of darkness, without warning or explanation, Judith was taken from the bed she shared with her sister, and placed in a Dickensian state institution for the "mentally retarded"—a great dark fortress of heat, offensive smells and small, twitching bodies.

We can only guess the misery, the anguish that Judith suffered through this traumatic separation, for she lacked the means to put her feelings into words. However, we can glimpse the impact through the powerful writings of her twin, who speaks of a single being inhabiting two bodies, a closeness and confusion of identity that would cause her agonising guilt and self-doubt.

*Entwined – Sisters and Secrets in the Silent World of Artist Judith Scott,* Joyce's memoir of their lives, weaves a glowing tapestry that draws together several disparate threads to create a powerful picture of Judith's life and the forces that gave it form. At its most elemental level, *Entwined* can be read as simple biography. But *Entwined* actually offers the reader much deeper meaning. Beyond the inspiring story of limitless love and devotion, and the improbable emergence of a world renowned artist, *Entwined* carries profound messages.

Judith's sudden, apocalyptic disappearance is a turning point, launching the story on a descent into darkness as we follow the family's consequential decline —the mother's breakdown, the father's premature death and the author's on going life of unassuaged grief and self-blame. The agony of separation and loss is repeated when Joyce is forced to give up the daughter to whom she gave birth while in college, leaving her with two secret grief's to be carried alone and in silence.

The reader might be forgiven for wondering how any possible escape might be found from the wasteland of sorrow into which the story has descended. The unexpected appearance of a fairy godmother—a college professor with faith in Joyce, her abilities and future —marks the start of a slow ascent as Joyce rebuilds her life. The bond with her twin never lessens. Through visits to the institution, however infrequent, we get windows, powerful vignettes, into Judith's unfulfilling parallel life, of which there are but few, faint records—a symptom of official neglect and lack of concern in which her deafness went long unnoticed and all her teeth were pulled without cause. We learn that when, on the one occasion the future artist tried to draw with crayons they were forcibly removed, leaving Judith rushing from the room in tears.

The twin secrets that Joyce carries with her in silence, paired threads running through the book, eventually lead to resolution. We follow the tangled path leading to Joyce's reunion with her daughter, while at the same time sharing the epiphanal realization that she might become her sister's legal guardian, a realization that will eventually lead to Judith's release from institutional life. From this point onwards Judith now dominates the story. We meet a remarkably strong and resilient personality, with an impish sense of humor, who survived her flight across the country alone and unaccompanied, and who quickly adapted to her new family life. We learn of her enrolment in the Creative Growth Art Center, where her compulsive creativity remained hidden for two years, before suddenly erupting once the necessary fiber medium became available to her.

Another small miracle occurs when John MacGregor enters her life. A distinguished art historian and psychoanalyst, Dr MacGregor came to Creative Growth to study Dwight Macintyre, a Creative Growth artist about whom he was writing a book. Chancing to see Judith at work, he immediately recognised the compelling quality of her work, and determined to study her in depth. For two years he watched Judith intently as she laboured away at her workbench, before writing *Metamorphosis – The Fiber Art of Judith Scott*, whose publication was timed to coincide with the first public showing of Judith's sculptures. This beautiful book was instrumental in bringing her work to a wider audience, leading to her growing recognition, and eventual acclaim. For some years Judith's fame was as an 'Outsider Artist'—that is as a self-taught artist on the fringes of society, whose creativity springs from some deep inner compulsion, but with no concept of material gain or recognition. Today Judith is acclaimed as a leading 'contemporary artist', a brilliant and wholly original creative virtuoso who garners international applause, her disabilities now being consigned to a mere biographical footnote. Judith's powerful sculptures are found in museum collections around the world, and in countless galleries and exhibitions from Japan to Sweden, from New York to Tasmania, while articles about her appear with increasing regularity in newspapers and magazines.

Throughout *Entwined* there are numerous sub-texts, many of them serving to whet our appetite. We learn of the penalties demanded by society from those unfortunate enough to give birth outside of marriage, of the black market in adoptions, of the secret options open to parents for finding their children given up for adoption at a time when it was illegal to search. Viewed from today's perspective, attitudes to disability when Judith and Joyce were born, and the conditions under which infants with disability were institutionalized are thrown into bold, unflattering relief. Few who are not born a twin can appreciate the impact of this relationship. Seen in this light, the author's autobiographical passages may be interpreted as another reflection of Judith's own voice, otherwise manifested eloquently through her sculptures.

Perhaps the most important message carried by *Entwined*, is that differentness is not disability and that differentness in no way lessens an individual's gifts or creative originality—and indeed may well enhance it. Frequently deficits in one ability are compensated—if not over-compensated—in others. No human being should be cast aside, for all have hidden talents to share. In a society that still discriminates against those individuals who are in any way different, *Entwined* carries a beacon of hope. For those families struggling with the silent stigma still implied by disability, *Entwined* bears a message of expectation and joy.

## Discursus Seventy-Three
# Random Recollections

As the manuscript of this volume was going through a final edit, further memories surfaced that seemed worthy of inclusion. Hence:

"Indian villages have changed little through the centuries. This timeless window into the soul of the nation was brought home to me most powerfully when I stayed with a Swedish Engineer and his most beautiful Indian family near Bareilly, some 250km East of Delhi, where he ran a match factory. Exquisitely beautiful, they were an outstanding demonstration of the power of hybrid vigour.

As is the custom in rural India, we slept on the roof. Before dawn the village slowly began to stir. It was the staccato, barely audible, unintelligible voices of the womenfolk as they lit their dung fires in the darkness that first wakened me, soon joined by the distant barking of countless dogs.

As the mist lifted, to be replaced by the smoke of many cooking fires, the first hint of a new day lightened the sky—a ritual repeated uncountable times over the centuries, nay millennia. The rich, gentle smells of the wakening community drift slowly upwards, a timeless gift from mother earth. Neighbouring rooftops begin to stir and the harsh calls of the peacocks prevent further thoughts of sleep. To me, it is this magical, timeless ritual that epitomises the essence of rural India.

I was in India during the 1960s, when there was widespread opposition, particularly in the South, against the imposition of Hindi as the national language. At the time, Indian banknotes showed their value in perhaps sixteen different languages. Curious, I would often ask people how many of these diverse scripts and languages they could identify. Even academics were seldom able to identify correctly more than half a dozen, if that.

It was not surprising to see numerous graffiti opposing the imposition of Hindi as the national tongue, but it was notable how many of them were written in English! Colonialism, however offensive, was clearly not without some benefits in so diverse a land!

In France, the TGVs (high speed trains) are renowned for punctuality, and it takes an exceptional event to cause any acceptable delay. There is one occasion on which the delay was deemed unquestionably understandable.

Now it must be understood that Frenchmen, like the Scots, are not easily parted from their wallets, so when a passenger dropped his wallet down the toilet of the TGV, he was mortified. Reaching down, he endeavoured to recover it, but slowly, inevitably, the wallet remained elusive, slowly moving further down the drain at each attempt to grasp it.

It was not long before the victim had inserted his arm so far that he was trapped, unable to withdraw it. Once his predicament had attracted attention, at the next stop the *pompiers* were summoned. The only solution was to saw the toilet through to carefully remove it from its base. The world was rewarded by photographs of the victim lying helpless on the platform, his arm still firmly encased within the liberated toilet. This was considered a legitimate excuse for the TGV running behind schedule.

.Returning once again to memories of children, John recalled an event, soon after the family had moved from England to Connecticut.

> "We were down on the shore at Squam Lake in New Hampshire, swimming in shallow water, when Joanna, then about three year old, suddenly vanished beneath the surface. I was several yards away, and suffered agonies of apprehension as I tried to wade to help her. It was a nightmare sensation, the water slowing me down as if wading through molasses. Reaching the spot where she was last seen, I spotted a tangle of blond hair and seized it in desperation. Once brought to the surface I had expected wails of dismay, but was greeted only by the off-hand comment "I was talking to the fishes!"

On another occasion, Joanna, a voluble talker, was frustrated by the grown-ups inability to understand her. Finally, in desperation, she threw her hands up and declared "but I don't know anymore words."

When the family drove from New York to the Natural History Museum's Southwestern Research station in Arizona, they took a circuitous route, combining the search for spiders with sightseeing at the many National Parks along the way. A key aid in determining the route was a guide to campgrounds that listed facilities available; hot water, tent sites, trailer sites etc.

> "Occasionally we would be tempted by the thought of hot showers and washing machines, but generally we would head for the sites with the fewest amenities. Following

the North Rim of the Grand Canyon we were drawn irresistibly to the Toroweap Overlook, which apparently had just two tent sites and no other facilities. It was a sixty-mile diversion on dirt roads from Fredonia, and when we got a flat tire from a bullet lying in the dust, the children were delighted that we had seemingly been attacked by Indians.

On arrival at the campsite, we found it even more magical than we had dared to imagine. With Richard, barely two, secure in a harness, the children sat on the lip of a 3000 ft drop sheer to the Colorado river beneath, overwhelmed by the grandeur of the view. We pitched our tent a short distance away and prepared for the night. One of my prime pictures is of the tent, glowing from a pressure lamp within, set in a vast wilderness brightly lit by the light of a full moon, with multiple lightening strikes from an electrical storm raging in the distance.

When Lilia was about three-years-old she had a rough, croaky voice. One day, when someone commented on this, she said "There's a male mallard in there. Look! Can you see his green head?"

John will often comment on the improbability of any child ever reaching adulthood, considering the potential for disaster along the way. As an example he recalls, with a shudder, the time he was building a tree house in the garden in Oxford when he was about ten. He repeatedly told his little sister, Judy, to keep away, but she continually ignored him. Eventually disaster struck. The hatchet he was using slipped from his belt and landed on Judy's head far below. It was a nasty wound, to be sure, but nothing like it might have been if it had landed blade-first, unquestionably penetrating her skull in consequence. John cannot shake the images of carnage that would have resulted, even seventy years later.

When Judy married a Church of Scotland minister, she determined on having a dozen children. On his £400 per annum salary it soon became clear that this was not to be, and she drew the line at six. Even this left them with financial difficulties, which they eventually overcame by joining the army, Bruce becoming chaplain to the Black Watch. When Judy, a keen horsewoman, suffered a serious back injury, the family were flown from their posting in Germany, back to the UK. When Helen, the oldest child, began clearing up their military transport in preparation for landing she was heard to say, quite rightfully, "You mustn't leave a mess in somebody else's aircraft."

When the family lived in Old Greenwich, Connecticut, John's wife. Sue, turned her sewing skills to good use and established a dress-making business that flourished. One day she was approached by a forceful Italian lady, the wife of a local Mafia boss. On being told that her dress would not be ready for a couple of weeks, she responded "You do-a me first; I pay you more!" When the job was finished, John offered to deliver it.

The Don's estate in Stamford was guarded by massive iron gates and fully armed henchmen. It was a scene straight out of the *Godfather*, and he breathed a deep sigh of relief once the delivery had been made and he could escape.

During John's undergraduate years at Oxford he would not infrequently be found in North Wales on climbing expeditions. It was a fine morning when John and several friends piled into a pickup truck to drive to cliffs in Tremadoc. The driver, John Cole, was in a hurry, and it was not long before the passengers in the back became apprehensive as they squealed around sharp bends on the winding mountain road. In preparation for the awaiting accident, John wedged himself tight against the cab, and when it came he alone remained as the truck turned over. While the other passengers had been thrown clear, John was trapped beneath the upturned vehicle, his head firmly embedded in the tarmac, and drenched in petrol. The driver and passenger found themselves suspended upside down above a precipitous drop into the valley below.

In due course John was called as a witness to the accident at the Tremadoc magistrates court, where John Cole was charged with dangerous driving. It was an entertaining experience. In an earlier case, as a Welsh farmer was charged with obstructing traffic, he made an impassioned appeal to the court saying "But it wasn't me holding up the traffic. It was the policeman there, standing in the middle of the road with his arms out".

John Cole had claimed he was driving at 25, perhaps 30 mph, to which the prosecution, holding a plan of the crash site, responded: "Mr Cole, skid mark A is106 feet in length, skid mark B is 97 feet in length— to be followed by three more marks of similar size. Do you think it probable, Mr Cole, that you would have made these skid marks, and have demolished sixty feet of dry stone walling had you been travelling at twenty-five, or shall we say thirty, miles per hour?. There was no logical response, and John was convicted. He was fined £5! Those were the days.

"Planning a vacation in Turkey, we had decided to meet up at Ephesus. I arrived first and settled in at a small *pension* some distance from the ruins. Joyce and Ilana, travelling separately from Rome, were to arrive soon afterwards by way of Istanbul, and Izmir, travelling by bus and train. It was an audacious plan, with innumerable opportunities for delay and confusion. Meditating on the distances and times involved, I selected a potential ETA and sat out on the porch as evening approached. Lo and behold! At the appointed hour, there were Joyce and Ilana arriving by taxi! Sometimes the fates can be unbelievably cooperative.

It was a memorable vacation. Each morning at first light we would head for the ruins before guards or visitors were awake, and were able to wander at will enjoying the solitude of the remains. Again, at dusk we would return to enjoy the sunset alone.

In love with Turkey, we have vowed many times to return, for there is so much to see and do in this cradle of civilisation. Somehow the years have slipped by and today the political environment renders Turkey less and less attractive, but we shall never forget the overnight train journey from Central Anatolia to Izmir, travelling first class for $5 each in a luxurious car that might have come from the fabulous Orient Express of yore, guarded by an attendant seated outside or compartment the whole way." We retain happy memories, come what may."

# SUBLIME LUNACY

# Discursus Seventy-Four
## A Natural Odyssey

J ohn was in a meditative mood one evening, and was easily persuaded to explain the origins of his delight in spiders. "There is nothing in the family archives to indicate when I first became interested in Natural History, but it certainly pre-dates my own earliest memories. When I was three, or perhaps four, years old, it is reported that on one occasion when, the contents of my over-filled pockets—snail shells, pebbles and tangled lengths of string etc.—were set out in recriminatory array, my only comment was: "There should have been a beetle in there!".This early attraction to Coleoptera received a boost some years later when it was suggested that I take an attractive reddish-brown carabid beetle discovered beneath a stone in our North Oxford garden, to the Entomology Department at the University Museum It was a pivotal moment as I watched how to key out the identification of my capture in the massive two-volumes of Norman Joy's *Practical Handbook of British Beetles*, and even more so when I experienced for the first time, the special thrill of having discovered a rare species—and in my very own garden!

My earliest conscious memories of entomological excitement date from my wartime sojourn in Connecticut from age five to nine, not all of them calculated to instill a love of insects. The family I lived with at this time were hard-working and self-sufficient. In addition to having my own little vegetable garden, I had expressed an interest having my own bee hives. In an unguarded moment of gluttonous curiosity I foolishly lifted the lid of a hive to see how the honey was doing, thereby antagonizing the colony. The multitude of stings swelled my face so much that I could barely see my way back to the house. I now treat bees with great respect.

Beetles again figured in these early memories when I chose to sleep in a tent in the garden, where the lawn bordered the woods. The warm summer Connecticut nights swarmed with fireflies, or 'lightening bugs', and I was convinced that if I collected a sufficient number, they might emit enough light for me to read within my tent. I was wrong!

Living in the country, I was faced with a mile-long walk from the nearest bus stop, and part of my route lay across waste ground, where insects abounded..I can still feel the rush of excitement that embraced me when I found my first Preying Mantis, which I carefully carried home to be fed on the banquet of flies I provided.

Like many little boys I was fascinated by the way orb-weaving spiders could quickly locate a fly struggling in its web, and immediately wrap it in swathes of silk, its movement quieted by the injection of venom. I noted that wasps were often allowed to break free without being approached, and that certain insects would be treated as distasteful and cut from the web. Nevertheless, I do not consider such encounters as early evidence of my later fascination with spiders. On the other hand I can vividly recall my first encounter with *Dysdera crocata,* a spider on which many years later I was destined to write my doctoral thesis . It is a large spider (as British spiders go) bright mahogany red in colour, with mouse-grey abdomen and long, ferocious fangs..Even now, seventy-five years later, I can still see clearly the stone beneath which it was hidden..I did not, at that time, appreciate that the fearsome fangs were an adaptation to capturing the woodlice on which it particularly feeds.

There have been many moments of supreme happiness in my arachnological journey. One major event occurred after an interminable interval of withdrawal brought about by the realization that my future depended on mastering sufficient Latin to gain admission to Oxford. All spider books and equipment were strong-mindedly locked away until I had proved myself.

When eventually successful, my father had promised me the reward of a microscope of my own. It was to be a basic instrument, but I negotiated that I might upgrade it to the standard I desired at my own expense. So it was that I got the Watson stereoscopic instrument that was to serve through out my professional career. Were it not for the criminal tenants we admitted to our Dutch Flat sanctuary I would have it yet. The loss, though painful, is in practical terms relatively unimportant as I am no longer physically able to spend hours examining spiders.

Spiders have figured prominently in many of the high points of my life and the search for spiders has brought hours of happiness and peace of mind tramping over the mountains of North Wales and the highlands of Scotland. The search for spiders has also given rise to a number of anecdotes worthy of repetition.

Many years ago I was searching for *Segestria*

*florentina*, a large spider of rather limited distribution in Britain. It constructs a silken tube, particularly in crevices in stonework, opening into a series of long, radiating trip-lines flush with the surface. Knowing that the species had been found around Westminster Abbey, I was busy examining walls in Place Yard, and periodically luring spiders out by touching a trip line with a vibrating tuning fork. Once enticed from the sanctuary of their silken tubes, they could then be persuaded into a glass tube to be carried home. Totally absorbed in my quest, I had failed to notice the small crowd that had gathered round to watch—it was, after all, a somewhat unusual sight on the streets of the capital. When I eventually looked up, I was not a little surprised to find I was entertaining a throng of gaitered Commonwealth bishops in their episcopal finery, apparently in London attending an ecclesiastical conference."

Warming to his subject, John recounted another anecdote from his fund of spider stories. "One of the collecting techniques sometimes used by arachnologists," he explained, " is to hold an open umbrella upside down while the foliage above is struck hard with a stick to dislodge any hidden spiders. One day my friend John Parker was progressing slowly up a glen in Scotland, beating the vegetation along the way as he went. His wife, Nan, was some distance behind, when she was accosted by two worried women walking the opposite direction, who said to her, "if that's your husband up the glen, he seems to be havin' a wee spot o' bother wi his parasol!"

Another memorable episode involved the search

for a spider described in 1916 as a new species from Northumberland by the Rev. J.E. Hull under the name *Diplocentria saxetorum*. Cantankerous and somewhat eccentric, Hull's description was sparse and inadequate, so that in time, in the absence of further specimens, the name was dropped from the British list on the grounds that it could not be recognised from the original description.

In the 1960s I was teaching a course on spiders at the Flatford Mill Field station, and heard a rumour, later proved correct, that the remnants of Hull's collection was lying neglected in a disused East Anglian church. Gaining access to what remained of the collection, I found some dried-out shrivelled remains and a slide-mounted specimen that I immediately recognized as a species not on the British list. My curiosity thus ignited, I determined to visit the original locality given by Hull; the confluence of the East and West Allen Rivers, not far from his vicarage in the village of Ninebanks. Here I discovered why Hull's species had remained unverified for so long—its chosen habitat was on the river's sandy banks beneath large embedded boulders that were essentially too big to turn over! Here, in the damp, narrow space between the rock and the sand grains, this tiny, colourless spider was abundant. Having once discovered its hiding place, armed with crowbar and pick, I was able to locate it in several similar locations in England, Scotland and Wales, all within one month.

Once I had discovered where it lived, I had to determine its true taxonomic identity. I felt justifiably pleased when I discovered a closely related species from caves in Romania, for which the genus *Lessertiella* had been created. However, since being fully described and illustrated in 1967, *Lessertiella saxetorum* has since been moved to a different genus, and is now called *Caviphantes saxetorum*. At least the 'trivial' name that Hull had given it, meaning "of a rocky place", persists in recognition of his neglected contribution to knowledge.

The discovery of a lone male *C. saxetorum* in Oregon should not be considered too surprising. Although caught in a pitfall trap, and its precise microhabitat hence unrecorded, it was close to embedded boulders on a river bed, as in Britain. In time it will undoubtedly prove to be a widely distributed Holarctic species as it has since also been found in several scattered European locations."

## Discursus Seventy-Five
# Life Changes

John has long maintained that he is happiest in the wilderness, and feels alienated from society in the concrete jungles of big cities. Nowhere does he feel this more than in the canyons of New York, and yet he is the first to admit that his sojourn there provided gateways to some of the most important, defining experience in his life—not least his marriage to Joyce.

"Although I left the Natural History Museum in New York at odds with the administration, I still retained many personal friendships from my time as a curator, and it was through these that some life-changing events were born. On my return to the US after leaving OSF, I brought with me copies of several films I had worked one. Foremost among these was 'Sexual Encounters of the Floral Kind', our prize-winning exploration of the remarkable deceits and strategies plants have evolved to ensure their pollination. Through casually describing this film to a friend in the museum's education department over drinks, I was invited to give a presentation in the museum's impressive auditorium.

Now I have always hated public speaking, and when forced to do so, have felt very dubious about the outcome. However, despite facing a huge audience on the museum stage, I felt less daunted than usual because the film stood on its own merits and had no need of support from me. Indeed, at a later presentation, I once actually fell asleep on stage during the film, awaking suddenly and briefly not knowing where I was.

One outcome of showing 'Sexual Encounters' at the AMNH was an invitation to participate in National Audubon Society's winter lecture program. I was already familiar with this as several OSF colleagues had participated in previous years. It would be a tight, demanding progression of one-night stands through the southern, eastern and central states, with a side trip to Bermuda, and I happily accepted, even though the financial rewards were minimal.

It would prove to be a transformative baptism by fire, in which anything that could go wrong, went wrong, and my abilities to improvise and ad lib were tested to the limit. It was in a beautiful lecture theatre in Tallahassee, for example, that shortly before I was scheduled to start, I suddenly noticed to my horror that the large, professional projector did not have a lens in it. By good fortune one of the early arrivals in the audience caught wind of the agitated discussions taking place after this discovery and volunteered that he had a 16mm movie projector at home—a twenty-minute drive away. The program began a little late, and I gave a very protracted introduction, until I saw the replacement projector being hurriedly set up at the back of the hall. On another occasion it transpired that the controls for the audio system were locked in the head teacher's office—and he was not present. At another school, the wiring for the sound system had been burnt out through being inadvertently connected to the mains. In sunny Bermuda there were no curtains in the hall, and hence no way to darken it, making the film virtually impossible to see. In Lancaster, Pennsylvania—the Amish heartland—on peering through the curtain at the assembling audience, I saw a vista of little old ladies in old-fashioned bonnets and suddenly realized that this was not a typical Midwestern audience. With great presence of mind I had to perform major surgery on the film's commentary, which was delivered live over an 'effects' soundtrack. My standard commentary, dealing with sex and evolution, and filled with *double-entendres*, would clearly not appeal to an audience that I now took to be somewhat fundamentalist.

As it turned out, many of the audience proved to be new-order Mennonites, who were much more receptive. My hosts on this occasion proved to be a Mennonite family, with whom I had stimulating religious discussions late into the night, and whose church service the next morning was bright and musical, with none of the heavy-duty religiosity I had misguidedly expected."

The Audubon tour completely cured John of any remaining hesitancy in public speaking, and indeed led him to become quite a ham actor. He discovered the deep satisfaction that can be gained by having the audience completely under one's control, responding on cue as required.

The most significant outcome of the Audubon tour was an invitation to participate as guest lecturer on a month-long cruise for wealthy museum patrons. It should be explained that museum membership is considered a prestigious association among the wealthy New York social elite, who are invited to participate in a variety of fund-raising activities.

"So it was that I found myself in Bombay to join the Illyria on the second half of her month-long cruise from Singapore to Athens, my brief being to mix with the guests and lecture on Natural History and Photography (although instructed not to become overly friendly!) The first shipboard activity in which I participated on arrival was an excursion to the Elephanta Caves. Now designated a UNESCO World Heritage site, the caves have been hewn out of solid basalt, and consist of pillared temples filled with Hindu (and some Buddhist) carvings. The caves are reached by a long series of steps, and as I was climbing I saw an old betel nut vendor in conversation with a visitor from the Illyria. Pausing to do my duty as an official host, we soon found ourselves in conversation, and sharing a leaf-wrapped serving of betel nut. Joyce, as I quickly learnt her name, immediately caught my attention as someone with special qualities, and together we continued up to explore the caves together. Little did I suspect that Joyce's betel nut would become Eve's apple."

For many years Joyce believed that it was a happy coincidence of fate that they found themselves together again that evening, seated next to each other at dinner, unaware that John had been in a position to engineer the seating plan. Over the days that followed, John paid more attention to Joyce than to the other guests on board as they found themselves visiting Oman, Yemen, Petra, and St. Catharine's Monastery. By the time they watched *son et lumiere* in Luxor, it was clear that their futures were inescapably entwined.

After a wrenching farewell in Athens, John returned

reluctantly to New York, while Joyce took a train to Europe before flying to her home in Berkeley, California. While travelling at night through Yugoslavia, all her belongings were stolen in the darkness, leaving her with only the underwear in which she had slept, an event she took in her stride. On her return to California she acted quickly.

"I had barely had time to return to the chaos that is New York, and was consumed by visions of an absent soul mate still waving at the train station in Athens. In the depths of my growing depression, sudden joyous relief appeared in the form of a letter bearing a California postmark. In it I learned that Joyce had persuaded the Berkeley Camera club to invite me to come and give a talk. It did not strike me, at the time, that it was curious that the invitation and accompanying ticket should have come from Joyce and not from the club itself. I have often wondered since…! After two unbearably long weeks of waiting, I boarded a plane to what would prove to be the gateway to a new, and wonderful phase of my life."

After two blissful weeks together, John once more said goodbye—but this time with a much lighter heart. He was returning to New York to fulfill two final commitments.

At the Natural History Museum John had become good friends with Dick Van Gelder, Chairman of the Mammals Department—and like him, a thorn in the administration's flesh. Dick had been reluctantly pressured into overseeing a new Hall of Mammals. The report that he prepared for the Trustees was a masterpiece.

He pointed out that most people only see a whale

when its corpse is washed up on the beach. All that is normally visible of a dead whale is its head and its tail. Thus, by having the bulk of the whale's body out of sight beneath the surf, it would greatly reduce the cost of the exhibit. Waxing lyrical as he expanded on his proposal, he described in detail the cries of the flocks of gulls pecking at the corpse, and the roar of the waves breaking against it. But above all would be the stench of rotting flesh. This latter embellishment had been suggested because a trustee who owned an artificial fragrance business had already manage to have his products sprayed elsewhere in the museum, ostensibly to enhance the sensation of being in a pine forest or desert after rain. The general opinion was that it made the museum smell like a poorly maintained public toilet. Stifling the urge to vomit, the trustees had no difficulty in rejecting Dick's proposal.

"In the event it was decided that the new Mammal Hall should be dominated by a massive Blue Whale in the act of diving, suspended from a single support on the ceiling. This design resulted in some serious engineering problems. Constructed of Styrofoam over a steel supporting skeleton, it was calculated that just one extra coating of paint on the massive whale would make it exceed the permitted load at its attachment point on the roof of the Hall. As the exhibit was slowly assembled and painted, the designer was suffering agonies of doubt in case his calculations had been wrong, Thus each morning he would come in and measure the distance from the whale's nose to the floor to check that there had been no movement overnight. Dick, observing this daily ritual with a wooden measuring stick, decided to doctor the stick each evening. Dipping the end in glue, he then dusted on some sawdust, so that the stick gradually, very slowly, increased in length. Thus making it appear to the tormented designer that the whale was slowly sagging."

Dick Van Gelder was a great field naturalist, and from time to time organized tour groups to East Africa. Soon after he had resigned from the Museum, Dick invited John to join him to lead some wildlife photographic tours to Kenya. He was already seriously ill from the effects of drug-resistant malaria, and greatly inconvenienced by a colostomy bag, which in no way dampened his enthusiasm. His knowledge of animal behaviour made him a boon to photographers, who would told what their subjects were about to do next, and could prepare to record it.

No sooner had the tours with Dick ended than John was again on safari. This time it was again with the Natural History Museum, and again they were high-end excursions. Organized on behalf of the Museum and their well-heeled supporters by Abercrombie & Fitch, John one again found himself travelling in luxury. When crossing into Zambia, the group were greeted personally at the frontier by the President, Kenneth Kaunda himself. The highlight of the Zambia trip was sitting silently in the moonlight outside his tent and watching a procession of elephant, zebra, lion, giraffe and other wildlife walk by only yards away. However, the Zambia experience was totally overshadowed later by Botswana.

"Flying in a miniscule high-winged plane at low altitude, we headed into the Okavango swamp, a vast delta system that is home to the last great African wildlife wilderness. From the air, the grassland and its associated ponds were criss-crossed by trails made by elephants and other game. We eventually reached Xaxaba Camp, an oasis of luxury, as expected by the clients, set in a magnificent landscape teeming with wildlife. My happiest memories associated with this peak experience were exploring the swamps alone in a small dugout canoe, from which I would periodically disembark to wade shoulder-deep to photograph insects, spiders and flowers, choosing to ignore the possibility of crocodiles lurking out of sight. The resulting images were well worth the risk."

On John's return from Africa, plans were swiftly made to head for a new life in California. Joyce flew East and they bought, from a friend an old 12-seater van, which they packed tight from floor to ceiling with books and photographic equipment.

With a chameleon rescued from the departure lounge of Zambia's Lusaka airport riding on the rear-view mirror, they set off across the country for a new and fruitful life together that has already lasted over thirty joyous years.

Lightning Source UK Ltd.
Milton Keynes UK
UKHW011516050620
364505UK00001B/13